Sultry Climates

Sultry Climates

TRAVEL & SEX

Ian Littlewood

DA CAPO PRESS
A Member of the Perseus Books Group

Cataloging in Publication data is available from the Library of Congress.

First Da Capo Press edition 2002
Reprinted by arrangement with John Murray (Publishers) Ltd.
ISBN 0–306–81221–5

Published by Da Capo Press
A Member of the Perseus Books Group
http://www.dacapopress.com

Da Capo Press books are available at special discounts for bulk purchases in the U.S. by corporations, institutions, and other organizations. For more information, please contact the Special Markets Department at the Perseus Books Group, 11 Cambridge Center, Cambridge, MA 02142, or call (800) 255-1514 or (617) 252-5298, or e-mail j.mccrary@perseusbooks.com.

1 2 3 4 5 6 7 8 9 10—06 05 04 03

For Ayumi and Hanako

Contents

What men call gallantry, and gods adultery,
Is much more common where the climate's sultry.
Byron, *Don Juan*, canto I, st. 63

Introduction

'All of us wanderers are made like this. A good part of our wandering and homelessness is love, eroticism.'

Hermann Hesse

The official line rarely tells the whole truth about anything, let alone anything that involves sex. The story of tourism is no exception. Some years ago I worked on a pair of literary companions to Paris and Venice. Both were places that had attracted tourists for centuries, spawning a vast literature of handbooks, histories and general information. But it soon became clear that the literature and the experience were often worlds apart. On one side, the talk was all of art and culture; on the other, there was a stream of more personal writing – letters, diaries, memoirs, poems, novels – that pointed to quite different enticements. The public version of tourism as a cultural venture was challenged by a private version, largely unacknowledged, which suggested that it was also a sexual venture.

To see where this leads, we need a way into the history of tourism that bypasses the usual preoccupations with social change or technological progress. What links the cultural and the sexual motives of travel has more to do with the workings of the imagination. With this in mind, I have tried to classify various kinds of tourism according to the imaginative role they offer the traveller, arguing that by the end of the nineteenth century there were three basic identities: the Connoisseur, the Pilgrim and the Rebel. For eighteenth-century Grand Tourists the principal model was the cultural connoisseur, whose business was to pick his way through Europe gathering information and artefacts, developing his understanding of social institutions, refining his manners along with his appreciation of the arts. In the nineteenth century this tended to give way to a perception of the tourist as engaged on a more personal quest for fulfilment; the typical journey to the Mediterranean was a kind of pilgrimage both in terms of its destination – the holy places of classical and Renaissance civilisation – and in terms of the spirit of self-discovery in which it was frequently undertaken. During the second half of the century, easier foreign travel encouraged a tourism of escape. For those who had the means, it was now possible to reject at will the social and moral restrictions of life at home: the rebel could become a tourist.

These identities are not mutually exclusive, nor do they follow quite the neat historical sequence I have implied, but they do correspond to recurrent patterns of motivation, behaviour and satisfaction. Though the focus of the book is mainly on the tourism of earlier periods, I have tried in each section to highlight the continuities that give this a bearing on our own experience at the start of the twenty-first century. In particular, this is the concern of the final chapter, which looks at the role of sun-worship in reshaping the identities handed on by the nineteenth century.

My choice of travellers has been dictated in some cases by their historical importance, in others by their typicality, in others again by the scarcity of written evidence elsewhere. It is perhaps inevitable, given the imbalance of published accounts, that there should be more men than women, but over the past few years much has been done to bring to light the writings of women travellers in the eighteenth and nineteenth centuries, and I have drawn freely on this work. If the majority of travellers are also British, this is partly for reasons of coherence, because patterns of tourism evolved differently from country to country across Europe, partly because, until after the First World War, America developed only a narrow tradition of leisure travel abroad. But this is not a story that could be told just in terms of the British. The influence of Goethe in Italy, Gauguin in the South Seas, Gide in North Africa, or American expatriates in the south of France is a fair indication of how much depends on both Europeans and Americans.

The book's geographical emphasis on France and Italy has been determined by my wish to keep in view the outlines of mainstream tourism. The case for Tahiti is slightly different. 'Discovered' in the eighteenth century and colonised by France in the nineteenth, it inherited much of the erotic legacy of European orientalism, providing fertile ground for the romantic mythology that has since enveloped island tourism in general. Its importance goes way beyond the relatively small numbers who have actually reached it; Tahiti has been a seed-bed for the tourist fantasies of the mass market.

Regardless of who the travellers are or where they are going, there is one sense in which a sexual resonance is always in the background. Freud's comment on 'the compulsive link ... between railway-travel and sexuality' is a reminder of how far the physical business of travel is itself erotically charged. Steam trains were just the most recent example of a phenomenon, 'clearly derived from the pleasurable character of the sensations of movement', that takes in almost every imaginable means of conveyance. ('Could any man have written it,' Byron asked of *Don Juan*, 'who had not lived in the world? – and tooled in a post-chaise? in a hackney coach? in a Gondola? Against a wall? in a court carriage? in a vis a vis? – on a table? – and under it?') Different forms of transport – ships, coaches, trains, planes – have long been favourite sites for pornography. They are both a context for sexual encounters and a facilitator of them, from the horse-drawn carriage that bore off runaway lovers to the automobile that has haunted the memory of generations of Americans.

The practical circumstances of travel have also been a spur to sexual activity. Journeying in cramped coaches, eating at communal tables, sleeping in public inns all contributed to the sense of opportunity. Casanova refers approvingly to 'those very free *tête-à-têtes* afforded by travel', and E.S. Bates's *Touring in 1600* mentions a much reprinted work of the seventeenth century, *Traité de la civilité qui se pratique parmi les honnêtes gens*, which laid down the etiquette to be followed if, like Laurence Sterne in *A Sentimental Journey*, you happened to be sharing a bedroom with a stranger of the opposite sex. This has been a feature of tourism since it first entered British culture with the medieval pilgrimage. In his *Travel in Early Modern Europe* (1978), Antoni Mączak concludes from the diaries and memoirs of the period that 'travel somehow unleashed interests, which had been previously suppressed and, in a general sense, allowed the traveller greater sexual freedom'. It is no accident that Chaucer's amorous Wife of Bath was the most sexually knowledgeable member of the group and also its most experienced pilgrim. As early as the eighth century, St Boniface blames foreign pilgrimages for the fact that 'there are few cities in Lombardy, or France, or Gaul in which there is not an adulteress or prostitute of the English nation'.

But neither the practical links nor the imaginative ones have had much impact on discussions of the history of tourism. This is both because the tourists themselves have presented their travels as a cultural narrative rather than a sexual one – letters home commonly tell of the churches visited, not the brothels – and also because tourism is an approved social activity that needs to guard its own respectability. In so far as sex is recognised as an aspect of tourism, the response takes two forms. From one direction, it is argued that people have always taken advantage of foreign travel for sex but that this scarcely warrants attention since it's no more than an after-hours truancy, marginal to the real concerns of tourism – what Boswell got up to after dark may be mildly interesting but it tells us nothing significant about the Grand Tour. Alternatively, there is the argument that sex is of course linked to tourism, but to the special, modern and unacceptable kind we call sex tourism, readily distinguishable from the sort of mainstream tourism that engages the rest of us. In answer to these points, I have set out to make the following case: first, far from being marginal to what tourism is about, the sexual element is vital to it. If we want to understand the Grand Tour and its relation to modern tourism, it is quite as important to take account of Boswell's visits to Dresden streetwalkers and Venetian courtesans as of his visits to the Dresden picture gallery and the Doge's Palace. Second, the convenient line between sex tourism and mainstream tourism does more to obscure reality than define it. Historically, the tourist's sexual interests have been a reflection of corresponding cultural interests. Because we like to pretend they are separate, the history of tourism has left out the sex, and contemporary responses to sex tourism have left out the history.

Both these arguments imply a degree of scepticism about the current orthodoxy which sees sex tourism as a malign extension of the sexual urge, doubly dangerous because it escapes the sanctions of home. Instead, we might consider the possibility that sex tourism expresses the impulses of the tourist as much as those of the sexual predator. This approach does not make the business of travelling for sex more or less acceptable, nor does it say anything about the lot of those who provide the sexual services, but it does bring the underlying imperatives of sex and travel very much closer together. In this, it perhaps also exposes realities about the nature of tourism that are usually veiled by the rhetoric of cultural and personal benefit.

Modern sex tourism in fact plays little part in the chapters that follow, for its entry into the mass-market has added nothing to what is revealed by earlier travellers; but the questions it raises have obvious relevance. Most of the figures with a major role in this book behaved in ways that now excite public indignation: they went abroad and paid for sex, often with young people. It is pointless either to disguise this fact or to dress it up as something else. I have no interest in writing an apology for eighteenth- and nineteenth-century sex tourism, but nor do I intend to spend much time condemning it. Adult readers can presumably make their own moral judgements without reassurance from the author. For what it's worth, I find some of the behaviour described repulsive, some not; but I am suspicious of moral outrage that finds sexual targets more congenial than others. Why, for example, does sexual exploitation trouble us so much more than the various kinds of exploitation that provide us with cheaper consumer goods? The process by which other people's lives are blighted for our convenience is not, after all, peculiar to the sex trade.

The truth is perhaps that we have adopted sex tourism as a lightning conductor for guilt that might otherwise taint the rest of society. At a comfortable distance from the seedy world of pimps and prostitutes and shifty men in floral shirts, we can deplore this rough commerce in human beings, confident of our own moral decency. In doing so, we fail to grasp that it is only the most visible expression of a relationship between travel and sex that reaches far deeper. What lies below the surface is the subject of this book. Two things, I hope, will emerge: first, the strength of a continuing thread of experience which has for the most part been neglected or ignored, and second, a sense of how closely this sexual thread is intertwined with the same imaginative impulses that have motivated cultural tourism. One way or another, the erotic lines of force that have run through our habits of travel since the eighteenth century involve all of us who go abroad for pleasure.

A word perhaps needs to be said about the definition of tourism. In commercial terms, it can include more or less any excursion from the place where one normally lives and works; but my concern here is not with people who travel in their own country or who go abroad as a requirement of their job. I use the word to cover foreign travel that is undertaken voluntarily and for personal rather than professional reasons. It does not greatly bother me that this will sometimes overlap with exile, or that it makes no contribution to the sterile debate about distinctions between traveller and tourist. More regrettable is the need to leave out the kinds of semi-tourist experience associated with business travel, military service, colonial administration and the like; they would have expanded the book too far. As for historical boundaries, there has been tourism of a sort since classical times, but modern tourism may reasonably be said to date from the spread of the Grand Tour in the eighteenth century. That is what I have taken as my starting point.

PART ONE

Connoisseurs

I

The Unofficial Tour

In 1996 the Tate Gallery mounted an exhibition with the title *Grand Tour: The Lure of Italy in the Eighteenth Century*. It ranged widely across different features of the Tour, offering persuasive confirmation that this was one of the great cultural enterprises of the eighteenth century. 'The main purpose of the Grand Tour,' according to the catalogue, 'was to experience and study foreign cultures and incorporate aspects of them into one's own society.' Over two hundred and fifty paintings and sculptures had been brought together to reinforce the message in a handsome parade of aristocratic wealth and taste. Richly dressed young nobles posed against a background of Roman ruins, fashionable tourists were pictured contemplating works of art, majestic landscapes offered the spectator a dignified window on classical antiquity. It was an exhibition the travellers themselves would have been happy to sponsor. In a sense that's what they had done, since these were the paintings they had commissioned and the objects they had bought; it was the version of the Grand Tour they had bequeathed to the world.

Or it would have been, if the exhibition catalogue had not kept casting faint shadows across this serene display, hints of just the kind of discrepancy referred to at the start of the Introduction. On one page it was a comment from Lady Mary Wortley Montagu that the young tourists 'only remember where they met with the best Wine or the prettyest Women', on another a reminder that the caricaturist Thomas Patch had been expelled from Rome for 'homosexual indiscretion', elsewhere a note that the tutor of the young 8th Duke of Hamilton 'had some difficulty in restraining his charge's amorous adventures'. Trivial observations, but also signs of a reality that was hard to discern among the pictures on exhibition. And then there was the Frenchman Charles de Brosses, who arrived in Rome in November 1739 to find it seething with English. 'The money the English spend in Rome and their custom of making a journey there as part of their education is of scant benefit to the majority of them,' he wrote, adding that there were some 'who will leave the city without having seen anyone but other Englishmen and without knowing where the Colosseum is.' So much for experiencing and studying foreign cultures. To have yourself painted in front of the Colosseum was apparently no guarantee of an inclination to visit it. The English tourists of whom de Brosses was writing – 'the majority' – seem to have had concerns rather different from either the cultural pursuits captured on canvas or the 'understanding of international politics and the acquisition of valuable contacts' which the catalogue tells us was the other important goal of the Tour. For these tourists the lure of Italy obviously lay elsewhere, in attractions quite unrepresented by the exhibits in the Tate. It is this gap in the record that I would like to explore.

Since the early Middle Ages the roads of Europe had seen a varied traffic of princes, pilgrims, pedlars, scholars, merchants, masons, diplomats and assorted hangers-on. A glance at the range of travel writing before the eighteenth century turns up accounts by travellers from all over the Continent, and whatever their avowed purpose, many of them were clearly prompted as much by tourist curiosity as by any practical consideration. A Polish cleric on the way to Italy, an eccentric Englishman tramping across Europe on foot, a French politician gathering information about the Spanish economy – all of them were tourists of a sort, but in an incidental fashion.* What distinguished the Grand Tour from earlier forms of travel was its elevation of tourism among the British aristocracy to the status of a cultural institution. The term itself is first recorded in Richard Lassels' *The Voyage of Italy* (1670), though twenty years earlier the diarist John Evelyn had been able to talk of a traveller on a journey through Europe 'making the tour as they call it'. From being simply descriptive of common tourist practice, this concept of the Tour became through the second half of the seventeenth century increasingly *pre*scriptive. Male, upper-class and predominantly English, it defined an experience of travel that was argued by many to be essential to the proper education of a gentleman. There was no set route for the Grand Tour and no fixed duration, but in general it was expected to last at least a couple of years and to include France, Switzerland and Italy, probably taking in Germany and the Netherlands on the way home.

By the early eighteenth century, this period of foreign travel was a recognised feature of British aristocratic life. The purpose envisaged for it was summed up by the scholar and antiquarian Thomas Nugent in his popular guidebook, *The Grand Tour* (1749): 'to enrich the mind with knowledge, to rectify the judgement, to remove the prejudices of education, to compose the outward manners, and in a word to form the complete gentleman'. This is the official version of the Tour. Its stated aim is educative: the young man, usually accompanied by a tutor, his so-called 'bearleader', sets out on his travels to observe, to discriminate, to improve. The validity of the journey is measured in terms of things seen, learnt and collected. On his return, the tourist will be able to lay claim to at

---

* Stanisław Reszka, travelling in the late sixteenth century, Thomas Coryate in the early seventeenth and François Bertaud (or Bertaut) in the mid-seventeenth are picked at random – very different figures, each of whom left an account of his travels.

least the basic elements of connoisseurship – a word that found its way into the language at just the time the Grand Tour was entering its heyday. His business abroad has been to school himself socially and to acquire the cultural capital that will define him as a civilised person. In establishing the identity of tourist-as-connoisseur, the Tour gives a pattern to what has remained the standard form of culturally approved tourism. Today's guidebook, with its list of monuments and its advice on local purchases, is a direct descendant of Nugent's.

But from the start there was another side to the project, glimpsed in those extracts from the Tate Gallery's *Grand Tour* catalogue. It was noted by Lassels in his Preface to *The Voyage of Italy*: 'Others desire to go into *Italy*, onely because they heare there are fine *Curtisanes* in Venice . . . these men travel a whole month together, to *Venice*, for a nights lodgeing with an impudent woman. And thus by a false ayming at breeding abroad, they returne with those diseases which hinder them from breeding at home.' The pun on breeding nicely plays off the social agenda against the sexual. Though the tourists themselves may have had little to say about it, there is plenty of evidence from elsewhere to confirm this more ambiguous version of the Tour. Its twin aspects were epitomised by Alexander Pope in his picture of the typical Grand Tourist:

> . . . he saunter'd Europe round,
> And gather'd ev'ry Vice on Christian ground;
> Saw ev'ry Court, heard ev'ry King declare
> His royal Sense, of Op'ra's or the Fair;
> The Stews and Palace equally explor'd,
> Intrigu'd with glory, and with spirit whor'd;

This is the figure who remains invisible in the tourists' own accounts of decorous hospitality and dutiful sightseeing but who regularly turns up in the accounts of critical third parties. Eighteenth-century polemics point repeatedly to young travellers who are 'immers'd in all manner of Lewdness and Debauchery', who 'acquire neither Virtue nor Learning, but Habits of all sorts of Debauchery, as we are taught by every day's experience', who go abroad 'to get ill Habits or foul Diseases . . . and to fall at last into ill Company or the worst Corruptions of all Virtue, Justice and Religion'.

It was these fears that sustained the long-running argument about the benefits and dangers of the Tour. The problem lay partly in just the worthy objectives that Nugent outlined with such confidence. The educative functions that he stresses make it clear that at one level the Tour was intended to act as a rite of passage: the traveller went out an unformed youth and came back a 'complete gentleman'. And it's equally clear that there was a tacitly understood sexual dimension to this process. Lord Chesterfield's letters leave no doubt that liaisons of the right sort could be regarded as an appropriate educational aspect of the Tour. He was hopeful, for example, that they might help to make something of his illegitimate and rather unpromising son, Lord Stanhope: 'The Princess of Borghese was so kind as to put him a little upon his haunches, by putting him frequently upon her own. Nothing dresses a young fellow more than having been between such pillars, with an experienced mistress . . .' His letters to Stanhope betray an anxious parental concern that he should make best use of the sexual opportunities around him on the Tour: 'if you have [an attachment], *il faut bien payer d'attentions et de petits soins*, if you would have your sacrifice propitiously received'; 'tell me . . . , if you will trust me with so important an affair, what *belle passion* inflames you'; 'Have you *un goût vif*, or a passion for any body? I do not ask for whom; an Iphigenia would both give you the desire, and teach you the means to please.'

Sexual liaisons of one sort or another were to be expected. '*Un arrangement*,' Chesterfield writes, 'which is in plain English a gallantry, is, at Paris, as necessary a part of a woman of fashion's establishment, as her house, table, coach, etc. A young fellow must therefore be a very awkward one to be reduced to, or of a very singular taste, to prefer drabs and danger to a commerce (in the course of the world not disgraceful) with a woman of health, education, and rank.' Not everyone would have taken such a relaxed attitude as Chesterfield, or been willing to make it so explicit, but his views reflect a reality of the Tour.

The difficulty was to draw a line between the acceptable and the unacceptable. From a parent's perspective, the distinction between drabs and danger on the one hand and 'a woman of health, education, and rank' on the other is crucial. To a youth in his teens, the same distinction is likely to carry less weight. On the loose for the first time, he may even find the dangerous drab a more enticing proposition than the society hostess. Chesterfield's surprise that a young nobleman of his acquaintance should have been 'reduced to keep an opera whore in such a place as Paris, where so many women of fashion generously serve as volunteers', shows uncharacteristic obtuseness. Women of fashion may have much to recommend them, but for a young and privileged tourist the opera whore would have other sorts of glamour.

Chesterfield himself is at other times well aware of this. Picturing his son in Rome, a model of studious youth, he recognises that as such the boy would be in sharp contrast to many of his compatriots – 'a number of idle, sauntering, illiterate English, as there commonly is there, living entirely with one another, supping, drinking, and sitting up late at each other's lodgings; commonly in riots and scrapes when drunk; and never in good company when sober.' He imagines Stanhope resisting the temptation to ill company with the argument that modest women at least do one no harm, which is more than can be said of the other sort. To this the Englishman briskly replies, 'That's true, I own; but, for all that, I would rather keep company with my surgeon, half the year, than with your women of fashion the year round'. Sexually transmitted disease was an occupational hazard of the Grand Tour, and the surgeon (i.e. physician), who would probably have prescribed an uncomfortable course of mercury treatment, was an essential member of the supporting cast. 'Some of our Company did purchase their repentance at a deare rate, after their returne,' wrote John Evelyn, commenting on the appeal of the Neapolitan courtesans. As the historian Jeremy Black puts it, 'A long series of distinguished tourists remembered their travels for years afterwards for reasons that bore little relation to the restrained portraits by Batoni that decorated their libraries.'

If critics of the Tour dwell with particular venom on the prevalence of disease, it is because one of the main functions of the Grand Tourist when he got home was to breed sons to continue the family line – Lassels's warning about Venetian courtesans went to the heart of the problem. But the company of women of fashion was no guarantee of a better outcome. 'I don't doubt,' noted one British tourist, 'but a great many of our gentlemen travellers have reason enough to be cross on account of some modish distemper the Italian ladies may have bestowed on them with the rest of their favours.'

These would have been the sort of gentlemen travellers who, unable to speak any language but English, descended in droves on Lady Mary Wortley Montagu's home in Venice, 'their whole business abroad (as far as I can perceive) being to buy new cloaths, in which they shine in some obscure coffee-house, where they are sure of meeting only one another; and after the important conquest of some waiting gentlewoman of an Opera Queen, who perhaps they remember as long as they live, return to England excellent judges of men and manners'. Later in the century Tobias Smollett published his *Travels through France and Italy* (1766), which contains a sketch of the Grand Tourist that points up how far reality tended to diverge from the ideal:

I have seen in different parts of Italy, a number of raw boys, whom Britain seemed to have poured forth on purpose to bring her national character into contempt: ignorant, petulant, rash, and profligate, without any knowledge or experience of their own, without any director to improve their understanding, or superintend their conduct. One engages in play with an infamous gamester, and is stripped perhaps in the very first partie: another is poxed and pillaged by an antiquated canta- trice: a third is bubbled by a knavish antiquarian; and a fourth is laid under contribution by a dealer in pictures. Some turn fiddlers, and pretend to compose: but all of them talk familiarly of the arts, and return finished con- noisseurs and coxcombs, to their own country.

As Montagu and Smollett suggest, the cantatrice, or opera singer, has a starring role in the Grand Tour throughout the century. Writing to James Boswell in 1764, with quaintly mis- placed faith in his romantic sensitivity, the Reverend Charles de Guiffardière warns him that if he goes to France he must devote himself to courting women of fashion, 'Otherwise you will see nothing but cabarets and *filles de joie*. I well know that many of your countrymen are reduced to that, but you have too much delicacy and taste to plunge into that kind of debauchery.' Nonetheless, he imagines Boswell in Paris, 'flying away to the opera in a chariot blazing with gold, to frolic with the prettiest of actresses behind the scenes'. Twenty years on, William Bennet writes from Paris of 'Madame de Gazon, a lively little opera singer well known to many young Englishmen who have shared her favours, and as *Gazon* sig- nifies turf, are said by the wits to have been on the *turf*'.

Smollett's reference to 'raw boys' highlights an aspect of the rite of passage that was of persistent concern to moralists: the youths sent out to become men were often just that – raw boys. In *Some Thoughts Concerning Education* (1693), Locke had specified the normal age for those undertaking the Grand Tour as 'from Sixteen to One and Twenty', and the tourists' youth was a flashpoint for hostility to the Tour. Bishop Hurd's *Dialogue on the Uses of Foreign Travel* (1764) puts into Locke's mouth a complaint against the dangerous combination of 'raw, ignorant, ungovernable boys, on the one hand, and of shallow, servile, and interested governors, on the other'. These, according to *The Gentleman's Calling* (1660), were the adolescent travellers who, through their governors' negligence or their own headiness, 'run a full career in all debaucht pleasures'. 'It is evident', wrote Thomas Sheridan in *British Education* (1756), 'that there can be no greater evil than the sending our youth abroad at so improper and dangerous a season'. Thomas Brand is still making the same point at the end of the century when he inveighs against the practice of sending 'not young men, but *boys* to travel through Europe', with the result that they are 'launched into vicious society before they know even any theory of virtue and morality'.

The assumption is that older travellers will have acquired a more solid grounding in native morality and thus be better able to resist the temptations of a foreign land; but this cuts across another central objective of the Tour – the idea that it will, in Nugent's words, 'remove the prejudices of education'. The point is made in a letter that Boswell's friend William Johnson Temple sent him a few days before his departure for the Continent in 1763:

> You have a fine prospect before you. You set out with a genteel allowance, and with letters of recommendation to several persons of fortune and character. Your end is the improvement of your mind. You go to rid yourself of ill-habits and of national prejudices, to fix upon a system of conduct, to acquire a knowledge of foreign literature, to examine the laws, manners and customs of different nations, and to compare them with those of your own; you go to qualify yourself against your return, to act a part in life, and to be of service to your country.

Like Nugent, Temple sees the trip as a formative experience,* and this emphasis marks a slight but significant departure from earlier notions of the kind Francis Bacon was expressing at the end of the sixteenth century in his essay 'Of Travel'. Bacon too sees travel as educational, but his formidable list of 'things to be seen and observed' implies little personal involvement in the process. His concern is with a checklist of objects and institutions – courts, churches, fortifications, antiquities, libraries, colleges, shipping, arsenals and so on – whereas Temple stresses a programme of self-development: the study of foreign manners and customs is part of the general project to 'rid yourself of ill-habits and of national prejudices' and 'to fix upon a system of conduct'. Bacon certainly expects the traveller to gain personal advantages from his experience, but it's clear that the function of information-gathering is essentially public. What develops across the following century and a half is a concept of private travel for enjoyment and personal improvement. The public function is still there – Boswell is qualifying himself to act a part in life and to be of service to his country – but its sustaining impulse is private.

The effect of this is to aggravate what has always been the greatest source of unease for moralists: travel tends to undermine moral absolutes. Montaigne noted in his essay on cannibals that we have no hold on truth and reason other than what comes from the customs and beliefs of our native country. It's a point that applies equally to our standards of social behaviour. Tyrants never like their subjects to travel: as long as there are no grounds of comparison, there is no basis from which to challenge the existing order. Anything that provides images of a different way of life poses a potential threat. The banning of

---

* This earnest letter was followed by another from Temple three weeks later (23 August) which shows the reverse side of the coin by quizzing Boswell, in a series of *double entendres*, about the sexual opportunities of Holland.

travel goes hand in hand with the banning of books and the censorship of other sources of information. To invite the traveller to 'examine the laws, manners and customs of different nations, and to compare them with those of your own', or even just to 'remove the prejudices of education', is a risky undertaking.

In terms of social and political organisation, the confident eighteenth-century assumption that comparisons are bound to work to the advantage of England was probably well-founded. Few of the tourists were likely to quarrel with a system that had put them at the top of the pyramid. But in terms of personal behaviour, there was no guarantee at all that foreign customs might not seem rather more attractive than one's own. If nothing else, comparison shows up the provisional nature of any particular cultural arrangement, and by making it the traveller's business to compare, the Grand Tour had opened another door to moral truancy.

No doubt there were many who fulfilled the programme of the official Tour, led blameless lives, learned foreign languages, acquired valuable knowledge of cities and societies, refined their artistic taste and generally did everything people claimed to have done when they wrote home, but the temptations of the unofficial Tour were strong. And they were supported by a sophisticated infrastructure. The Grand Tour had rapidly mobilised a disreputable army with its own interest in encouraging the traveller's natural tendencies. Philip Thicknesse, a former soldier with a somewhat prickly temperament ('he would sniff an injury from afar', remarked one contemporary), was into his fifties when he made his European journey in 1776, but he was alert to the moral pitfalls awaiting younger compatriots. By this time, the tourist visiting any of the major towns between London and Rome ran a well-established gauntlet of sexual temptation, orchestrated by 'artful, designing, wicked men, and profligate, abandoned, and prostitute women', whose traps were 'principally set to catch the young

Englishman of fortune from the age of eighteen to five and twenty.' According to Thicknesse, they were on the lookout for 'every *bird of passage* – but particularly the English *gold-finch*'. The arts by which the gold-finch is snared have changed so little over the centuries that Thicknesse's account is worth summarising.

The minute one of these young men arrives at either Paris or Lyon, some *laquais de place* has been paid to pass the word. The tourist is soon accosted by a charming French Marquis or English *Chevalier* who shows him the sights, accompanies him to Versailles and Marly, and generally convinces him that he has found a friend. The Chevalier 'carries him to see French Ladies of the *first distinction*, (and such who certainly *live in that style*) and makes the young man giddy with joy'. At play after supper the tourist wins a few guineas and promptly uses them to buy a trifle for the Countess. She is quite ashamed of the trouble he has given himself – 'but, says she, you Englishmen are so charming, – so generous, . . . and so . . . so . . . and looks so sweet upon him, that while her tongue faulters, *egad* he ventures to cover her confusion by a kiss; – when, instead of giving him the two broad sides of her cheek, she is so *off her guard*, and so overcome, as to present him *unawares*, with a pretty handsome dash of red pomatum, from her lovely pouting lips, – and insists upon it that he sups with her, *tete a tete*, that very evening, – when all this happiness is compleated.' What follows is entirely predictable to everyone but the young man himself. A few nights later, after drinking too much at supper with the Countess, he is stripped of all his money at play. Next day the Countess coolly advises him to leave Paris and head south, where in due course another stage of his ruin is accomplished.

This is not, Thicknesse assures us, an imaginary picture; it depicts the reality into which fond parents in England are sending their sons: 'Upon the whole, I think it is next to an impossibility for a young man of fortune to pass a year or two in *Paris*, the southern parts of France, Italy, &c. without running a great risque of being beggared by sharpers, or seduced by artful women.' The only safeguard is a wise and knowledgeable tutor. In confirmation of the moral dangers that await the traveller, he describes his own, quite innocent, visit to a picture shop in Lyon, where the pretty wife of the shopkeeper produces from her prayer-book 'a picture, so indecent, that I defy the most debauched imagination to conceive any thing more so'. After examining it with some attention, Thicknesse allows himself to be led by the woman into a bedroom hung with pornographic pictures, not one of which 'would not have brought a blush in the face of an English Lady, even of the most easy virtue'.

The depravity of Continental morals is evidenced as much by the casualness of the woman and her other customers as by the pictures themselves. Erotic interests are a matter of course.* Thicknesse concludes his letter with the account of a French gentleman in the same neighbourhood who, having invited a young English nobleman to spend the day at his château, 'took occasion to tell his Lordship, that in order to render the day as agreeable as possible to his company, he had provided some young people of *both sexes* to attend, and desired to know his Lordship's *gout*'. When the same question was put to the rest of the company in order of rank, the last 'an *humble Frenchman*, replied, it was to him *egal l'un et l'autre*, just as it proved most convenient'. Anecdotes of this kind are offered by English writers partly to stress the moral gulf that separates one side of the Channel from the other but also because they do in fact indicate the sexual context within which the Grand Tour took place. In this case the young nobleman tells his host 'that he was not fashionable enough to

---

* One of the first things Dr John Polidori noticed on his arrival in Ostend with Lord Byron was 'books in every bookseller's window of the most obscene nature' (Polidori, 33).

walk out of the paths of nature', but the episode is a useful reminder that the erotic opportunities of the Tour were homosexual as well as heterosexual.

What Thicknesse gives us is a snapshot of the correspondences between the cultural focus of the Grand Tour and its sexual focus. As a rite of passage it leads to the pursuit of sexual initiation; as a display of economic power it invites the attention of sexual predators; as an acquisitive project it lends itself to the sampling of sexual as well as cultural products; and as a revelation of foreign life-styles it encourages the adoption of foreign sexual mores.

Throughout the eighteenth and nineteenth centuries there was one dominant feature of European travel that reinforced these correspondences: its primary destination was Italy. In 1617, right at the start of the vogue for European tourism, Bishop Joseph Hall had summed up the problem: 'The world is wide and open, but our ordinarie travell is southward, into the jawes of danger: for so farre hath Satan's policie prevailed, that those parts which are onely thought worth our viewing are most contagious.' Hall's concern here is primarily religious, but he had voiced a fear about the Janus face of Mediterranean travel that would resonate through the next three centuries. The cultural pivot of British tourism, the home of Europe's greatest artistic treasures, was also, notoriously, the home of every kind of sexual iniquity. To follow the cultural agenda of the Tour was to put oneself in the way of sexual temptation. 'This Italy is indeed a Sink of Sin,' wrote Johnson's friend, Mrs Thrale; 'and whoever lives long in it, *must* be a little tainted.' 'This Italy' – no other country has been so long and consistently associated with erotic freedom. From the Renaissance until well into the twentieth century its identity for British travellers was shaped by a reputation for transgressive pleasure that stretched back to the more colourful Roman emperors. In particular, there was the native inclination to 'beastly sodomy', from which, according to the Scottish traveller William Lithgow at the start of the seventeenth century, not one of the cities was exempt, 'nor yet the smallest village of Italy'. This was the proclivity that Mrs Thrale had in mind, and it had been a common theme among earlier commentators. In 1699 the Dean of Norwich complained of a young man returning from the Tour 'all over Italiz'd . . . an Italian I doubt [i.e. suspect] in his moralls, for he cannot be perswaded to marry'. A couple of years later, in 'The True-Born Englishman' (1701), Daniel Defoe caught the prevailing attitude when he matched a series of countries with their characteristic sin: '*Lust* chose the Torrid Zone of Italy,/Where Blood ferments in Rapes and Sodomy.'

The national threat posed by homosexuality was enlarged upon at length in an early eighteenth-century tract roundly entitled *Plain Reasons for the Growth of Sodomy in England* (c. 1728). Its author paints a nostalgic picture of the full-blooded English youth of former times who was accustomed to the healthy rough and tumble of school life ('No matter if his Hands and Face were now and then a little Dirty, so his Understanding was clean') as against the present-day specimen who is molly-coddled, taught dancing and exposed to effeminate customs from abroad – 'none more hateful, predominant and pernicious than that of Men's *Kissing* each other. This *Fashion* was brought over from *Italy*, (the *Mother* and *Nurse* of *Sodomy*).' The French are included in his censure, notably the French nuns, who are 'criminally *amorous* of each other, in a *Method* too gross for Expression', but it is Italy, the goal of increasing numbers of young English travellers, that is the real target of his attack:

> How famous, or rather infamous *Italy* has been in all Ages, and still continues in the Odious Practice of *Sodomy* needs no explanation, it is there esteemed so trivial, and withal so modish a Sin, that not a Cardinal

nor Churchman but has his *Ganymede*; no sooner does a
Stranger of Condition set his Foot in *Rome*, but he is surrounded by a Crowd of *Pandars*, who ask him if he chuses
a *Woman* or a *Boy*, and procure for him accordingly.

Though sodomy might be reckoned the nation's speciality,
Italy was associated generally with sex and sensuality. Venice,
above all. During nine days there in the mid-sixteenth
century, the scholar Roger Ascham, who acted as private tutor
to Queen Elizabeth I, claimed to have found 'more libertie to
sinne, than ever I heard tell of in our noble Citie of London
in ix yeare', a point echoed a century and a half later by
another traveller, Charles Baldwyn, who observed in 1712 that
the 'whole City may well be term'd the Brothell house of
Europe'. The mythology surrounding Venice's courtesans was
part of the shared culture of the Tour. The city is one of the
principal resorts of Pope's dissipated tourist. 'But chief her
shrine where naked Venus keeps,/And Cupids ride the Lyon
of the Deeps'. The reference to naked Venus is itself a pun on
the city's name, since eighteenth-century pronunciation
brought the two conveniently together. But Venice's association with Venus long pre-dated the Grand Tour. From the fif-
teenth century onwards travellers were bringing back reports
of the number and beauty of its courtesans – 'the best flesh-
shambles in Italy', as it is called in John Day's *Humour out of
Breath* (1608). Thomas Coryate put the number of courtesans
in the early seventeenth century at twenty thousand, 'whereof
many are esteemed so loose, that they are said to open their
quivers to every arrow'. While insisting that he himself visited
them merely 'to see the manner of their life, and observe their
behaviour', and noting that every other writer on Venice has
kept quiet about them, he nonetheless makes it clear that their
services were a major tourist attraction: 'For so infinite are the
allurements of these amorous Calypsoes, that the fame of them
hath drawn many to Venice from some of the remotest parts

of Christendome, to contemplate their beauties, and enjoy their pleasing dalliances.'

No one setting out for Italy in the seventeenth or eighteenth century could be unaware of this background. Sensual abandon was part of the country's history, climate and geography. As Goldsmith put it, with a suitably moral disclaimer: 'But small the bliss that sense alone bestows,/And sensual bliss is all the nation knows'. Less piously Byron declared in *Beppo*: 'With all its sinful doings, I must say,/That Italy's a pleasant place to me'. The sinful doings are part of the pleasantness, an element of the region's imaginative landscape that is inseparable from its classical and artistic heritage. It was this heady mixture of the cultural and the sexual that constituted the real 'lure of Italy' and exercised a shaping influence on the character of the Grand Tour. To see what it meant in practice, we can look more closely at the travels of one particular tourist.

2

The Travels of James Boswell

Case studies in this area are not easy to come by. Published accounts of the Tour rarely went into details that would be likely to reflect discredit on the writer, and private papers tended to fall into the hands of family or friends who were more careful of the writer's good name than of posterity's claim to the truth. This is the basis on which a sanitised version of the Tour gets handed down to later generations. We are therefore doubly fortunate to have the writings of James Boswell. More vividly than any of the Tour's critics, he conveys the sexual undertow not just of eighteenth-century tourism but of the whole strand of tourism I have associated with the ideal of the connoisseur. Boswell was far from being the pathetic gull described by Thicknesse, but he demonstrates with wonderful candour what Thicknesse had identified – the sexual corollaries of the four main cultural functions of the Tour: as a rite of passage, as an exposure to different social mores, as an opportunity for collecting artefacts, and as a display of the tourist's (and his nation's) economic power.

First, the rite of passage. At twenty-two Boswell was older than most of those who undertook the Grand Tour. He had already twice exchanged his native Scotland for the excitements of London. On the first occasion he had run away to become a Roman Catholic monk, before rapidly discovering seductions of another kind: the social and literary life of the capital, freedom from parental constraint, and, at the Blue Periwig in Southampton Street, 'the melting and transporting rites of love'. After three months of dissipation he returned home having abandoned Roman Catholicism but contracted gonorrhoea. Over the next two years relations with his father, a prominent Scottish judge and the Laird of Auchinleck, worsened to the point where the Laird threatened to disinherit him. His desultory study of the law took second place to rakish diversions in Edinburgh, the writing of indifferent verse and dreams of getting a commission in the Guards. By the time he got his father's reluctant consent to go back to London, Boswell was on the point of becoming a father himself, after an affair with a 'curious young little pretty' called Peggy Doig. In the course of the following nine months, the period recorded in his *London Journal*, he plunged again into the pleasures of the capital. Well connected, personable and talented, he had no difficulty in broadening the range of his literary and social acquaintance. The young man who set out for Utrecht was supposedly destined for the law, and had indeed passed his exam in Civil Law before leaving Scotland, but his heart was elsewhere.

On the face of it, Boswell's Tour got off to a textbook start. He had travelled from London to Harwich with the great Dr Johnson, he had discussed with him the programme of study to be followed when he reached Utrecht, he had said his prayers at the local church. On an August evening in 1763 he and Johnson walked down to the beach, where they 'embraced and parted with tenderness'. Boswell went aboard and from the deck looked back at his revered friend: 'As the vessel put out to sea, I kept my eyes upon him for a considerable time, while he remained rolling his majestic frame in his usual manner: and at last I perceived him walk back into the town, and he disappeared.' Despite the note of melancholy, it was an auspicious departure. The ideals of the Grand Tour, restated a few days earlier in the letter from William Temple, were fresh in Boswell's mind.

What followed can be divided into three distinct periods covering just under two and a half years. First, ten months' study in Holland, then six months travelling in Germany and Switzerland, and finally, climactically, a year spent mostly in Italy, with a few crucial weeks in Corsica and a return journey through France. It is the Utrecht period that most clearly highlights the tension between the educational objectives of the Tour and its function as a rite of passage. As Temple had indicated, Boswell was going to Holland for the improvement of his mind, and his journal in the week before he leaves is peppered with reminders of the fact: 'Resolve now study in earnest . . . Learn to be reserved . . . Prepare like Father . . . Mark this and keep in pocket . . . You have a worthy father whose happiness depends on your behaving so as at least to give no offence . . . Be reserved and calm, and sustain a consistent character . . . get into grave humour for journey, and write out instructions . . . Set out for Harwich like Father, grave and comfortable . . . Be in earnest to improve. It is not you alone concerned, but your worthy father . . . Go abroad with a manly resolution to improve, and correspond with Johnson . . . See to attain a fixed and consistent character, to have dignity.' And so on. The overpowering presence of his father in this programme is obvious; but the aim of the rite of passage is precisely to mark adult independence from the parent. Even if Boswell's relationship with his father had been less stormy than it was, those repeated references would still have seemed a little strained.

Within hours of his arrival in Utrecht the cracks had begun to appear. Almost at once Boswell fell into the sort of black melancholy that afflicted him periodically throughout his life. The problem had less to do with being abroad than with being in Utrecht. 'My enthusiastic love of London,' he explained in a letter to a friend, 'made me leave it with a heavy heart. It might not have been the case, had I been setting out on an immediate tour thro' the gay regions of Italy and France. But to comply with my Father's inclinations . . .' Utrecht is heavy with the deadening weight of paternal approval; the gay regions of Italy and France are the proper destination of the young Grand

Tourist. And when another friend, George Dempster, the MP for the Perth burghs, heard of his plight, he suggested that rather than staying in Utrecht Boswell would do better to go to a French academy. 'In the mean time, I should think you might amuse yourself in acquiring the French, keeping a journal and writing your friends, and debauching a Dutch girl.'

This was just the sort of advice that Boswell in more robust spirits might have been happy to take, but his stay in Holland, from August 1763 to June 1764, is marked by unusual sobriety. It is almost as though his journey from London to Utrecht, instead of taking him further from his father, has brought him more deeply into the Laird's shadow. The daunting programmes of study he laid out for himself, the fierce injunctions against backsliding, the occasional words of self-commendation all tell the same story. Boswell in Holland is doing his best to be the dutiful traveller that his earnest memoranda directed him to be. His studies are leavened by a teasing relationship with the delightful Belle de Zuylen, the intellectual and unconventional daughter of one of the governors of the Province, and by a brief and unconsummated passion for a young Dutch widow, but these are innocent enough distractions. In the words of his biographer, 'During those ten months he was by heroic effort modest, studious, frugal, reserved, and chaste.'

He is rowing against the tide. The attempt to please his father is under increasing strain from the contrary impulses of the youthful traveller. And the focus of these impulses is invariably sexual. On the day he records the arrival of 'excellent letter from worthy father', he notes 'Think if GOD really forbids girls', and a week later, 'Maintain character gained at Utrecht, nor ever rave. Mem. Father. If you whore, all ideas change.' Two or three times at this stage of the journal, entries that begin to broach sexual possibilities have been crossed out, as though he feels the need to censor even his thoughts. Amsterdam is never far from his mind. 'Go not to Amsterdam,' he notes on 21st March. 'Read more law. Write Father neat clear little letter.' But the weeks of intermittent melancholy take their toll. 'Whore not except fine; Amsterdam, private',* he tells himself, indicating the attraction of Amsterdam's anonymity. The journal entry for 21 May concludes: 'Also go to Amsterdam and try Dutch girl Friday, and see what moderate Venus will do.' The following day: 'No Amsterdam yet. *Retenue* [Restraint].'

Desperate to break loose, he could never quite manage it. The sexual adventures which would be his assertion of independence were blocked by the requirements of the dutiful son. Even when the trip to Amsterdam came off, it turned into a curiously half-hearted affair. The 'sweet and lively' thoughts with which he started the journey quickly gave way to gloom, and by the time he got to his lodging in the city, he was feeling restless and fretful. That afternoon he duly headed for a brothel, but the combined stimulants of a girl and a bottle of claret failed to stir him – 'so sickly was my brain that I had the low scruples of an Edinburgh divine'. Later he went on to a music house, 'but could find no girl that elicited my inclinations'. The next day, Sunday, he was due to return home. After two visits to church, he went for yet another inconclusive encounter with the city's low-life: 'I then strolled through mean brothels in dirty lanes. I was quite splenetic. I still wanted armour [condom].' By the early hours of Monday morning he was back in Utrecht, 'changeful and uneasy', without having found any sexual release.

The fact is that Boswell had not really started travelling yet. Utrecht was a ten-month purgatory imposed by his father as a condition of being allowed to travel. The journal for this period shows the whole context of his life governed by his father's will. Even the two relationships mentioned above were framed by a dominant concern with marriage. Boswell was

---

* i.e. only frequent the better sort of whore, and do it in Amsterdam where you are not known.

trying hard to persuade himself to leave behind the irresponsibility of youth and join the ranks of the Fathers – not as the
scapegrace father of an illegitimate child but as the future
Laird of Auchinleck, whose patriarchal business it was to
marry and prolong the line. It is clear that his desire to maintain the character of the ideal Grand Tourist involved a
massive effort of suppression. Time and again the word *'retenu'*
recurs in his journal: 'Be prudent and *retenu*', 'Be *retenu* with
Gordon', 'You was *retenu* at dinner', 'But you had not *retenue*
enough', etc. Just how much of himself had been denied in the
service of this ideal becomes apparent as soon as his coach rolls
out of Utrecht towards Germany.

The change of gear is unmistakable. His journal entry for
Monday 18 June 1764 begins, 'At seven we set out in a coach
and four. My blood circulated just as briskly as in my days of
youth.' From someone who is only twenty-three, this reference
to recovered youth speaks eloquently of the oppressive respectability of life in Utrecht. The blood stirs; a new Boswell is entering the picture. The day after his arrival in Berlin he joins a
party at the country-house of his bankers: 'I was firm and gay
and sound as ever. Am I indeed the dull dog of Utrecht?' And
the following day, 'If ever man underwent an alteration, it is the
man who writeth this journal. I drank punch at the lodgings of
Captain Wake, a Scots privateer. At night I was Young Boswell
of Auchinleck upon his travels, and had with me Macpherson,
a brave Highlander. He was quite the man for me.'

The entries that follow show Boswell throwing himself into
a social round that quite banishes the studious activities of
Utrecht. He was lodging in Berlin at the house of Carl David
Kircheisen, President of the City Council, whose family
became the hub of many of his social pleasures. One week in
July will give the flavour of his life there. On Monday 16 July
he dines with the Dutch minister, then returns for tea with his
landlord and a drive in the Park before supper with the rest of
the Kircheisen family, 'and after supper went with the ladies and

the young Kircheisen and walked *sous les marronniers* [under the chestnut trees]. Is not this living? It is. I am quite a new man.' Next day the family take him to a ball at the house of a member of the War Council: 'I eat much and drank much and found animal life of very great consequence. I danced a great deal, and was an easy man, without affectation and timid consequence. We went home late.' The rest of the week is largely taken up with a wedding party and the extended celebrations that follow it. The journal entries mark Boswell's increasing self-confidence. 'Prodigious!' he writes after listening to his landlord's fulsome compliments. 'Is this the gloomy wretch who not long ago laid it down as an impossibility that he could ever have a happy hour? After this can I dare to oppose sickly theory to bold practice? I hope not. I hope to be free of sickly theory.'

The praise of animal life, the rejection of 'sickly theory', the sense that this at last is living, are of a piece with his abandonment of books in favour of lessons in fencing and horsemanship. 'I was rather too singular,' he notes after one of the marriage celebrations; but instead of using the episode for self-recrimination, he goes on, 'Why not? I am in reality an original character . . . Let me then be Boswell and render him as fine a fellow as possible.' Boswell is becoming his own man. 'Why fear the censure of those whom I despise?' he asks a few weeks later. 'Let me boldly pursue my own plan.' And three days after that, commenting on a night at the opera where he was 'fine with the ladies of the Court', 'I saw my error in suffering so much from the contemplation of others. I can never be them, therefore let me not vainly attempt it in imagination . . . I must be Mr Boswell of Auchinleck, and no other. Let me make him as perfect as possible.'

We could not ask for a clearer example of the Tour's significance as a rite of passage. Reviewing his behaviour at the wedding festivities, Boswell now puts traditional virtues second to the essential requirement to be himself. 'Be self. Be original. Be happy. You *was* so, certainly. Add to this learning and taste and devotion and *retenue*. Marry not, but think to have fine Saxon girls. &c., and to be with Temple.' This is one of a number of memoranda which reflect the link between his new-found sense of self and a growing determination to enjoy sexual freedom. Though he continued to preach chastity to himself in the style of the Dutch journal, his resistance was waning. This period in the second half of July seems to have marked a watershed. 'Now my mean scruples are gone,' he writes to Temple on 23 July, 'but rational morality directs me to do no harm to others or to myself. I have not yet had an opportunity of indulging my amorous genius. But I have hopes.'

A visit with friends to a Berlin brothel a few weeks later, apparently just as a spectator ('We found a poor little house, an old bawd, and one whore. I was satisfied with what I saw'), was soon followed by a more decisive encounter at his lodgings. From time to time Boswell showed a curious ability to stay up all night and find himself refreshed rather than exhausted. This was his state on the morning of 11 September:

> I was quite drunk with brisk spirits, and about eight, in came a woman with a basket of chocolate to sell. I toyed with her and found she was with child. Oho! a safe piece. Into my closet. 'Habs er ein Man?' 'Ja, in den Gards bei Potsdam.' ['Have you a husband?' 'Yes, in the Guards in Potsdam.'] To bed directly. In a minute – over. I rose cool and astonished, half angry, half laughing. I sent her off.

Boswell was in truth so far from having divested himself of 'mean scruples' that the episode caused him a good deal of soul-searching, but the way was now open for further adventures that soon followed. Clear of Utrecht, emerging from his father's shadow, this was young Boswell of Auchinleck upon his travels.

It was not quite so simple, of course. Boswell was certainly moving away from the role he had adopted in Utrecht, but he kept on looking for models, measuring himself against others, attaching himself to surrogate father-figures, and sinking into periodic bouts of self-questioning melancholy. His erotic pursuits were still framed by a punishing awareness of the moral code with which he had been brought up. 'Wrong, low ... Resume reins. Let Father force you to be a man,' he urges himself after a hasty transaction with street-walkers in Dresden – which doesn't prevent him seeking them out again next day and again upbraiding himself for it afterwards: 'Support Utrecht character. Command self.' Such entries are evidence of a continuing tension, but the ideals of the Utrecht period, though Boswell never entirely lost sight of them, were a fading force. Before long he would be heading south, to Switzerland first, and then, with the Laird's grudging agreement, on to the traditional climax of the Grand Tour. As long as he was north of the Alps, Boswell remained at least half under the influence of his father's will, but beyond the mountains was Italy.

At this point, the question of exposure to foreign ways takes on a new urgency. 'After much wandering,' wrote the nineteenth-century explorer Richard Burton, 'we are almost tempted to believe the bad doctrine that morality is a matter of geography . . .' To go to a different country is to enter a different moral world. The creeping relativism that threatens the moral standards of the traveller was, as we have seen, at the heart of contemporary misgivings about the Tour. No less corrupting than the snares against which Thicknesse warned was the blithe acceptance of sexual immorality as a normal condition of daily life. What horrified him most about the sale of pornographic pictures in Lyon was the complete shamelessness of the business; the woman's fashionable customers 'talked with her about the several pieces, without betraying the least degree of surprize at the subjects, or the woman who shewed them . . . and I verily believe the woman was so totally a stranger to sentiment or decency, that she considered herself employed in the ordinary way of shop-keepers . . .' Nowhere was this state of things more evident than in Italy. It was the home of bad doctrine in both a religious and a moral sense. Boswell himself neatly combines the two when he excuses his behaviour in Rome: 'I remembered the rakish deeds of Horace and other amorous Roman poets, and I thought that one might well allow one's self indulgence in a city where there are prostitutes licensed by the Cardinal Vicar.' When in Rome . . .

The facetious tone masks a serious point. Boswell is offering a flamboyant demonstration of precisely what Burton was talking about. A change in place becomes a justification for a change in morals. 'When I go to France and Italy,' he asks the philosopher Jean-Jacques Rousseau, 'may I not indulge in the gallantries usual to those countries, where the husbands do not resent your making love to their wives?' The lax atmosphere of Italy provides a context in which the sexual prohibitions he has brought with him from Scotland can be discarded. It was no more than people expected. The evening after he gets to Turin, he goes to a ball and dances with the Spanish Ambassadress:

> There was here many fine women. The counts and other pretty gentlemen told me whenever I admired a lady, 'Sir, you can have her. It would not be difficult.' I thought at first they were joking and waggishly amusing themselves with a stranger. But I at last discovered that they were really in earnest and that the manners here were so openly debauched that adultery was carried on without the least disguise.

It is to all appearances a sexual Kingdom of Cockaigne, and Boswell's response anticipates the enthusiastic double standards of generations of tourists who were to come after him: 'My desire to know the world made me resolve to intrigue a little while in Italy, where the women are so debauched that they are hardly to be considered as moral agents, but as inferior beings.'

Moral agents or not, the fashionable women of Turin had enough taste to reject the young tourist's rather crude addresses. The third evening after his arrival he decided to move in on Mme de St Gilles,* one of the leading figures in Turin society ('I thought an oldish lady most proper, as I should have an easy attack'). Having thrown out a few hints, such as pressing his legs against hers at the opera, Boswell concluded a couple of evenings later that the time had come. 'Night before last,' he records on 14 January, 'I plainly proposed matters to Mme St Gilles. "I am young, strong, vigorous. I offer my services as a duty, and I think that the Comtesse de St Gilles will do very well to accept them."' She managed to decline the invitation, as did the Countesses Burgaretta and Skarnavis on whom he also set his sights during his fortnight in Turin. Rejected by the *beau monde*, Boswell was obliged to fall back on the services of 'honest' Captain Billon, who was happy to procure local girls for him. The implication that it was merely his discovery of the prevailing immorality that had led him astray was absurdly disingenuous. Well before his departure from Scotland, Boswell had taken Italy as the erotic focus of his tourist daydreams. 'Indeed my Friend,' he writes back to John Johnston the following year, 'I have experienced all the delicious enjoyment of Italian Gallantry, which I used to fancy in gay prospect while eating your Currant Jelly on a Summer afternoon.' The Laird of Auchinleck had fair reason to be suspicious of his son's eagerness for 'that intoxicating Region'.

From the start of his journey, Boswell had been aware that the opportunities for connoisseurship were sexual as well as artistic. For travellers to eighteenth-century Italy, the two were closely related. Writing to his brother from Florence at the

---

* Caterina Maria Theresa di San Gillio.

beginning of 1752, the soldier and statesman Henry Seymour Conway had claimed, 'There are but two things at all thought of here – love and antiquities, of which the former predominates so greatly that I think it seems to make the whole history and the whole business of this place . . .'* The ease with which both could be accommodated within the same perspective of the Connoisseur is suggested later in the century by Goethe, who visited Sir William Hamilton in Naples and observed his passion for Emily Hart, later Emma Hamilton, his wife and Nelson's mistress: 'The old knight idolizes her and is enthusiastic about everything she does. In her, he has found all the antiquities, all the profiles of Sicilian coins, even the Apollo Belvedere.' His love could not have attached itself to a more appropriate object. With her celebrated 'Attitudes', the *tableaux vivants* that entranced Neapolitan society, Emma Hamilton had adroitly united the twin interests of the Grand Tour, fusing erotic spectacle with the artistic appeal of classical imagery: love and antiquities.

The varied scenes of travel opened new prospects to Boswell, and he repeatedly excited himself with thoughts of adding to his own sexual collection. 'I was in the humour of gallantry tonight,' he writes after flirting with a Turkish woman in his party. 'I was pleased with the romantic idea of making love to a Turk'. Shortly afterwards he notes another brush with exotic possibilities in the streets of Berlin: 'Black girl† – had no condom. Walked, came home.' A week later, 'Marry not, but think to have fine Saxon girls.' And three months after that, at a coach stop on the journey from Leipzig,

---

* In a letter to his friend Horace Walpole, written at about the same time, he remarks that Florence is 'a scene of cicisbeship, of intrigue and lewdness beyond anything, in all kinds of people of all orders, ages, and conditions and in all ways' (23 January 1752).

† This may have today's meaning, but in the eighteenth century it could have referred to a girl with noticeably dark hair or complexion.

'I strolled about in a village in search of the ugliest woman I could find. I restrained myself. Such inclinations are caused by disease.' A couple of months further on, in his memo of topics to discuss with Rousseau, whose acquaintance he was determined to make, '. . . will have Swiss girl, amiable, &c. Quite adventure.' In Italy the same projects continue, but as Boswell's impulses are given increasingly free rein, the role of collector becomes more engrossing. 'The whim seized me of having an intrigue with an Italian countess,' he remarks in Turin. A few weeks later, unable quite to limit himself to 'one a week girl', he adds 'if not fine Roman'. In Rome, his thoughts jump on to the next stage: 'Now swear no *libertinage*, except Florentine lady'. On his arrival in Venice another excitement beckons, 'My fancy was stirred by the brilliant stories I had heard of Venetian courtesans'. And in the course of the year he does indeed secure the sexual spoils on which he had set his heart – an Italian noblewoman, several fine Romans, a Venetian courtesan and many others. The sex tourist in Italy is a gourmet at the board. 'I'm determined,' Boswell writes, 'to try all experiments with a soul and body.' Even the inclinations he repressed on the road from Leipzig can now be explored: 'Old woman; few words, business done. Quite brutish. . . .,' he notes of a woman in Rome, itemised in his accounts simply as 'monstre' costing about five shillings. On the same day as his brief passage with the 'monstre', Boswell left for Naples where, according to the account he wrote for Rousseau, he exercised little restraint: '. . . my passions were violent. I indulged them; my mind had almost nothing to do with it. I found some very pretty girls. I escaped all danger.'

If the rite of passage, the lesson in comparative morality and the pleasures of the collector are all aspects of the Tour whose sexual ramifications are clearly shown in Boswell's journal, so also is the Tour's function as a display of the tourist's economic and cultural power. Boswell himself was not particularly rich, and he was a mark for predators only in the way that all tourists are – he had the usual problems with extortionate innkeepers, and his pocket was picked on two successive nights by 'those easy street girls' in Dresden – but he nonetheless demonstrates clearly enough how the tourist's economic position enhanced the erotic possibilities of the Tour. The sultanesque fantasies that recur in his journal are a sexual expression of the Grand Tourist's confident sense of a world that offers itself for his satisfaction.

For Boswell the most potent image of this was Lord Baltimore, the British proprietor of Maryland, who was at the time, according to what Boswell heard in Berlin, 'living at Constantinople as a Turk, with his seraglio around him'.* Baltimore later died in Naples, leaving, in the words of Sir Horace Mann, the British envoy in Florence, 'a whole *seraglio* of white, black etc. to provide for'. His example fired Boswell's imagination: 'Lord Baltimore was a beacon to me. I trembled to think of my wild schemes.' These schemes are partly revealed to Rousseau a few months later, when Boswell, having at last got into the philosopher's presence, broaches his inclination to 'follow the oriental usage':

> But consider: if I am rich, I can take a number of girls; I get them with child; propagation is thus increased. I give them dowries, and I marry them off to good peasants who are very happy to have them. Thus they become wives at the same age as would have been the case if they had remained virgins, and I, on my side, have had the benefit of enjoying a great variety of women.

Boswell was not just trailing his coat here. Three days earlier at an inn he visited while laying siege to Rousseau, he had taken

---

* Predictably, Lord Baltimore's own account of his tour gives no hint of any sexual irregularity. Such is his delicacy that even the word 'whores' is rendered wh---s.

a fancy to one of the innkeeper's daughters who had just served him dinner: 'I asked her, "Would you like to go to Scotland?" She said, "Yes, Sir. I don't want to stay here." She pleased me.' The following day he returned to the inn and she assured him that she had been serious. '"But you understand on what footing you will be with me? I do not wish to deceive you." "Yes, Sir; you will dispose of me as you see fit." She had two pretty children and was a fine fresh Swiss lass. I said, "Well, I make no promises; but if I find it suitable, I shall write to you."'

For a traveller with money in his purse, working-class women casually encountered along the way were an available trophy. The analogy with the tourist practice of picking up desirable artefacts from the countries visited could hardly be more obvious. As Boswell's conversation with Rousseau makes clear, it is a form of conspicuous consumption that exhibits the tourist's powers of acquisition as well as his taste. In Brunswick earlier in the year Boswell had contemplated a similar project:

> There came into my room this morning the sweetest girl I ever saw, a *blanchisseuse* [laundress], eighteen, fresh, gay. I spoke German to her with unusual ease, and told her that I would not for the world debauch her to give myself a few days' pleasure, but if she would go with me to England and then to Scotland, I would be very kind to her. She was really innocent. Her beauty thrilled my frame. I thought that I might be an old patriarch upon occasions and could not see any harm in taking her with me. She refused to go, but promised to come back from time to time.

The image of patriarchy reflects both the tourist's status and the sexual privileges that go with it.

These various threads that make up the sexual fabric of the Tour come together in a single episode towards the end of

Boswell's time in Italy. Suffering in Florence from yet another bout of venereal disease to add to those contracted in Rome and Venice, he wisely reminded himself to 'ask condoms for Siena', but as it turned out, his visit to Siena broke the pattern established in Turin, introducing a new and romantic element into his travels.

Armed with a letter of introduction from Lord Mountstuart* to his former mistress, Porzia Sansedoni, Boswell lost no time in proposing himself as a successor to the young nobleman. His argument that far from causing any distress to Mountstuart, it would bring the two of them closer together, was backed up with characteristic protestations: 'Believe me, I shall admire you more for generosity and a noble frankness than for any nicely calculated reserve. The romantic man really worthy of you is at Siena. Do not lose him. Time passes. A moment of despair may remove me for ever. Think seriously. I adore you. Be quite frank. Ah, Madame – I dare say no more.' It was a more sustained campaign than usual, but the results were equally unsatisfactory. Meanwhile, however, Boswell had turned at least half his attention to another noblewoman, Girolama Piccolomini (referred to as Moma or Momina), the pretty 37-year-old wife of the mayor of Siena. The progress of their relationship is described in Boswell's letter to Rousseau:

> I was wicked enough to wait at the same time on a very amiable little woman to whom I made declarations of the most sincere passion, as can be easily done when one feels only a slight inclination. . . . Behold me, then, very busy indeed, with two affairs going at the same time. It required an unparalleled dexterity, and I had it. . . . This amiable person, whose heart was already touched, listened

---

* Boswell had travelled to Venice with Mountstuart and his entourage after the two men met in Rome.

to me kindly and granted me all, saying, 'Ebbene, mi fido a voi com' a un galantuomo' ['Well then, I put my trust in you as a man of honour']. . . . I studied her character. I found many good qualities in her. I even found charms in her which the dissipation of my spirit had caused me to overlook previously; and with extraordinary joy I found myself truly in love with her. . . . I was utterly happy and I risked nothing.

Moma's devotion to Boswell was genuine and long out-lasted the weeks he spent in Siena. For him, it was a realised fantasy ('I enjoyed . . . the exquisite pleasure of Italian gallantry, whose enchantments I had heard so much of'); for her, some-thing much more. On the morning of his departure Boswell went to see her: 'She was quite tendered down, for she had not slept. You told her you was resolved. She said: "You go to greater and greater happiness, but you leave me here to go continually from bad to worse; for after a few years my youth will be gone, &c., and I am among people for whom I care nothing."' But Boswell's thoughts were now on the trip he had decided to make to Corsica. Moma's tears were met with a hollow promise of 'eternal friendship' ('You was like Spanish cavalier,' he notes of his behaviour). 'Leave quite in confusion. At twelve found chaise at Porta. Half well, half ill all day. Night, bad inn.' The traveller moves on, leaving the emotional debris to be picked over by the one who stays behind.

His relationship with Moma was the romantic highlight of Boswell's travels, but it also epitomised the unseen side of the Grand Tour, embracing a spectrum of motives and satisfac-tions that were crucial to the tourist experience but were usually passed over in discreet silence – as they have been ever since. Boswell had at last got his high-born Italian woman, a perfect item for the connoisseur's display cabinet; in addition, he had asserted his independence by doing so in the teeth of his father's increasingly peremptory commands to return home. Moreover, in contrast to the disappointments of Turin, the episode had shown him dealing urbanely with the free and easy morality of sophisticated Italian society; and finally, its conclusion had been a gratifying confirmation of his sexual power.

Boswell was now on his way to visit the Corsican leader Pascal Paoli, a meeting which led to his *Account of Corsica* and which was to be the basis of his celebrity as 'Corsica Boswell' when he returned to England. His main concerns for the rest of the Tour were in one way or another political, and not much of sexual interest is recorded until we reach his affair with Rousseau's mistress, Thérèse Le Vasseur. This is worth pausing on, if only because it re-emphasises how easily the sexual realities of the Tour could be suppressed.

Charged with accompanying Thérèse from Paris to London on his way home, Boswell was quick to take advantage of the situation. By the second night they were sharing a bed, and for the rest of the journey Thérèse did her best to bring a little more refinement to Boswell's performance – though his journal entry on reaching Dover suggests that he was still more concerned with quantity than quality: 'Yesterday morning had gone to bed very early, and had done it once: thirteen in all'. In fact, the journal entries for the first eleven days of February, which contained Boswell's account of the affair, were destroyed. A note with the words 'Reprehensible Passage', written by one of his literary executors, was found in their place. That we know some of the details – Boswell's initial humiliation, Thérèse's attempts to comfort and instruct him, his less than gallant assessment of her own ardours – is due merely to chance: the earliest editor of the papers had read the passage before it was destroyed and noted its contents.

In other cases, there is no such memorial. The journal Boswell kept of his travels is a striking indication of how much gets left out of the official version of the Tour. Like most

Grand Tourists, he took in the recommended sights – visited the Borghese Palace and the Vatican library, had his portrait painted by the fashionable Gavin Hamilton, admired the countryside described by Horace and noted the mosaics of St Mark's – but there is no reason to suppose that his other experiences were any less common. On the contrary, it seems probable that his unofficial tour followed a course that was as standard as the official one. This is suggested by the actions and assumptions of pretty well everyone he came across along the way, from Lord Mountstuart, who followed him to the Venetian courtesans and took the same infection from the same girl, to the pair of 'English gentlemen' whose acquaintance he made in Turin: 'After the opera Norton and Heath insisted I should go home with them and sup. I went, like a simpleton. They carried me into a low room of their inn, where they romped with two girls and gave me a most pitiful supper. This, now was true English.' On his way back through France he stopped long enough in Marseille to try the recommendation of a fellow traveller he had met earlier in the month: 'The gallant Duncan Drummond had told me at Genoa of a very good girl whom he had kept a long time, and had with him eight months at Minorca.' Boswell duly called on Mlle Susette: 'I sacrificed to the graces. I think I did no harm.' During the two weeks he spent in Paris, which were overshadowed by news of his mother's death, his pursuits were mainly social rather than sexual, but it's notable that the couple of brothels he did try were again both recommended by a fellow traveller. On 25 January he had been obliged to spend most of the day at the customs recovering a trunk. 'Was dull a little,' he comments in his memorandum. 'Met there a young fellow who gave you names of good bordellos.'

Boswell's travels do more than illuminate aspects of the Grand Tour. In so far as the Tour becomes the blueprint for a certain kind of leisure travel, what he records has implications that reach into the next two centuries. The outlines of Connoisseur tourism are clear. The Connoisseur, usually male, goes to foreign countries as to a treasure-house. His guidebook functions as a catalogue, indicating where his gaze should rest, what special experiences he should try, what special items he should buy. He looks, he tastes and, one way or another, he takes possession, perhaps simply by adding to the list of things seen and done, perhaps by purchasing replicas, souvenirs or local artefacts, perhaps even by buying the objects themselves and taking them home. These are his satisfactions. To end this chapter I would like to glance at them in slightly more detail and to suggest how the patterns established by the Grand Tour are reproduced by later tourists.

In the first place, the Connoisseur is a spectator. The traveller goes to look, and his discriminating gaze is an instrument of aesthetic rather than moral observation. Present at the scene yet detached from it, he has the power of the figure who looks down from the balcony. Everything is grist to his mill because nothing is more than spectacle. (His modern descendant travels with a camera: like a journal, it authenticates the tourist's experience; like a sketchbook, it takes possession of what has been seen.) On his way out of Turin after a last abortive attempt at a love affair, Boswell happens upon the execution of a criminal – one of the sights Bacon lists as 'not to be neglected'. He crowds close to the gallows and watches the thief tossed over and strangled by the hangman, who puts his feet on the man's head and neck in order to do it. Immediately afterwards Boswell goes into a church and kneels 'with great devotion' before a splendidly lit altar: 'I Icrc then I felt three scenes: raging love – gloomy horror – grand devotion. The horror indeed I only *should* have felt. I jogged on slowly with my *vetturino*, and had a grievous inn at night.' The horror is unreal because Boswell's chaise is waiting a few yards away to transport him at a steady jog to the next place, the next uncomfortable inn. It is one of the seductions of travel that it allows us to enjoy the extremes of human emotion and experience in the knowledge that next morning we shall wake in a different place, having left them behind. In the normal way of things, sex, death and religion may be fascinating but they are also embroiling; their social context imposes responsibilities and requirements. On the tourist they have no lasting claim; tomorrow will be another scene. This detachment allows them to become objects of spectacle, along with everything else.*

I pick the example of an execution because of its ambiguity: the watcher is situated uneasily between tourist as legitimate spectator and tourist as voyeur. Travellers' accounts of torture and execution shimmer with a half-suppressed sexual excitement that underlines the tinge of eroticism in the tourist's quest for spectacle. The day before he left Rome in 1817, Byron saw three robbers guillotined, and the scene, 'including the *masqued* priests – the half-naked executioners – the bandaged criminals – the black Christ & his banner – the scaffold – the soldiery – the slow procession – & the quick rattle and heavy fall of the axe – the splash of the blood – & the ghastliness of the exposed heads', clearly excited him: 'The first turned me quite hot and thirsty – & made me shake so that I could hardly hold the opera-glass ...' The sexual connection is made explicit by Casanova in his account of the execution of Damiens, which he watches from a window overlooking the place de Grève in the eager company of two women, one of whom is being buggered by his friend as the spectacle unfolds.

---

* Executions were of course a public spectacle in England at the time as well. It might be argued that one of their attractions was precisely that they took death out of its everyday context and turned it into a tourist pleasure for the population at large – though Boswell himself, in contrast to his reaction here, had been much affected by an execution at Tyburn some three months before his departure.

It is the tourist's business to take in unfamiliar sights, and the shift from cultural observer to sexual voyeur is a commonplace of the unofficial tourist world. The avid snaps of slums and shanty-towns belong to the same category of tourist experience as the evening trawl through the red-light district that has been a standard part of the itinerary for as long as there have been tourists and red-light districts. (Visitors were already praising the splendour of arrangements at Valencia by the beginning of the sixteenth century.) We can see a starker version of this slippage between observer and voyeur in Flaubert's travel notes on his Egyptian journey. His description of the syphilis cases in a Cairo hospital comes under the heading of (just about) respectable tourist observation, but it is exactly the same impulse that prompts his detached scrutiny of Kuchuk Hanem's body or the brutal copulation of his old donkey-driver with a roadside prostitute.

In a foreign place the Connoisseur's natural voyeurism readily combines with economic power and sexual curiosity to nurture an element of sadism. It glints through the descriptions already mentioned and reappears in the experiences of later travellers. 'I went first to Paris,' writes the Victorian author of *My Secret Life*, 'where I ran a course of baudy house amusements, saw a big dog fuck a woman who turned her rump towards it as if she were a bitch.' And Evelyn Waugh at a brothel in the same city: 'I arranged a tableau by which my boy should be enjoyed by a large negro who was there but at the last minute, after we had ascended to a squalid divan at the top of the house and he was lying waiting for the negro's advances, the price proved prohibitive . . .' In both cases the reference to size – 'a big dog', 'a large negro' – serves to emphasise the sadistic undertones, while the language remains studiedly neutral. To propose other places and people as spectacle, which is what tourism does, promotes an essentially amoral response to experience, and sexual spectacles are just one aspect of the general tourist imperative. The package tourist who takes in the sex shows of Bangkok is at the end of a long line.

For the Connoisseur, seeing is a form of consumption. Dr John Moore, who acted as bearleader to the 8th Duke of Hamilton on his Grand Tour, records the instance of a young Englishman in Rome, determined to fulfil his tourist obligations with a minimum of inconvenience, who ordered a coach and four early in the morning and by driving through 'churches, palaces, villas and ruins, with all possible expedition', managed to see in two days everything that Moore's party had seen in six weeks. 'I found afterwards,' noted Moore, 'by the list he kept of what he had seen, that we had not the advantage of him in a single picture, or the most mutilated remnant of a statue.' This is Connoisseur tourism pared to the bone, a paradigm for all the whistle-stop tours that have since danced tourists through cities and countries at a speed which just about enables the landmarks to be recognised and crossed off the list. But that is what, at its crudest, one kind of tourism is about. The aim of the visitor is not to understand a place, or even to experience it, but just to taste it, specifically those aspects of it that have been arranged for tourist consumption. This is perfectly demonstrated in our use of the holiday brochure. It is the modern tourist's prerogative to sample countries without having to cope with any of their awkwardness or ugliness, without being vulnerable to them or dependent on them. We simply flick through the pictures in the brochure, check the cost and make our choice. As tourists we are kings for the day, able to enjoy the sense, lost since childhood, of a world that exists to gratify our desires. From this perspective, sexual indulgence, whether on the part of the Grand Tourist or the package tourist, is merely an extension of the habitual relationship to the countries visited. The murmured invitations of the street-corner touts do no more than confirm that everything is at the tourist's disposal. 'Sir, you can have her . . .'

The gourmet's curiosity that sends Boswell off in search of the ugliest woman he can find during a brief coach-stop is a predictable feature of Connoisseur travel. A century and a half later, Cyril Connolly, on a student holiday in 1922, takes the opportunity to visit a brothel in Budapest. In his diary he tells how, after a long conversation with an English officer about the immortality of the soul, he went upstairs with a girl who became 'very passionate and took her stockings off – she enjoyed it I think. I love it I must say and said I had never been so happy before – tried several "ways of love" afterwards, "*comme animal* etc.".' Like Boswell, Connolly wants to take advantage of the licence travel gives to 'try all experiments with a soul and body'. It is part of the Connoisseur's programme. Where this leads, if pursued coldly enough across a long enough period, can be seen in Graham Greene, whose travelling days began at about the same time as Connolly's. By the time he went to the Congo to research material for what became *A Burnt Out Case* (1961), his credentials as a connoisseur were well established and openly displayed: 'I can never get used to the beautiful even colour of the young African women – the most beautiful *backs* of any race. Here there are elaborate crossroads of partings on the scalp, the hair is twisted in thin cords to form a kind of bird's cage. The big toes are often made up.' He records the details fastidiously. And his knowledge goes further: 'A black woman takes more care about the cleanness of her parts than a European. She is far more *pudique*, but on the other hand she is uncomplicated and in a relationship will never deny her man.' The clinical tone insists on discrimination. For birds of passage like himself, he explains, 'a taxi driver will always fetch a succession of girls, but it is necessary to be particular in description'.

Anthony Burgess strikes the same note in his autobiography. Places, people and events are there to be sampled: 'A Malay female body, musky, shapely, golden-brown, was always a delight . . .' His sexual catalogue roves through the different races of the East – Chinese girls ('thin, lithe, sinuous, but disappointingly uninvolved in the act'), Thais, 'Tamil women blacker than Africans, including a girl who could not have been older than twelve', and so on. The traveller's constant movement ensures variety. And when a sample is approved, it can usually be acquired. At a village on the way up-river Greene sees 'a lovely young woman in green with a fish' and asks Father Georges, the Belgian priest accompanying him, 'whether perhaps I could buy her as a wife for the trip, but he explained that it would be hardly worthwhile'. The whims of the Connoisseur overlap with those of the sultan. Just as the country lays itself out for the leisured inspection of the tourist, who enjoys what he chooses and then passes on, so the country's women offer themselves for the tourist's delectation; they constitute local specialities that can be collected in the same way as other foreign trinkets. In this respect there is little change, whether we are looking at Boswell's proposition to the *blanchisseuse*, Greene's response to the village girl, or the tidy arrangement of a British officer on the Nile in 1884 who 'bought a very lady like little girl for £16' for the duration of his voyage. Or come to that, the sex tourist brochure at the end of the twentieth century: 'in the Philippines the man is still king. It would be a sin to leave all these flowers unpicked . . .'

It is, as always, a language of supreme detachment. The satisfactions of the Connoisseur are based on a degree of social, emotional and financial security that dispenses with any need for personal involvement. This was the natural assumption underlying the Grand Tour, but towards the end of the eighteenth century a new kind of traveller was appearing for whom both the cultural and sexual attractions of travel would have a different meaning.

PART TWO

Pilgrims

3

A New Concept of Travel

By the time Boswell died in 1795, the Grand Tour in its classic form was more or less over, killed off by the French Revolution and the continuing hostilities between France and England. Young Victorian males who showed signs of restlessness were more likely to find themselves shipped off to the colonies, where they could indulge their various appetites while bringing civilisation to races less fortunate than their own. The Grand Tour enjoyed a brief revival in the nineteenth century (Disraeli, duly infected with venereal disease, returned from a late version of it in 1831), but tourism was entering a new phase. Railways brought with them the age of the package tour and the guidebook. This was obviously not the end of the line for the Connoisseur – the guidebook itself is evidence of that – but the dominant characteristics of tourism had changed. It was no longer primarily a young man's enterprise, and it no longer had the same cultural function.

For some time, attitudes to travel had been affected by a revolution in sensibility that was turning conventional notions about the European tour upside-down. The narrator of Laurence Sterne's *A Sentimental Journey Through France and Italy* (1768) has done none of the things expected of a dutiful tourist. He explains to a French nobleman that he has not seen the Palais Royal or the Luxembourg Palace or the façade of the Louvre, nor has he tried to add to the catalogues of pictures, monuments and churches; his concern is with knowledge of the individual heart:

The thirst of this, continued I, as impatient as that which inflames the breast of the connoisseur, has led me from my own home into France – and from France will lead me through Italy – 'tis a quiet journey of the heart in pursuit of NATURE, and those affections which arise out of her, which make us love each other – and the world, better than we do.

Sterne quite deliberately contrasts his own priorities with those of the connoisseur: he is pursuing nature rather than art; his is a journey of the heart rather than the intellect. Where earlier travel books had been expected to supply the sort of dusty information that often made them look more like an encyclopedia than a personal narrative, *A Sentimental Journey* is blithely indifferent to such material. Sterne shifts the whole emphasis from the exterior to the interior journey. He is less interested in places than people and less interested in both than in their impact on the consciousness of the traveller.

In this he was part of a wider trend. Rousseau's *La nouvelle Héloïse, Du contrat social*, and *Emile* had all been published in the early 1760s, and they heralded the cultural sea-change brought about in the closing years of the century by the Romantic movement. *A Sentimental Journey*, with its cult of sensibility and its stress on the personal and the spontaneous, is foreshadowing a new theory of travel. For the Romantic, travel was not simply about seeing new sights, acquiring new information, making new contacts; it could also be about becoming a new person. What happens to the mind and heart of the traveller in the course of the journey is as important as the physical tally of incident and observation. In many cases the places visited and objects seen were the same, but the sense of travelling for observation was overtaken by a sense of travelling for enlightenment. The destination was envisaged less as a gallery than a shrine. A new identity, recast from an earlier age, had opened up for the tourist – that of Pilgrim.

Twenty years after Sterne, Goethe made the epic trip recorded in his *Italian Journey*. It stands as a manifesto for the liberating nature of Italian travel and for the status of the journey south as a pilgrimage. 'My purpose in making this wonderful journey,' he declares at the start, 'is not to delude myself but to discover myself in the objects I see.' What his journey also does is confirm the intimation, clear enough in *A Sentimental Journey*, that the move towards the Mediterranean was a sensual as well as a spiritual pilgrimage. The rhythm of Sterne's narrative, with its recurring peaks of amorous excitement – a chance encounter in the coachyard, a few moments with a beautiful milliner in Paris, a sentimental interlude with a girl in the countryside – links the transforming experience of travel with the tremors of erotic possibility that are part of its texture. Goethe was more discreet, but there is no mistaking a similar drift. 'I ate some nice pears,' he notes in Regensburg, 'but I am longing for grapes and figs', and his comment anticipates the exhilaration with which he will later respond to the sensual allurements of the south, imaged in the wide baskets of fruit, the warmth of the sun, the discarding of clothes – 'for I am now only concerned with the sensuous impressions that no book or picture can give me'. In a letter of February 1787 he mentions the complaisance of the painters' models in Rome, which he would have taken advantage of, had not the threat of syphilis made 'even this Paradise unsafe'. Whether he succumbed in Naples is uncertain – he destroyed the letters and diaries relating to his stay there – but his surviving comments leave no doubt about his general response to its atmosphere: 'Naples is a Paradise; everyone lives in a kind of intoxicated self-forgetfulness, myself included. I seem to be a quite different person, whom I hardly recognise.'

Back in Rome, Goethe took up with the woman he calls Faustina, the daughter of a local innkeeper. This was his first documented sexual relationship. 'It is only here in Rome,' writes Richard Friedenthal, 'at the age of 40, that Goethe finds complete erotic freedom, only now that his experience of love is complete . . . He looks at things differently now, more sensuously.' There were other strands to the process of self-discovery on which Goethe had embarked: his days were spent searching for Roman antiquities, studying the behaviour of the people, acquiring knowledge of Renaissance art and architecture; but the erotic component of his travels was nonetheless central to their meaning – so much so that his most reliable biographer, commenting on the change brought about by his affair with Faustina, can suggest, 'Perhaps, after all, it was for this, more than anything else, that he had come to Italy in the first place'.

Goethe had presented his Italian journey in a way that would find sympathetic echoes throughout the nineteenth century. The promise of revelation was confirmed by the travels of the British Romantics, and of Byron in particular. Allan Massie makes a useful distinction between the effect of travel on the average Grand Tourist, for whom it was just a diverting episode, and its effect on Byron, for whom it was altogether more decisive: 'Henceforth he lived emotionally and intellectually, in what he called "the clime of the East". He had discovered habits of thinking and feeling which seemed to him truer and more admirable than those he found in England.' The distinction applies to others as well. This experience of self-discovery, catalysed in Byron's case by his sexual encounters in Greece and Turkey, is fundamental to the new kind of travel. Byron himself, as I shall argue later, took on the identity of Rebel rather than Pilgrim, but the emphasis he gave to travel as a personal odyssey, whose meaning was a matter of individual shifts in consciousness, had a crucial influence on tourist ideals.

To say that a passion for the Mediterranean was the defining feature of nineteenth-century tourism is to indicate both a

destination and a state of mind. If the journey south was a pilgrimage, it was a lover's pilgrimage. In *The Tender Passion*
(1986), Peter Gay has shown how Victorian sensuality was displaced into a range of activities from music and religion to
shopping and gardening. Travel is not a category he considers,
but for those with money it was a natural channel for displacement of this kind. In imagination, the Mediterranean was the
reverse of everything cold, damp, smog-ridden, buttoned-up
and repressive about Victorian England. 'Tis the hard grey
weather/Breeds hard English men', Charles Kingsley claimed
with evident approval, but to nature's hard grey weather the
nineteenth century had added a blanket of industrial pollution
that in London and elsewhere had turned grey to dingy
yellow. Just to get across the Channel was to escape from a
choking, depressing miasma that seemed to seep into the soul.
'I came here today with Percy Ffrench,' noted Ronald Gower
of his arrival in Paris, 'and am glad to leave the terribly depressing fog and darkness of London, a fog which during the last
day or two has entered into everything, including one's lungs
and, apparently, one's brain.' It was the murky atmosphere that
writers from Dickens to Lawrence expanded into a metaphor
for a certain way of life and cast of mind:

> Melancholy streets in a penitential garb of soot, steeped
> the souls of the people who were condemned to look at
> them out of windows, in dire despondency. In every
> thoroughfare, up almost every alley, and down almost
> every turning, some doleful bell was throbbing, jerking,
> tolling, as if the Plague were in the city and the dead-carts
> were going round. Everything was bolted and barred that
> could possibly furnish relief to an overworked people.

This is the world to which Arthur Clennam, newly arrived
from Marseille, returns one Sunday evening at the start of
Dickens's *Little Dorrit* (1855–57).

Not surprisingly, tourist reaction to the Mediterranean was often a hymn to light. The cultural historian John Pemble remarks on the number of nineteenth-century painters and writers, from Frederic Leighton and Edward Lear to John Ruskin and Vernon Lee, who were constantly struggling to convey its magic. Along with the escape into light went a sense of liberation from many of the restraints imposed by an atmosphere of gloom. The tourist heading south was moving from reflection to instinct, from the intellect to the senses. 'The vines are weighed down by their clusters, and the trees loaded with figs. Come and eat! Will you?' Mary Shelley had written back to a friend in England. It is a landscape of sensual indulgence, and Victorian enthusiasm for Italy and Greece often contained a strong undercurrent of erotic excitement. This had two aspects. In the first place, there were those tourists who were drawn by the sexual tolerance of Mediterranean countries, and took grateful advantage of it. In the second place, there were the far greater numbers for whom the erotic lure of the Mediterranean was much less specific – no more, perhaps, than a heightened sensual alertness, a liberating responsiveness to qualities of light, colour and texture, which spilled over into a kind of general sexual awareness.

For the first group the appeal of the Mediterranean was threefold. To start with, it was abroad, and therefore conferred all the freedoms traditionally enjoyed by the traveller; to be outside one's own society was to be beyond its immediate scrutiny. Secondly, Greece and Italy were sanctified for the educated classes by their classical heritage. The lingering presence of Homer, Herodotus, Virgil, Horace and all the other ghosts of antiquity lent colour to the sense of pilgrimage that marked visits to these countries. Moreover, it was just these classical associations that provided a moral rationale for sexual tastes which ran towards the bronzed limbs of Mediterranean boys. (The word 'bronzed' itself, much favoured by nineteenth-century pederasts, carried bracing echoes of a classical age.) It was a connection that reached deep into the psyche of many Victorians. The sunny landscapes of Italy and Greece offered a delicious conjunction of classical antiquity and supple young bodies, which took these travellers straight back to the public schools where their tastes had often been formed. (It was on a trip to Italy in the early 1870s that Edward Carpenter discovered the love of Greek sculpture that hastened his transition from respectable clergyman to homosexual dropout.) And thirdly, there was the fact that everything seemed so natural. Under the sinless blue skies of the Mediterranean, all was permitted. Life's horizons expanded. Aberrations that could scarcely be spoken of at home were here part of the currency of day-to-day life. The whole culture seemed to invite a relaxation of moral scruples.

This was overwhelmingly a male response, reflected, even among those who did not actually travel for sex, in the pervasive imagery of Italy as a woman, seductive and open to seduction. Henry James's 'beautiful disheveled nymph' was just one example of what the literary critic James Buzard refers to as 'the nineteenth century's habit of mapping Europe as a whole on a grid of sexual difference':

> Italy thus charted becomes a woman of incomparable physical charms and mysterious, imperfectly controlled poetic powers: all things Italian, including the indigenous population, exude this quality before the enamoured male spectator from the North.

The myth, which found its way into the public narratives and private fantasies of generations of tourists, was of the romantic male traveller taking possession of the languorous beauty of the South. Browning's lines addressed to Italy in 'By the Fire-Side' make it clear that she is figured as mistress rather than wife: 'Oh woman-country, wooed not wed,/Loved all the more by earth's male-lands,/Laid to their hearts instead!'

As with the parallel metaphor that set a feminised East over against the dominant male West,* there are wider cultural claims to masculine superiority just below the surface, but in both cases the immediate effect is to eroticise the role of the male tourist. 'I have really nothing to relate to you,' Henry James wrote to the literary critic Edmund Gosse, 'save that I sit here making love to Italy. At this divine moment she is perfectly irresistible, and this delicious little Florence is not the least sovereign of her charms'. Rarely can James have hit a note of such unequivocal lechery.

But the male tourist was not the only one making love to Italy. By the end of the nineteenth century there were more women tourists than men in southern Europe. Thomas Cook was of course partly responsible for this. In a much-discussed article for *Blackwood's Magazine* Charles Lever excoriated the ubiquitous tour groups. With their view of Europe as 'a great spectacle', their 'overbearing insolence' and 'purse-strong insistance', their derision of Catholic religious ceremonies, their distaste for foreign food and ignorance of foreign languages, they were flooding the Continent. Such tourist characteristics were hardly new. What had upset Lever was in reality a downmarket version of Connoisseur tourism which had come surging back to pollute the haunts of the Pilgrim. But when he claims that these groups are mainly composed of 'elderly, dreary, sad-looking' men and 'intensely lively, wide-awake, and facetious' younger women, his comments reveal another side to the story.

The contrast is worth pondering: unlike the subdued old men, these were women whom the opportunities of the

---

* Buzard's point that Italy after the Risorgimento could be seen from a northern perspective to undergo an ambiguous shift towards masculinity is matched by western perceptions of Japan in the wake of its wars against China (1894–95) and Russia (1904–05).

package tour had set free, and there is no doubt of the erotic element in their frequently expressed sense of liberation – it is there already in 'the continual sparkle of the eye and the uneasy quiver of the mouth' noted by the disapproving Lever. In increasing numbers they now had access to the dangerous world which before had been the preserve of a privileged few. Its excitements could be measured by the sort of disquiet that had led Frances Trollope, a generation earlier, to wonder in *A Visit to Italy* (1842) whether a long stay abroad, even with the best tutors, 'is, *on the whole*, advantageous to young women, whom their friends wish should remain *English*, and whose hopes are to become English wives and English mothers . . .' The insistent repetition of 'English' makes its own point about the dubious contrast offered by Continental ways.

For one group of earlier women travellers – Mary Wortley Montagu, Mary Shelley, Claire Clairmont, Lady Blessington, Mary Ellen Meredith, Elizabeth Barrett Browning and many others – this contrast had been the principal inducement: abroad, and especially in Italy, they could live lives that would have been barred by convention in England. More frequently, women travellers speak for the second category of tourists, who are confronted in the South by murmurs of a sexuality that has little place in the landscapes of home.

When Dorothea Brooke, the heroine of George Eliot's *Middlemarch*, goes to Rome for her honeymoon, it quickly becomes apparent that 'the gigantic broken revelations of that Imperial and Papal city thrust abruptly on the notions of a girl who had been brought up in English and Swiss Puritanism' carry intimations that are both feared and longed for:

> . . . all this vast wreck of ambitious ideals, sensuous and spiritual, mixed confusedly with the signs of breathing forgetfulness and degradation, at first jarred her as with an electric shock, and then urged themselves on her with that ache belonging to a glut of confused ideas which

check the flow of emotion. Forms both pale and glowing took possession of her young sense, and fixed themselves in her memory even when she was not thinking of them, preparing strange associations which remained through her after-years.

Eliot's language – ambiguous, metaphorical, suggestive – hints at a response that becomes clearer as we read the accounts of other nineteenth-century women: of Lady Morgan in the Uffizi, who experiences 'a rush of recollection, a fulness of hope, that almost amounts to a physical sensation; and the breath shortens, as imagination hurries from object to object, and knows not where to pause, or what to enjoy'; of Fanny Kemble in front of the Vatican Apollo: 'I could believe the legend of the girl who died for love of it; for myself, my eyes swam in tears and my knees knocked together, and I could hardly draw my breath while I stood before it'; of Elizabeth Sewell on the charm of Venice, able to recognise without misgiving 'a luxury in the mere feeling of existence'; of Anna Jameson on her balcony in Naples, 'looking out upon the lovely scene before me, with a kind of pensive dreamy rapture'.

The cultural was often no more than a step from the sensual. Matthew Arnold wrote of the Renaissance as in part 'a return to the life of the senses', and this was manifest in the swooning responses of many female tourists to the paintings and sculptures they were free to contemplate in Italy. Earlier in the century Anna Jameson had herself drawn attention to the perilous elision of Italian culture and Italian sensuality. At a performance of Vigano's ballet *Didone Abbandonata* in Milan she had noticed a young English girl 'apparently not fifteen, with laughing lips and dimpled cheeks, the very personification of blooming, innocent, *English* loveliness'. She watches her during the scene in which Dido and Aeneas are about to consummate their love in a cave: 'I saw her cheeks flush, her

eyes glisten, her bosom flutter, as if with sighs I could not over-
hear, till at length, overpowered with emotion, she turned
away her head, and covered her eyes with her hand.' Erotic
enticements are all around, and the risk, as Jameson warns, is
that the pursuit of culture will lead into moral danger:
'Mothers! – English mothers! who bring your daughters
abroad to finish their education – do ye well to expose them
to scenes like these, and *force* the young bud of early feeling in
such a precious hot bed as this? – Can a finer finger on the
piano, – a finer taste in painting, or any possible improvement
in foreign arts, and foreign graces, compensate for one taint on
that moral purity, which has ever been (and may it ever be!)
the boast, the charm of Englishwomen?'

Hostile to English restraint, the atmosphere of Italy encouraged an unfamiliar sense of 'luxury in the mere feeling of
existence'. Like Mary Shelley's reaction to the vines and fig-
trees ('Come and eat. Will you?'), Sewell's phrase suggests an
openness to experience, almost an abandonment to it, that has
been purged of the complications and restrictions of life at
home. So Frances Trollope describes 'abandoning myself in
delicious idleness to the gentle movement of our gondola,
floating here, and floating there, without any other end or
object than the enjoyment of that waking dream of beauty',
and Lady Morgan, likewise yielding to 'the exquisite indulgence' of Venetian life, recalls how pleasant it was 'to sink on
the down of the cushioned gondola ... enjoying existence for
existence sake'. That the gondola should be a focus for these
sensations is entirely appropriate. It would be hard to imagine
a form of conveyance more antithetical to the earnest, morally
charged tenor of Victorian life. With its sinuous glide which
brings the reclining passenger so close to the lapping water, it
invites a kind of relaxation unthinkable in the context of ordinary social duties. Just how close such responses bring the
traveller to forbidden ground can be measured by comparing
them with this passage from Burton's *Personal Narrative of a*

Pilgrimage to Al-Madinah and Meccah (1855–56). To explain the Arab word *kayf,* he is trying to summarise the state of mind of the Asiatic voluptuary:

> The savouring of animal existence; the passive enjoyment of mere sense; the pleasant languor, the dreamy tranquillity, the airy castle-building, which in Asia stand in lieu of the vigorous, intensive, passionate life of Europe. It is the result of a lively, impressible, excitable nature, and exquisite sensibility of nerve; it argues a voluptuousness unknown to northern regions, where happiness is placed in the exertion of mental and physical powers.

If this voluptuousness was unknown to northern regions, it clearly did not remain so to the lively, impressible, excitable travellers we've been considering. The revelation of foreign travel for these women was the range of emotional and sensual experience from which they were normally cut off.

'A short season of transport' was how Harriet Martineau described her stay in Cairo, adding that the traveller in Egypt must 'surrender himself to the most wonderful and romantic dream that can ever meet his waking senses'. The excitement of this sensual assault was borne in on Florence Nightingale when she too visited Egypt three years later. In 1849, to the dismay of her mother, she had rejected a proposal of marriage from the eligible Richard Monckton Milnes. Instead of going to the altar she went abroad, and by November of the same year she was in Cairo with her friends the Bracebridges. A couple of months later, after a thrilling ride up the cataracts of the Nile, she remarked on the contrast with what she had left behind: 'The inward excitement of European life is so great, its outward excitement so small, that a violent external call upon our senses and instincts to us is luxury and peace.'

Responding to this call could have powerful consequences. The literary critic Shirley Foster suggests that Italy acquired for

Victorian women travellers a particular symbolic meaning: 'Standing for the fulfilment of desire and the possibility of spiritual expansion beyond the confines of normal life, it promised release from the prosaic conditions of domesticity and enjoyment of an alternative reality which both permitted and encouraged self-gratification'. Foster goes on to point out how women who suffered nervous crises and chronic ill-health in England found themselves able to endure, and even enjoy, the hardships of crossing the Alps or climbing Vesuvius once they got away from the restraints of home. Emily Birchall's dismissal of the chair-bearers on Vesuvius who protested the difficulty of the ascent – 'It is too far for a lady . . . La signora would be much better in a chair' – stands as a declaration of independence from all the bonds of social expectation that condemned women to physical debility. 'At last we shook ourselves free of these wretches,' she writes, 'and proceeded on our way' – with smoke rising from the ground beneath their feet.

The argument that Italy presented an alternative, less prosaic reality, highlights a link, clearly evident in the lives of Victorian women, between the lure of travel and the fantasies of displacement offered by reading. Those who cannot move in any other way can at least be transported by novels and poems. In some cases the novels were themselves a spur to travel. Mme de Staël's *Corinne* (1807), for example, was hugely influential in promoting nineteenth-century sentiment for Italy, not least because it confirmed in vivid terms just the sort of symbolic status that Foster has in mind. For de Staël, the countryside around Naples was 'the image of the human passions': 'sulphurous and fertile, its dangers and pleasures seem born of those flaming volcanoes which give the air such charms and make the ground under our feet rumble with thunder'. Her words echoed in the imagination of readers through the next half-century and more.

One tourist who had read de Staël with passion was the American teacher and journalist, Margaret Fuller. No one provides a clearer image of the erotic potential of the Italian pilgrimage. Given a bookish upbringing by her father, she was soon aware that the rarefied atmosphere of intellectual New England offered little to the more romantic side of her nature. She had read Goethe as well as de Staël: Europe, Italy in particular, became the focus of her longings. 'Once I was almost all intellect; now I am almost all feeling,' she wrote to a friend in 1841. 'Nature vindicates her rights, and I feel all Italy glowing beneath the Saxon crust. This cannot last long; I shall burn to ashes if all this smoulders here much longer.' It smouldered on for another five years. After repeated delays, she finally set sail in the summer of 1846, an unmarried woman of letters, thirty-six years old, travelling as a correspondent for Horace Greeley's *New York Tribune*. The belated pilgrimage did not disappoint her. By November she could write from Paris: 'I find how true for me was the lure that always drew me towards Europe. It was no false instinct that said I might here find an atmosphere needed to develop me in ways *I* need.' A few months later the volcanic emotions awakened by the prospect of Italy were matched by personal experience. A meeting in Rome with the Marchese Giovanni Angelo Ossoli led to an affair, the birth of a son, and subsequently marriage. Her love for Ossoli, an ardent Republican, drew her further into the political turmoil of the time, adding to the romance of a story which ended in tragedy when both of them were drowned, along with their child, on the way back to America in July 1850.

Fuller was exceptional. What was involved for most of the women who made their way through Europe was not direct access to erotic experience but a whisper of it created by the impact of the physical world on their senses. The image of Italy's molten lava glowing beneath the Saxon crust is none the less apt. 'I have just seen the most magnificent sight,' writes Anna Jameson; 'one which I have often dreamed of, often longed to behold, and having beheld, never shall forget.

Mount Vesuvius is at this moment blazing like a huge furnace; throwing up every minute, or half minute, columns of fire and red hot stones, which fall in showers and bound down the side of the mountain . . . I can hardly write, my mind is so over-flowing with astonishment, admiration, and sublime pleasure.' The smouldering ground that threatens to burn through Birchall's boot, the red-hot boulder at which Jameson stops to warm her hands, and indeed the whole project of climbing the great volcano, with its dangerous columns of fire, generate an excitement that is unmistakably sexual. In its awesome natural power and the answering response it drew from Victorian women tourists, Vesuvius had an affinity, as Fanny Kemble noted, with another great tourist destination of the age, Niagara. Kemble's description of the 'terrible loveliness' of the waterfall conveys an explosive fascination:

> I feel half crazy whenever I think of it. I went three times under the sheet of water; once I had a guide as far as the entrance, and twice I went under entirely alone. If you fancy the sea tumbling down from the moon, you still have no idea of this glorious huge heap of tumbling waters . . . As I stood upon the brink of the abyss when I first saw it, the impulse to jump down seemed all but an irresistible necessity . . . I think it would be delightful to pass one's life by this wonderful creature's side, and quite pleasant to die and be buried in its bosom . . .

The water's plunge into foamy annihilation presents itself to many of the women who observe it as a kind of shocking invitation. Marianne Finch's wild impulse – 'I seemed to have caught the frenzy of the Rapids, and longed to precipitate myself into the Niagara; anything to *know* it – to *feel* its power' – and Jameson's image of the rapids 'whirling, boiling, dancing, sparkling along . . . rejoicing as if escaped from bondage', both express a response that links their own desires to the elemental freedom of the water. The idea of the water's destructive force, says Jameson, 'thrills the blood'. Kemble's reaction to a spectacular landscape near West Point sums up the longing for self-abandonment that characterises so much of this writing:

> I looked down, and for a moment my breath seemed to stop, the pulsation of my heart to cease – I was filled with awe. The beauty and wild sublimity of what I beheld seemed almost to crush my faculties, – I felt dizzy as though my senses were drowning, – I felt as though I had been carried into the immediate presence of God . . . I could have stretched out my arms, and shouted aloud – I could have fallen on my knees, and worshipped – I could have committed any extravagance that ecstasy could suggest.

Compare this with Kemble's response to her first train journey, which has a similarly orgasmic strain: 'I stood up and with my bonnet off "drank the air before me". The wind, which was strong, or perhaps the force of our own thrusting against it, absolutely weighed my eyelids down . . . A common sheet of paper is enough for love, but a foolscap can alone contain a railroad and my ecstasies.' There is, as we noted in the Introduction, a teasing kinship between the liberating effects of the physical and the imaginative sides of travels.

Kemble goes well beyond what most of the tourists would have been willing to put down on paper, but the sensation of being overwhelmed, and of being physically and emotionally released by that sensation, was for many of them central to the experience of travel. It is related to what the cultural critic Roland Barthes had in mind when he talked in 1977 of travel as 'linked to a kind of amorous awareness'. Lucie Duff Gordon (1821–69), who was obliged by ill-health to spend most of the last seven years of her life in Egypt, displays exactly this kind of awareness in her letters home, which burn with an intensity that her very British husband, in the familiar surroundings of Westminster, found it difficult to match. Tempting him to come out for a visit with a kaleidoscope of scenes that tempted him not at all, she imagined how he would 'revel' in ancient Cairo, peep up at lattice windows, gape at the sights of the bazaar, 'go wild over the mosques, laugh at portly Turks and dignified sheikhs on their white donkeys, drink sherbet in the streets, ride wildly about on a donkey, peer under black veils at beautiful eyes, and feel generally intoxicated'. Such images of wildness and intoxication give voice to an almost ecstatic release from the constraints of life in England. The impatience of convention that could at home be expressed only by a mild bohemianism in dress and behaviour (she was noted for smoking cigars and staying at her table for the port) has here expanded into a celebration of life's diversity that was quite beyond the reach of most of her contemporaries. As she discarded the various articles of clothing essential to the respectable Victorian lady – gloves, hat, underskirts, stockings and finally stays – she was drawn further and further into a different sensual and imaginative world. It was an experience that could only have been offered by a foreign country. Her awareness is so passionate and so physical that one is left with the impression of following a love affair – not just her love for Egypt but Egypt's for her. Unable to sleep one night at Philae, she went out to lie on the parapet of the temple:

What a night! What a lovely view! The stars gave as much light as the moon in Europe, and all but the cataract was still as death and glowing hot and the palm trees were more graceful and dreamy than ever. Then Omar woke and came and sat at my feet and rubbed them, and sang a song of a Turkish slave . . . Then the day broke deep crimson and I went down and bathed in the Nile and saw the girls on the island opposite in their summer fashions consisting of a leather fringe round their slender hips;

divinely graceful bearing huge . . . baskets of corn on their . . . heads, and I went up and sat at the end of the colonnade looking up into Ethiopia and dreamed dreams . . . until the great [sun god] Amun Ra kissed my northern face too hotly and drove me into the temple to breakfast and coffee and pipes.

The glowing heat of the night, the native servant rubbing her feet, the crimson daybreak, the girls on the island, the dreams, the god's embrace – all make the writing pulse with a sensuality that declares itself in every detail to be the antithesis of Englishness. Such fruits of travel must have been compensation of a sort for the consumption that forced her away from her family before killing her at the age of forty-eight.

Lucie Duff Gordon's engaging frankness was hers by nature, but travel gave it latitude. For her, as for so many women, being abroad extended the range of permissible responses. Fanny Kemble notices the mule and cattle drivers of the Campagna with their 'brilliant colouring and vivid expression peculiar to this singularly handsome race', but she also notices their tight breeches and leather gaiters showing off their 'straight and well-proportioned limbs'. The quality of admiration is untethered by moral concerns. When she catches sight of a strikingly beautiful group of girls on the way out of Tivoli, singing and laughing as they walk along with intertwined arms and bare heads, her reaction transforms moral negatives into aesthetic positives: 'they would have formed a splendid study for a painter, with their fine heads and full figures and free reckless bearing; they looked dirty and saucy, but most eminently picturesque'. Laughing, singing, free, reckless, dirty, saucy – these girls could hardly be more of an affront to Victorian notions of female decorum. To judge them positively, as Kemble is doing even while she maintains a semi-aesthetic distance from them, is to share imaginatively in the values of another world.

For both men and women that was the promise of the South, and also its danger. The Tivoli girls have the same kind of raw sensuality as the painters' models, 'with splendid heads and shoulders, and daggers thrust through the braids of their hair', that Kemble sees on the Spanish Steps in Rome: 'here they sit and stand, and lounge and loll in the sun, screaming, shouting, laughing, gesticulating, or dozing like cats with half-closed eyes upon the worn stone steps; or with true brotherly humanity exploring the animated nature of each other's elf-locks.' They are, she adds, in a phrase that catches all the ambivalence of the Victorian tourist, 'beautiful beastly creatures'. The Mediterranean's beauty and freedom is inextricable from its squalor and animal sexuality.

4

Symonds and Fusato

The double-edged attraction of the South has a special place in the life of John Addington Symonds, for whom the Mediterranean journey was a pilgrimage in all three senses: cultural, spiritual and sexual. In itself his story would be of limited interest, but by the second half of the nineteenth century a number of factors were combining to give it wider relevance. The view of travel as a personal odyssey had lent a new importance to relationships formed abroad. Moreover, modern transport meant that these relationships could now be renewed year by year; it was no longer the case, as when Boswell left Siena, that the parting was necessarily final. These changes coincided with a widening of sympathies in Victorian England, reflected in both its literature and its institutions. For lack of a better term, we can call it the birth of a modern social conscience. Among other things, this involves an imaginative awareness of what it means to be at the bottom of the heap, to be Joe the Crossing Sweeper in *Bleak House* or one of the needlewomen turned prostitute described by Henry Mayhew; and this in turn imposes new responsibilities towards such people. True, these shifts in sensibility affected only a fraction of the population directly, but they were part of the current of the time, and they give resonance to the efforts by Symonds to change the meaning that could be ascribed to his sexual encounters abroad. Against the grain of the previous couple of centuries, he wanted to reconcile the sensuous and the spiritual in his response to Italy.

In February 1877 he was giving a course of lectures on 'Florence and the Medici' at the Royal Institution. A married man of thirty-six, with four daughters, he was the author of a number of volumes of classical and literary studies and had already begun to publish the massive *Renaissance in Italy* on which his reputation was to rest. In spite of some unwelcome controversy that had blasted his chances of being elected Oxford Professor of Poetry, Symonds was well on the way to becoming an eminent Victorian. And for at least seventy years after his death, this is what, in the eyes of the public, he remained. As late as the 1970s, literary reference books were still making no mention of what Symonds himself described in his *Memoirs* as 'the underlying preoccupation of my life'. The reason for this was simple: the *Memoirs*, which deal in some detail with his homosexuality, were not published until 1984. In the care of the London Library, they had been consulted by a few scholars – Phyllis Grosskurth made use of them for her 1964 biography – but they had not been allowed into the public domain. Without them we should know little beyond the public façade of Symonds's life. (About literature, for example, to outward appearance his chief interest, he remarks, 'I have never been able to regard it very seriously'.) As it is, we find a private reality shaped by incidents and emotions that were scarcely permitted to ripple the surface he presented to the world. The travels which seemed a natural consequence of precarious health and a professional interest in Italy are revealed as having another level of motivation altogether. As so often in the history of tourism, there was a dimension of the story that had remained invisible.

For Symonds, the decisive moment came during this engagement at the Royal Institution when an acquaintance took him one day to a well-known male brothel near the Regent's Park Barracks, where he was introduced to a 'brawny young soldier' whom he arranged to meet later in a private room: 'For the first time in my experience I shared a bed with one so different from myself, so ardently desired by me, so supremely beautiful in my eyes, so attractive to my senses.' Afterwards they smoked and talked together. The soldier's conduct, 'comradely and natural' in Symonds's perception of it, 'taught me something I had never before conceived about illicit sexual relations'. It was a lesson in sex as adventure, discovery and companionship as well as sensual pleasure. The episode, he says, 'exercised a powerful effect upon my life'. In fact, it was to be a guiding influence on the foreign travels which began later the same year when ill-health forced him away from England.

The idea was to make for Egypt, where it was hoped that the dry air would mend his damaged lungs; but he stopped at Davos on the way. Within a few months he had fallen in love with a nineteen-year-old local youth, Christian Buol, 'one of the finest specimens of robust, handsome, intelligent and gentle adolescence I have ever met with'. Egypt was abandoned, and Davos became his base for the rest of his life.

Symonds gained a wide acquaintance among the local population – peasants, parsons, doctors, hunters, guides, shopkeepers, stableboys, artisans – and he makes no bones about the nature of his relations with them: 'Entering thus into their lives, I have brought, as I confessed above, my passions with me; and often have I enjoyed the sweetest fruits of privacy, with no back thoughts except such as must be always given to law and custom.' In this he was no different from a stream of other tourists who were happy to take advantage of the sexual opportunities afforded by Continental travel. For many, including friends of Symonds such as Ronald Gower, Roden Noel and Theo Marzials, this was one of the privately acknowledged reasons for going abroad. Members of the first generation that could benefit from the growing network of European railways, they no longer looked on Continental travel as an occasional adventure; it was part of their way of life.

But in the case of Symonds, the issue was less straight-forward. What he had taken away from his encounter with the guardsman was a feeling of sexual liberation that seemed to promise a resolution of the dilemma that had poisoned much of his early life. He had already outlined it in a pamphlet called *A Problem in Greek Ethics* (1883).* This study of ancient Greek attitudes to pederasty had concluded that there were 'two separate forms of masculine passion clearly marked in early Hellas – a noble and a base, a spiritual and a sensual'. For 'the paederast of nobler quality', this posed a problem summed up in Plato's *Phaedrus*:

> . . . he is drawn different ways, and is in doubt between two principles, the one exhorting him to enjoy the beauty of the youth, and the other forbidding him; for the one is a lover of the body and hungers after beauty like ripe fruit, and would fain satisfy himself without any regard to the character of the beloved; and the other holds the desire of the body to be a secondary matter, . . . and desiring the soul of the other in a becoming manner, regards the satisfaction of the bodily love as wantonness.

This describes just the situation in which Symonds had always found himself. His experience with the guardsman had opened up the possibility that sex might not after all be at odds with the ideal of wholesome male companionship he aspired to. He went abroad desperately wanting the release offered by casual sex with foreigners but wanting also to realise an ideal that would transcend the sordid commerce of brothels and backstreets. The quest was one that would lead him to define a new kind of relationship between travel and sex, and thereby,

---

* Symonds had written this in 1873 but did not publish it until ten years later.

77

for a substantial group of tourists, to redefine the meaning of travel.

It was of course the Mediterranean that drew him. In a way, he was sexually more comfortable in Switzerland, but this was because neither the dilemma nor the attempt to resolve it was so intense there. The relationship he describes with Christian Buol, cemented by loans amounting to £3,000 to help Christian's family out of financial difficulty, teeters on the edge of a sexuality that cannot quite be acknowledged because Symonds is determined not to slip from the role of noble lover. Sleeping in the same bed together, viewing 'the naked splendour of his perfect body', enjoying the 'innocent delights of privacy' are all contained within notions of comradeship and aesthetic appreciation. 'But neither in act nor deed, far less in words, did the least shadow of lust cloud the serenity of that masculine communion. (. . .) Anyone who has enjoyed the privilege of Christian's acquaintance will know that he could not have yielded a base pleasure to me, and that I could not have dared to demand it.'

It would be ungenerous not to believe this, particularly since Symonds is so candid about his other relationships in Davos and Italy. What it suggests is that, in spite of the discovery he claims to have made with the guardsman, he was still trapped in the Platonic dilemma, restricting his hunger for Christian to the soul and finding relief for the senses elsewhere. It is clear from his letters and memoirs that however wide-ranging his adventures in Davos, Italy was the place he identified with sensual fulfilment. From his Venetian *entresol* on the Zattere he had a window on a lovelier world. 'I am just above a bridge,' he wrote to Edmund Gosse, '. . . up & down wh go divine beings: sailors of the marine, soldiers, blue vested & trousered fishermen, swaggering gondoliers. I can almost see their faces as they top the bridge.' It was here in Venice, among so many objects of desire, that he at last managed to persuade himself that he had resolved the conflicting claims of the sexual and the spiritual.

In the spring of 1881 Symonds was drinking one afternoon with his friend Horatio Brown in a wineshop on the Lido when Brown pointed out a pair of men in the white uniform of gondoliers, one of them strikingly handsome. For Symonds, it was a *coup de foudre*. In breathless sentences written a few days after their first meeting, he notes the man's fiery eyes, dazzling teeth, short blond moustache and bronzed skin, which nonetheless showed 'white and delicate through open front and sleeves of lilac shirt'. With his 'wild glance of a Triton', he looked as though 'the sea waves and the sun had made him in some hour of secret and unquiet rapture'. (This bewitching physical vitality may be something more than a lover's fantasy. Eleven years later, the poet Arthur Symons, quite different from Symonds in character and sexual interests, met Fusato in London and found a man 'whose vivid and passionate glances, whose wild gestures, whose intense excitement, whose rapid interchange of words sent waves of sensation over me'.) Symonds's passion was instant and obsessive: 'This love at first sight for Angelo Fusato was an affair not merely of desire and instinct but also of imagination. He took hold of me by a hundred subtle threads of feeling, in which the powerful and radiant manhood of the splendid animal was intertwined with sentiment for Venice, a keen delight in the landscape of the lagoons, and something penetrative and pathetic in the man.' Fusato, who was twenty-four at the time, responded to the Englishman's overtures with a lack of scruple that Symonds found disconcerting. Next evening they met at nine by the Church of the Gesuati on the Zattere and went back to Symonds's apartment. In the words of the sonnet Symonds wrote on the episode, 'There on the counterpane, he bade me use/Even as I willed his body'. But Symonds was paralysed by the ideal role in which he had cast himself – 'Love forbade'. He turned down the offer in some confusion and left Venice the following day. After an uneasy summer tormented by thoughts of Fusato, he returned in the autumn, 'resolved to establish this now firmly rooted passion upon some more solid basis'.

That Symonds should have fallen for a gondolier is unsurprising. They were the staple fare of tourists in search of sexual adventure. 'The gondoliers of Venice are so accustomed to these demands,' Symonds notes, in a remark which says much about the routine nature of Victorian sex tourism, 'that they think little of gratifying the caprice of ephemeral lovers.' In a letter to Havelock Ellis, he recalls a male prostitute he came across at Naples who said that he was a Venetian 'but had come to Naples because at Venice he only found custom with Englishmen, Swedes and Russians whereas at Naples he could live in excellent Italian society and be abundantly supported'. It was to Venice that A.E. Housman made annual visits for his continuing affair with a one-eyed gondolier called Andrea, and from Venice that Corvo, a few years later, wrote enthusiastically to Charles Masson Foxe about the sexual possibilities of a city full of gondoliers. Tourists, both British and American, continued to be well served through at least the first half of the twentieth century: Cole Porter in the Twenties and Truman Capote in the Fifties were among many who took advantage of this tradition of tolerant compliance.

Not that it was a purely homosexual tradition. For women tourists, gondoliers offered a piquant combination of exoticism, physical charm, availability and discretion that was a strong incentive to female sex tourism. When Lady Chatterley and her sister reach Venice, they engage a gondolier who glances swiftly at Connie's card 'with his hot, southern blue eyes' and soon becomes devoted to them, 'as he had been devoted to cargoes of ladies in the past. He was perfectly ready to prostitute himself to them, if they wanted him: he secretly hoped they would want him. They would give him a handsome present, and it would come in very handy, as he was just going to be married.'

Such encounters, whether with men or women, were more or less part of the job, and Fusato was well practised in handling them. But Symonds wanted much more. While travelling in Northern Italy in 1868 he had written the first draft of a poem which, according to his *Memoirs*, had 'a deep significance for me'. Called 'Phallus Impudicus' after 'a singular and fetid fungus which exactly imitates in shape the *membrum virile* when erect', it draws on the sort of poignant sentimental/aesthetic experience of male Italian beauty common among Victorian homosexuals (which Symonds had had with particular intensity during a stay in Naples), and links it with the equally common experience of casual sex purchased by the wayside. Presented in three sections, the poem opens with the discovery of the fungus among the debris of a squalid wood. In the second part the scene changes to an inn at Naples where the poet goes at dawn into the adjoining room, as Symonds had done, and finds his carriage-driver, a 'tall Sorrento lad', sleeping naked on the bed. His enraptured response to the boy's body – 'rosy nipples', 'marble manspheres', 'lustrous gland' etc. – leads into a hectic declaration of spiritual joy. In the third part of the poem a middle-aged man is seen peering lustfully over a bridge in Venice at the half-clothed, muscular fishermen who are idling beneath it. The poet watches this degraded figure straining to get a view of those who stop to urinate against the wall. At length an especially handsome youth comes by, the man quickly strikes a bargain with him, and the two go off together.

The poem's 'deep significance' for Symonds is clear enough; it recasts in terms of his own sexual experience Plato's conflict between the two principles that pull against each other in the better sort of pederast. Symonds is both the poet roused to spiritual joy by the sleeping carriage-driver and the middle-aged lecher picking up Venetian fishermen. In Fusato he wanted to find the ideal figure who would enable him to unite the two, turning the base metal of physical lust to gold.

Their first assignation proved such an embarrassing failure because Fusato had at once classified Symonds as the middle-aged lecher and reacted accordingly.

In the process of vindicating his passion, Symonds bought Fusato a gondola of his own, supplied him with money, enabled him and his girlfriend to set up house, promoted their marriage, and finally took him on as his private gondolier at fixed wages. The result was a relationship he could regard with satisfaction: 'Though it began in folly and crime, according to the constitution of society, it has benefited him and proved a source of comfort and instruction to myself'. Symonds had purchased an increasingly large stake in Fusato's life and in doing so had successfully distinguished himself from the gondolier's usual clients, 'those other men to whose caprices he had sold his beauty'. But he had done more than this. His pursuit of Fusato, in marrying sex tourism to the quest for a romantic ideal, had produced a distinctively modern category of tourist experience that would later be explored by the kinds of traveller who are the subject of the next chapter.

One aspect of it is a rather un-British willingness to come to terms with the outlook and lifestyle of the local population. The casual exploitation of sexual opportunity among friends of Symonds like Gower and Noel belonged to the tradition of Connoisseur tourism that had been around since the Grand Tour and still predominates today; its paradigm, as we have seen, is the gourmet who selects particular dishes (places, people) without any motive beyond the satisfaction of the palate. It is a form of travel that may increase knowledge and refine taste but that leaves the traveller's basic assumptions undisturbed. To a large extent the tourist remains insulated within a national bubble that preserves intact the familiar distinctions of language, class, race, wealth, education and so on. This was how the English preferred it. 'Many English travellers remain four or five years abroad,' wrote John Moore in

1779, 'and have seldom, during all this space, been in any company, but that of their own countrymen.' Bishop Hurd had observed the same tendency of the English 'to flock together into little knots and clubs of their own countrymen'. In similar vein Lord Chesterfield satirised the young Englishman abroad who complains that his bearleader is 'always plaguing me to go into foreign companies'. In truth, he suggests, these tourists never leave home, for 'they go into no foreign company, at least none good; but dine and sup with one another only, at the tavern'. To Lady Blessington it appeared that the English travelled 'not so much for the purpose of studying the manners of other lands as for that of establishing and displaying their own'.

Changes in tourism later in the nineteenth century had little effect on this. Travellers, even the most intelligent of them, tended to regard the countries they visited as, in the words of John Pemble, 'museums, sanatoria, and asylums': 'Whether they stayed in Grand Hotels, in country inns, or under canvas, the British were almost all alike in that they had little interest in the idea of close contact with Mediterranean people'. There is an argument for saying that it was primarily through sexual relationships of the kind embarked on by Symonds that British tourists made any real contact with the local population at all. His wooing of Fusato put any sort of tourist insularity out of the question.

The *Memoirs* describe with pride his growing intimacy with the gondolier. It was, as he claims, 'an affair not merely of desire and instinct but also of imagination'. The progress of his love was inseparable from his imaginative response to its context – to Venice itself, to the unfamiliar society into which Fusato introduced him, to the sort of companionship he found there. In a letter to Charles Kains-Jackson, who had complained that he could not see the beauty of the Swiss, Symonds wrote from Venice, 'A friend of mine, an attaché at St Petersburg, says what is true: "You do not feel the beauty of a nation till you have slept with one of them"'.* At this point sex is not just an adjunct of travel, it is what gives travel its meaning. It is both the fulfilment of the journey and itself a mode of journeying – into another person, another culture, another social group, another way of life.

Today it is easy to make fun of the manoeuvres by which Symonds tried to justify and ennoble his illicit passions, but his attitude has little to do with what is crudely labelled Victorian hypocrisy. Then as now, the tension between sexual impulse and the demands of propriety did indeed produce a form of hypocrisy, in which Symonds undoubtedly shared, but the claims he makes for the relationships discussed in his *Memoirs* are not part of it. As Symonds himself realised, there may well be an element of self-delusion in these images of wholesome comradeship, widening horizons and mutual benefit, but they nonetheless represent a genuine attempt to reconcile the perceived contradiction between sexual appetite and human decency. And this troubled but humane endeavour was quite as characteristically Victorian as the practice of hypocrisy.

It signalled a radical break with the conventional attitudes of the British tourist. Beyond the knowledge and skills of the Connoisseur, beyond the store of personal experience, beyond even the emancipation of the senses, there is a new, often unconscious, goal for the traveller, which might be summed up in the words E.M. Forster took as the epigraph to *Howards*

---

* This belief that it is through sexual contact that one gets to the heart of a nation, though simplistic in its assumption of a unified entity waiting to be grasped by the traveller, has wide currency. Compare, for example, the comment of a young Sudanese on his experiences in Britain: 'One thing I noticed was that you can never understand a people well enough ... until you are in bed with a woman.' (Hopwood, 245.) Or the photographer Mirella Ricciardi on her affair with a black fisherman in Kenya: 'At one with him, I was at one with Africa.' (*Telegraph Magazine*, 21 October 2000, p. 44.)

End (1910), 'Only connect . . .'. Like Symonds, Forster's pilgrims to the Mediterranean find not just liberation but revelation, and if we are to trace the development of the pilgrim identity, we need to follow the line that leads through Forster into the twentieth century.

5

Sexual Pilgrims

Symonds's experience was at one level quintessentially Victorian, but it was also part of a continuing tradition that looks to the sexual possibilities of travel as a way of unlocking the personality. Both historically and temperamentally, E.M. Forster offers a link between the Victorian and the modern. Born in 1879 and brought up by an over-protective mother, he had little chance to escape the stifling atmosphere of late Victorian England. Apart from a brief visit to Northern France in April 1895, he did not get abroad until he was twenty-two. The journey was a turning point. 'I am getting to like Italy,' he wrote back to the Cambridge don Goldsworthy Lowes Dickinson in the spring of 1902. 'I was more horribly Northern than I thought and took some time to thaw.'*

This shift of allegiance from North to South was summed up in 'The Story of a Panic' (1904), which tells of a sulky adolescent, Eustace Robinson, transformed by an encounter with the god Pan while on holiday in Italy. The prim narrator exemplifies everything respectable, well-meaning and soul-destroying about the English middle classes. His recipe for the moody adolescent – 'what he really needed was discipline' – is brought

---

* It was Goldsworthy Lowes Dickinson who wrote the entry in the *Dictionary of National Biography* for Oscar Browning, the Eton schoolmaster whose sexual indiscretions led to his dismissal in 1875. Browning later retired to Rome, where, in Dickinson's arresting phrase, 'he helped young Italians, as he had done young Englishmen, towards the openings they desired'.

up against the fundamental Italian experience of anarchic sensuality. While the English tourists picnic stuffily in the woods above Ravello, Pan, the primitive fertility god, half-human, half-animal, sweeps down the hillside and scatters them in terror, all except Eustace, whom they find afterwards in a post-coital daze. Transfigured by the event, he gives himself up to wild displays of emotion and animalism, rolling like a dog in the goat's foot-marks Pan has left in the moist earth, wailing in front of the cathedral for Gennaro, the hotel waiter, leaping into his arms when they get back to the hotel, and finally escaping to freedom from the hotel room where the English have attempted to restrain him. The story ends with the distant sound of his shouts and laughter as he runs down the valley towards the sea.

Right at the start of Forster's career, 'The Story of a Panic' stands as a concise declaration of what were to be the central themes of both his life and work. On a larger canvas Eustace's story becomes that of Lucy Honeychurch, to whom Italy offers a modified version of the same revelation in *A Room with a View* (1908), and it is still there in Adela Quested's experience of India in Forster's last novel. On this first visit to Italy, accompanied by his mother, Forster's own revelation was a matter of perception and understanding rather than of any particular incident. While staying in Taormina he might, like Oscar Wilde a few years earlier, have been stirred by a visit to Baron Wilhelm von Gloeden, the German Count whose photographs of naked Sicilian youths had made him something of a celebrity, but the true impact of Italy was less tangible. For Forster, as for a long line of tourists from Goethe onwards, the meaning of the Italian journey lay in its seductive invitation to recognise aspects of himself that had been suppressed at home. Mr Emerson's advice to Lucy Honeychurch to 'Let yourself go' echoes the whispered temptation that Italy has always put to the English tourist. In Santa Croce, having left behind her Baedeker, Lucy finds that 'the pernicious charm of Italy worked on her, and, instead of acquiring information, she began to be happy'. The shift in priorities marks the difference between the Connoisseur and the Pilgrim, but also, in the terms of the novel, between the cautious, acquisitive North and the carefree South. To Forster, the sensual tones of Italy – its landscape, its climate, its sexual tolerance – expressed a world of possibilities that stood in direct opposition to the deadly proprieties of suburban England.

Just as Symonds had located his soul's home in Ancient Greece, so Forster, in the first of his stories to be published, 'Albergo Empedocle',* tells of a man, on holiday in Sicily with his fiancée and her family, who falls asleep one afternoon in the ruins of a Greek temple and dreams that he has lived there before. Harold is a stolid unimaginative sort of man, but his fiancée's father has already detected a deviant strain in him ('I'll have no queerness in a son-in-law!'). As in the case of Eustace, Harold's brush with classical antiquity releases a joyous responsiveness to the world around him, and he flings his arms round his fiancée – 'an embrace very different from the decorous peck by which he had marked the commencement of their engagement'. But when she asks him about his experience of love in his previous existence, it becomes clear that his love for her is a shadow of the different sort of love he enjoyed as an Ancient Greek:

> 'I loved very differently.' He was holding back the brambles to prevent them from tearing her dress as he spoke. One of the thorns scratched him on the hand. 'Yes, I loved better too,' he said, watching the little drops of blood swell out.

The vision that has overwhelmed him is an affront to both reason and religious propriety. In the face of the cold English

---

* Forster subsequently excluded the story from his canon, preferring to start with 'The Story of a Panic'.

scepticism of Mildred and her family, it cannot be sustained. Rather than lose it, Harold retreats into madness.

The drops of blood that swell from his hand, like the drops that spatter Lucy Honeychurch's art photographs in the Piazza Signoria, emphasise that the allegiance of the south is to blood rather than intellect. Lucy's ultra-civilised and quite bloodless fiancé, Cecil, who piques himself on his cosmopolitanism, is an image of all that has to be surrendered if the real message of Italy is to be understood – as Lucy surrenders to George Emerson's kiss when she falls, enveloped by light and beauty, on to the violet-covered terrace above Florence.

In reality, Forster found the liberation of the senses easier to preach than to practise. He had to travel far in order to achieve his first complete sexual relationship. The bare details of the affair – with a tram conductor called Mohammed el Adl whom Forster met in Alexandria during the First World War when he himself was almost thirty-nine – give some idea just how far. It was abroad in the geographical sense, but the wartime setting and the working-class lover suggest other ways in which Forster was abroad. War, like travel, upsets the comfortable certainties of ordinary life, breaks up routines, erodes inhibitions. It is a means of escaping the bonds that hold you to a particular place and a particular way of life. And one of these bonds is class. Slipping its leash, as Symonds too had found, was another kind of travel. (Christopher Isherwood later tried to explain its relevance to his own compulsion to get out of England: '. . . Christopher was suffering from an inhibition, then not unusual among upper-class homosexuals; he couldn't relax sexually with a member of his own class or nation. He needed a working-class foreigner.') The triple spur of Egypt, wartime, and a desirable partner, allied to the desperation of advancing age, was finally enough to push Forster over the brink.

His frustration, intensified by the sense of a new freedom away from his mother and within touching distance of the young soldiers on the beach ('down by the sea many of them spend half their days naked and unrebuked'), was conveyed in a letter to Edward Carpenter in April 1916, a few months after he got to Alexandria: 'I don't want to grouse, as so much is all right with me, but this physical loneliness has gone on for too many months, and with it springs and grows a wretched fastidiousness so that even if the opportunity for which I yearn was offered I fear I might refuse it . . . If I could get one solid night it would be something.' An unspecified episode in October, probably with one of the soldiers ('Yesterday, for the first time in my life I parted with respectability,' he wrote to his friend Florence Barger), did something to alleviate his pangs, but it was not until the following summer, when he got to know Mohammed el Adl, that Forster experienced the moment he had been longing for. The account of their relationship in his letters to Florence Barger chronicles a steadily increasing intimacy which culminates in his declaration on 8 October:

Dearest Florence, R[espectability] has been parted with, and in the simplest most inevitable way, just as you hoped. I am so happy – not for the actual pleasure but because the last barrier has fallen . . . I now know so much more. It is awful to think of the thousands who go through youth without ever knowing. I have known in a way before, but never like this.

As Forster later admitted to himself, the relationship was perhaps less splendid than he made it seem. Their meetings were sporadic and the passion was often one-sided. 'Determined my life should contain one success,' he noted in his *Journal* in 1922, 'I have concealed from myself and others M's frequent coldness towards me. And his occasional warmth may be due to politeness, gratitude, or pity.' But at the time it was a triumphant induction into the secret around which Forster's life had been circling for twenty years. This was the breaking down of barriers, the gaining of knowledge, the experience of liberation that had been at the centre of his writing from the start. It was what he had been travelling to find, and there could be no more revealing phrase to describe it than 'parting with respectability'. The words might well take us back to Forster's fascination with Italy. Respectability was what the Italians so signally lacked and the English possessed in such abundance. To escape from it was the prize of life that Italy held out to those, like Eustace Robinson, who were able to grasp it.

Symonds would not have thought of it in terms of a struggle against respectability, but Forster's tales of Mediterranean release echo the older man's beliefs and experiences. Indeed, Forster quotes extensively from Symonds's then unpublished *Memoirs* in his commonplace book. But along with the possibility of greater intimacy with the local population goes a corresponding nervousness about them. One of Forster's shrewdest perceptions about English tourists towards the end of the nineteenth century identifies a new insecurity that has entered their relations with the locals. Unlike the confident Grand Tourist of the previous century, the narrator of 'The Story of a Panic' and the Reverend Eager in *Room with a View* are uneasily conscious of the surrounding threat to their cultural standards. They are typical of a new breed of Englishman abroad, perpetually on the lookout for any encroachment from the natives. Like servants of empire dressing for dinner in the jungle, they detect a landscape that is hostile to their values and can only be held at bay by close attention to form.* The fate of Eustace is an object lesson in what happens to

---

* Kenneth Ballhatchet confirms the parallel in *Race, Sex and Class under the Raj* (1980), where he notes that towards the end of the nineteenth century there was 'growing official concern for prestige – a growing lack of official confidence in the ability of the British administration to convince people that its standards were the right ones' (p. 149).

those whose collars lose their starch. This anxiety to maintain standards of Englishness, which produced the Victorian tourist of caricature, is itself a tribute to the dangerous freedom of the South. The cultural pilgrims are all too aware how easily their pilgrimage can be subverted, how easy it is to stumble upon the wrong kind of revelation.

Moreover, Forster realises that the tourist's discovery of freedom has a price. When Symonds looked back on his relationship with Angelo Fusato, he could see nothing but what was positive: fulfilment for himself and material benefits for Fusato and his family. Our perspective has changed. The past thirty years have shown us how often the pressures of tourism – in Asia, Africa, Central and South America – can involve whole communities in the operation of a sexual market. What Symonds cannot acknowledge is that the decent satisfaction he took in promoting Fusato's marriage, providing a home for his family and securing his brother a job with P&O was gained at the cost of making them all complicit in his purchase of the gondolier's favour.

The sort of humane sex tourism that rejects a straight-forward commercial transaction, wanting to buy not just sex but friendship, community, landscape, and a personal stake in the alien and exotic, has become familiar to us now in many guises, but Forster was one of the first to see that its impact can be quite as far-reaching as the tourist's pursuit of casual pleasure. As James Buzard has pointed out, the Mediterranean pays for the enlightenment it offers: the waiter who helps Eustace to escape is killed by the jump from the hotel window, the passionate encounter witnessed by Lucy in the Piazza Signoria ends in death, the giant plane tree at Plataniste which affords a moment of epiphany to the old man in 'The Road from Colonus' crashes to the ground, killing the inn's inhabitants.

On a personal level, too, Forster knew well enough how muddy the waters of liberation could become. The journal entry quoted above displays a troubled awareness that the relationship with Mohammed el Adl which had made such an epoch in his life had probably been coloured by self-delusion on Forster's side and considerations of 'politeness, gratitude, or pity' on Mohammed's. The economic power of the tourist remains at the centre of the web of threads that link travel and sex. However resolutely this economic superiority is displaced into other, non-commercial kinds of assistance, its reality seeps back into the marrow of the relationship. When Forster made his second trip to India, in 1921, he was able to enjoy for the first time in his life a relationship that allowed him unrestricted sex; but it was a tainted freedom. After an unsatisfactory attempt to seduce a Hindu coolie, he confessed his predicament to the Maharajah of Dewas, for whom he worked, and was provided by His Highness with a young barber called Kanaya. Disappointed in any hope of companionship with this youth, who had 'the body and soul of a slave', and embarrassed by the spread of rumours around the Palace, Forster began to find that sex with Kanaya 'was now mixed with the desire to inflict pain':

> I've never had that desire with anyone else, before or after, and I wasn't trying to punish him – I knew his silly little soul was incurable. I just felt he was a slave, without rights, and I a despot whom no one could call to account . . .

This is a strange destination for the pilgrim to have reached. It offers a brief, unrepeated glimpse of where the inequalities of status between tourist and native can lead – unrepeated in Forster's life, but common enough in the history of tourism.

In different ways both Symonds and Forster recognised the ambiguities of a sex life that relied so much on the compliance of relatively powerless foreigners; they also recognised that what was bad did not necessarily invalidate what was good. The idealist contemplating the tall Sorrento lad is as real as the lecher on the Venetian bridge, the tender lover of Mohammed el Adl is as real as the brutal lover of Kanaya. To condemn the tourist's sexual contacts *en bloc* is not moral superiority but moral simplification.

Symonds and Forster have had some unlikely descendants. It is not difficult to see how the Mediterranean revelations celebrated by writers in the second half of the nineteenth century anticipate the erratic pursuit of self-discovery that characterised the post-war youth movements in the second half of the twentieth. 'I was a young writer and I wanted to take off,' says Jack Kerouac in the first chapter of *On the Road* (1957). 'Somewhere along the line I knew there'd be girls, visions, everything; somewhere along the line the pearl would be handed to me.' Ten years later, among the long-haired pilgrims who were already crowding the roadsides across Europe, there was scarcely a rucksack that did not have its worn copy of *On the Road*.

Kerouac's book depicts a world in which the metaphor of life as a journey has become literal truth: 'Our battered suitcases were piled on the sidewalk again; we had longer ways to go. But no matter, the road is life.' The highways that cross America are the veins through which its blood circulates. No one has tried so hard to catch the sheer exhilaration of being on the move. Dean and the narrator turn towards New Orleans, and suddenly they see 'the whole country like an oyster for us to open, and the pearl was there, the pearl was there. Off we roared south'. A couple of pages later Dean is steering them rhapsodically through the city – '"Ah! God! Life!" He swung around a trolley. "Yes!" He darted the car and looked in every direction for girls.'

In *On the Road*, travel, sex and the quest for enlightenment are woven into a youthful trinity that was to stamp its mark not just on the Beat generation but also on their successors. The hippie trail to Katmandu and beyond was a celebration of freedom in which, for both the pilgrims and their gurus, the spiritual was often tied to the sexual. Richard Neville's *Playpower* (1970) was a manifesto that now reads more like an elegy. It situates the overland trail of the Pilgrim in direct opposition to the cultural preoccupations of the Connoisseur: 'You might miss the Topkapi Museum and the Taj Whateveritis; instead you can paddle your own canoe down the Mekong River, nibble aphrodisiac chocolate in a South Thailand teenage brothel, be massaged in a steaming Moroccan bathing-dungeon by a fastidious Arab. Drift with the current and end up in places you never knew existed . . .' And what this offers, in contrast to the package holidays of the masses, is the experience of self-discovery – 'on a lonely trek from Marrakesh to Agadir, in the Atlas Mountains, or 17,000 feet up the Himalayas, there is no one *but* yourself to come face to face with'.

These are the authentic tones of the Pilgrim, but they assume a quite different relationship between travel and sex from the one we've been looking at. If there is a gateway to the shrine for these travellers, it is through drugs: 'Any self-enlightenment is often ushered in by drugs . . . how can you refuse a joint extended by a dazzling blonde tramp at a char-coal fire-side in Kabul, having just survived a two-hundred-mile desert journey?' The dazzling blonde, like the Thai brothel, like the girls who slip in and out of Kerouac's odyssey, are mere stations along the way. Sex is part of the pilgrimage because it is part of travel.

The idea that it might be more than this, that sex might itself be the source of enlightenment, belongs to a separate tradition, which runs strongest in those travellers, often women or homosexuals, whose erotic interests at home have been most severely curtailed. Writing of his time in Vienna between the wars, John Lehmann frames his response to its homosexual opportunities in terms that suggest an obvious kinship with Symonds. He acknowledges, as Symonds does of Venice, that his interest in the city's history and culture, his sympathy with its people, 'were suffused with sexual desire', and, as does Symonds, he defines his sexual relationships as a kind of pilgrimage towards knowledge and understanding:

> I wanted to mingle with them physically as a way of knowing them intimately. In fact, it seemed to me impossible to know them intimately without a sensual coming together . . . my sensual adventures with Austrian youth seemed to deepen perception . . . This pursuit of illumination through sex began gradually to create a barrier between myself and those homosexuals who were interested simply in satisfying a physical need . . .

In the tradition of the Pilgrim tourist, he protests the holiness of these relationships, assuring the reader that he never used the boys as *objects*: 'they were always living human individuals to me, with urgent problems in the solution of which I tried to help; and was rewarded by their confidence and uncomplicated affection. How I hope that I was right in this belief.'

We know today how much self-deception and exploitation such language can mask. Even if the book were less badly written, it would be easy to dismiss Lehmann's protestations. This, after all, is the language of the modern sex tourist who has struck lucky among the bar-girls: 'She has made my life sweet in my fifties and sixties and now at 66 I am grateful. And I think she is grateful to me . . . I don't want to hear any crap about Bangkok being sex and sleaze and all the rest of it. You can find happiness anywhere in the world and wherever it is, that place is holy.' It is, to put it mildly, a contentious area. To many, the language of mutual affection and newly-discovered companionship seems grotesque in the context of sex tourism, an obscene gloss on one of the nastier forms of exploitation.

Yet this language reflects an emotional pattern that has a long history. How do we judge at what point the pilgrim's quest shades into that of the sex tourist? While walking hand in hand with the catamite provided by his Maharajah, Forster claims to be struck by the fact that it is 'the companionship one really seeks, although it presents itself as a physical urge'. It's not an easy claim to judge. And why should it be any easier when we turn to the grim optimists, drawn from all over the world, who try to repair their fractured lives in the bars of Manila and Bangkok? To call them sex tourists is accurate but unhelpful, except in so far as it facilitates condemnation. Among them is the usual complement of tourists after sex at bargain prices, but there are also those whose motivation is less clear-cut. Repressed, unfulfilled, disillusioned, they board their planes for South-East Asia or Central America in search of release, fulfilment, fresh illusions. The brothel may seem an odd place to look for love, but both literature and film confirm it as an enduring fantasy. Whether we're talking about Graham Greene's South America, Richard Mason's Hong Kong, Henry Miller's Paris, or the Piraeus waterfront of *Never on Sunday*, the whore with the heart of gold is waiting to offer the stranger from another country not just sexual satisfaction but a vision of emotional fulfilment. 'In Europe men and women have intercourse because they love each other,' wrote Gauguin, 'In the South Seas they love each other because they have had intercourse.' Travel far enough and you'll find a place where love can simply be gathered from the street. This is precisely the dream that the casual, half-disguised forms of prostitution in many of the countries visited by sex tourists are designed to reinforce. And occasionally, since that is the promise which a strange world makes to the traveller, the dream comes true.

The western tourist whose life is changed by a foreign prostitute is part of a tradition of sexual pilgrims that goes back to the later years of the nineteenth century, but not much further. It depends on a belief, which only gains currency towards the end of the century, that sexual expression is a central aspect of selfhood, and conversely that sexual repression is a denial of the self. In his relationship with Fusato, Symonds stands at the head of this tradition, which runs on through the following century to places where he himself would certainly not have wished to follow. Desperate to idealise his relationship, the male sexual pilgrim is an easy target. In the end, though, there is probably no more self-delusion and no more unkindness among these stubborn, defensive romantics than among the angry moralists who, often in contrast to the prostitutes themselves, insist that it must be seen as a relationship of victim and villain.

Few people are so concerned about the other main group that has swelled the ranks of sexual pilgrims. Women, as we've seen, were among those who responded most passionately to the sensual stimuli of the Mediterranean. It was almost as though travel, by offering them a new world of colours and sensations, had brought to life the metaphor that hovers in the background of Victorian thinking about women and finds its classic embodiment in Charlotte Brontë's *Jane Eyre* (1847): the madwoman in the attic, whose dangerous, foreign sensuality has to be locked away out of sight, could now begin to emerge. But this release, though it was often sexual in character, was rarely given sexual expression. Plenty of women lived abroad in order to enjoy sexual liaisons that would have been unacceptable in England, but there were few Victorian women tourists who would have contemplated sex with the locals – few, anyway, who would have gone beyond contemplating it.

There is, of course, a line of splendid exceptions, which includes Margaret Fuller. Jane Digby (1807–81), for instance, cut a scandalous romantic swathe across Europe in the first half of the nineteenth century, before settling in Damascus as the wife of a Syrian sheikh; Emily Keene met the Sharif of Wazan in Morocco in 1872, fell in love with him, married him and settled there for the rest of her long life; Isabelle Eberhardt

(1877–1904), notorious for her casual liaisons among the Arabs of Tunisia and Algeria, consummated her passion for North Africa through marriage to a young *spahi* officer three years before she was drowned in a flash flood in western Algeria. But the biographies of these extraordinary women tell us little about the normal run of nineteenth-century tourism. It was not until after the First World War that the attitudes and behaviour of a significant number of women travellers began to change.

The gondolier's ready expectation of trade from the Chatterley sisters is one indication of this change, as are some of the sexual episodes that have become part of Twenties mythology. Lawrence's wife Frieda was herself the source of a number of them. Recalling his stay with the couple in Germany in 1912, David Garnett wrote, 'I found out that summer – Lawrence must have told me – that after they had had a row, she [Frieda] had gone down to the Isar and swum over to where a woodcutter was working, had made love with him and had swum back – just to show Lawrence she was free to do what she liked.' Figures like Nancy Cunard, Natalie Barney, Zelda Fitzgerald, Caresse Crosby, Duff Twysden (the model for Hemingway's Brett Ashley in *The Sun Also Rises*) and many others, testify to ways in which being abroad could offer women kinds of sexual licence unavailable at home. Sometimes this was merely the tourist's freedom to buy exotic sexual experiences, but it could also be a chance to realise facets of themselves that would otherwise have been denied. Either way, these new patterns of behaviour among women abroad affected mainly the rich and the bohemian – not least because they, more readily than women from other backgrounds, could take advantage of practical changes such as twentieth century developments in contraception and a gradual weakening of the stigma attached to sexual promiscuity.

If behaviour remained on the whole circumspect, fantasy ran riot. The success of E.M. Hull's *The Sheik* (1919), in which a wilful but frigid English girl ('that side of life does not exist for me') is abducted and raped by a desert sheikh with whom she then falls desperately in love, was sealed by the adulation heaped on Rudolf Valentino, who starred in the film two years later. His role as the dark foreign lover who sweeps the civilised western woman into a world of dangerous passion tapped a vein of fantasy that for most female tourists had to wait another half-century before it could be tested against reality.

If we are looking for a modern descendant of those Victorian women for whom Mediterranean travel was both a liberation of the senses and a discovery of self, we could do worse than go to the fictional heroine of *Shirley Valentine* (1989). One of the most popular British films of the 1980s, it came out four years after another highly successful British film, the Merchant/Ivory production of *A Room with a View*. Taken together, the two films testify to the role of the Mediterranean pilgrimage as one of our abiding cultural fantasies. *Shirley Valentine* tells the story of a middle-aged suburban housewife, locked into a routine of domestic drudgery that has buried her real self. The chance of a holiday without her immensely boring husband takes her to one of the Greek islands, where she has a brief affair with the owner of the local taverna. This romance is the core of the film, but its real importance is the effect it has on the heroine's sense of her own identity. Sex with the charming Greek, who quickly moves on to another holidaymaker, has given her back the key to herself. Jumping naked into the sea, shopping confidently in the local market, sitting by the beach to watch the sunset, she is now her own woman: 'I used to be the wife, I used to be the mother. But now I'm Shirley Valentine again.'

At the end of the holiday the plane leaves for Manchester, but the heroine remains behind. What had started as a rapturous fling has turned into a permanent revelation. This is the fictional climax of a vital strand of tourism in which self-discovery and sexual discovery are twin sides of the same coin.

The power of the myth embodied in *Shirley Valentine* is endlessly reflected in the dreams of today's holidaymakers. In 1994 the *Sun* newspaper ran a series of features on British women who had taken up with local men as a result of holidays in the Gambia, glossing one of the stories with the caption, 'It's like a mix of Shirley Valentine and Out of Africa . . . with more romance', and describing another of the women as doing a 'Shirley-Valentine runner into the arms of a Gambian lover'. At about the same time *Coronation Street* ran a plot line which had Deirdre Barlow marrying the Arab lover she'd met on holiday. A couple of years later, British television's Channel 4 took up the Shirley Valentine theme with a series called *Island of Dreams*, which followed the stories of half-a-dozen British women who had each gone on holiday to the same Greek island of Zakynthos and ended up trying to make a life there with one of the local men. They had fallen in love with the country, the atmosphere, the climate, but their dreams of escape and fulfilment in a foreign place were inseparable from the dream of romance with a foreign man.

Among younger women, travelling for sex is now commonplace, an accepted part of the holiday carnival. ('Girls, Can we interest you in a package holiday?' ran the slogan for a Club 18–30 poster, above a photograph of a man with a prominent bulge in his boxer shorts.) But the sexual pilgrims want something more: they are still in pursuit of the pearl. Now as in the past, the Mediterranean offers an erotic promise of personal fulfilment. People still go abroad hoping for a sexual experience that will change their lives, and still claim to find it.

PART THREE

Rebels

6

Byron Abroad

What makes people travel? At its most basic, the desire to get *to* somewhere or to escape *from* somewhere. There are those in pursuit and those in flight. Both the Connoisseurs and the Pilgrims belong primarily to the first group. The tourists in the second group I have called Rebels.

But our motives are rarely as simple as the categories that try to explain them. It is sometimes hard to draw a line between desire for what is foreign and revolt against what is familiar. Even in the culturally sanctioned Grand Tour, the rebel identity was present. The tension between an official tour and an unofficial tour is really that between the dutiful son and the rebellious son. It is no accident that his father looms so large in Boswell's attempts to keep himself in check, or that parental influence is finally ineffective. The whole project of a rite of passage involves an assertion of adult independence from the authority of the parents. And in the case of the Pilgrim, rebellion is often the other side of revelation. Forster himself was in quiet ways a rebel. From the start, he recognised that the personal barriers to self-fulfilment are ultimately cultural. When the sunlight and sensuality of the Mediterranean countries go to work, it is a whole class-bound English culture of grey skies and lace curtains that they undermine. In *Where Angels Fear to Tread* (1905), Miss Abbot remarks of her experience of Italy:

All that winter I seemed to be waking up to beauty and splendour and I don't know what; and when the spring came, I wanted to fight against the things I hated, – mediocrity and dullness and spitefulness and society. I actually hated society for a day or two at Monteriano.

For that day or two the experience of travel has turned Miss Abbot into a rebel.

One way or another there are stirrings of rebellion, however muted, in almost any tourist venture. When our spirits lift at the start of a journey, there is usually an element of relief to be leaving things behind. Travel releases us from the treadmill of domestic habit. Even if it goes no further than our choice of clothes, there is an impulse of defiance. But again it's a question of emphasis. Boswell's defiance is not at the heart of the tourist enterprise, Byron's is. Although the link between travel and rebellion may be long-standing, the tourist-as-rebel was established as a popular identity only at the beginning of the nineteenth century, and like the tourist as pilgrim it owed its popularity in large measure to the Romantic Movement. If Romanticism helped to shift the focus of tourism from social goals to personal ones, its stress on the primacy of individual response also made it easier to challenge social assumptions in the name of personal truths. From time to time, moral and religious convictions had always driven people abroad, but at this point there emerged a new kind of traveller, inspired by a purely personal antagonism to social constraints, whose motives provide a register of what society has chosen to repress. The more tightly offending impulses are nailed down, the more likely they are to resurface across the border, beyond the frontier, on the other side of the Channel. And because what is repressed, at least in England, generally has something to do with sex, the category of Rebel, even more decisively than that of Connoisseur or Pilgrim, has a sexual bias. A long and important tradition of rebel tourism is motivated by sexual dissatisfaction.

At the head of this tradition is Byron. In our own age, when so many popular icons compete for attention and are so quickly replaced by others, it is hard to grasp the sustained extent of Byron's influence. His celebrity was such that for two centuries he became the embodiment of a particular tourist identity. In a manner that was infinitely seductive, even to the circumstances of his death, he brought together the images of traveller and sexual rebel.

Until the late eighteenth century, youthful travel (apart from a few strategic absences during the Civil War) had been seen as a preparation for one's role in society. After a spirited run on the Continent, the prodigal son was expected to return home and take his rightful place in the community, just as Boswell had done. But for one group the choice was less straightforward. In early nineteenth-century England men convicted of homosexual acts were still being pilloried and hanged before enthusiastic crowds. Indeed, the period of the Napoleonic wars had seen an increase in prosecutions for a crime which was regarded not just as a violation of the natural order but also, by extension, as a rebellion against the social order, and which therefore seemed doubly threatening at a time of national crisis. In the course of the eighteenth and early nineteenth centuries, a steady trickle of clergymen and aristocrats had chosen exile in preference to the law courts. Montgomery Hyde, in his survey of homosexuality in Britain, lists a string of notable figures who ended up scattered across Europe, most often in Italy – tending to confirm Richard Burton's assertion that for many years 'England sent her pederasts to Italy, and especially to Naples, whence originated the term "the English Vice"'. Rather than risk the shame of enforced exile at some time in the future, not a few Grand Tourists prudently decided to prolong their stay abroad. This has led the scholar G.S. Rousseau to argue that 'the first sign . . . of English homosexuals in Italy is that, in greater numbers than heterosexual men, they elect to live abroad *permanently*'. Eighteenth-century Florence, in particular, had a thriving colony of expatriates.

The dangers of life in England had been graphically illustrated towards the end of the century by the fate of William Beckford, 'the great Apostle of Paederasty', as Byron dubbed him. Reputed to be the richest man in England, he had been forced into exile as a result of his passion for the young son of Lord and Lady Courtenay. Byron himself received news while on his travels that John Edleston, the Trinity choirboy with whom he'd been in love at Cambridge, had been accused of indecency. This was not something to be taken lightly. Another of Byron's Cambridge friends, Charles Skinner Matthews, put the advantages of being abroad with unanswerable force when he congratulated Byron in a letter of 13 January 1811 on his opportunities for pleasure among 'your friends the Turcomans', and added a telling reminder of conditions at home: 'that wch you get for £5 we must risque our necks for'.

Matthews' remark does not come out of the blue. The moral climate in England had been a central factor in Byron's plans for this first journey, which took him from Lisbon and Cintra through Seville, Cadiz and Gibraltar to Malta and thence to Albania, Greece and Asia Minor. Whatever his other motives for going abroad – financial embarrassment, disenchantment with England, an adventurous disposition – he had set out with the clear intention of using the trip to sample homosexual pleasures that were illegal at home. While waiting in Falmouth to sail on the Lisbon packet, he wrote to Matthews in July 1809 that he was 'surrounded by Hyacinths & other flowers of the most fragrant [na]ture, & I have every intention of culling a handsome bouquet to compare with the exotics we expect to meet in Asia' – Hyacinth being the beautiful Greek youth loved by Apollo.* The trip seems to

---

* Oscar Wilde was later to make the same reference in a letter to Lord Alfred Douglas, used in Wilde's trials: 'I know Hyacinthus, whom Apollo loved so madly, was you in Greek days.' (? January 1893).

have lived up to expectations. His wife – not, admittedly, the most reliable source – later noted what Lady Caroline Lamb had told her of Byron's taste for sodomy, 'Ly C.L- did not believe that he had committed this crime since his return to England, though he practised it unrestrictedly in Turkey'; and in a letter of 4 October 1810 he lays claim rather bizarrely (he was keeping count?) to over two hundred acts of homosexual intercourse while abroad.

The tracks he left in Greece and Asia Minor have been well followed in too many books for it to be worth going over the same ground again. What matters to the present argument is the point made by Allan Massie that Byron's experience of the journey confirmed him in his own mind as someone whose allegiances of thought and feeling were not those of the ordinary Englishman. It was a distinction measured partly in sexual terms. However widespread homosexual practices may have been in reality, they were defined by the law as un-English, and Byron chose to use them as a mark of his own un-Englishness. After eleven months he took leave in Greece of his Cambridge friend John Cam Hobhouse, who had been his travelling companion. When Tom Moore came to write the first biography of Byron, he blandly explained this parting by the poet's love of solitude, but Hobhouse noted acidly in the margin of his copy, 'He has not the remotest grasp of the real reason which induced Lord B. to prefer having no Englishman immediately and constantly near him'. The 'real reason' was not a desire for solitude but for other, less respectable, kinds of company.

The following nine months were the period of Byron's most clearly documented homosexual affairs, first with Eustathios Georgiou and then with Nicolo Giraud. Georgiou was a boy he picked up in Vostitza, beautiful, affected and soon tiresome. 'I found the dear soul upon horseback,' Byron noted of one incident in a letter to Hobhouse, 'clothed very sprucely in Greek Garments, with those ambrosial curls hanging down his amiable back, and to my utter astonishment, and the great abomination of Fletcher [Byron's manservant], a *parasol* in his hand to save his complexion from the heat'. Before long, the tears, protestations and sentimental attentions wearied Byron, who sent him home. More lasting was his fondness for the fifteen-year-old Giraud, half-Greek, half-French, whom he had met in Constantinople. Back in Athens, Byron moved into the Franciscan monastery that served both as a hotel for travellers and a boys' boarding school at which Giraud was a pupil. They nursed each other through illness, and Giraud accompanied Byron as far as Malta on his journey home. There were strong enough feelings for Byron to leave him a generous £7,000 in the will he drew up in August 1811, after his return to England.

Apart from Giraud and the other boys in the monastery ('We have nothing but riot from Noon till night'), there were the usual tourist amusements. 'I had a number of Greek and Turkish women,' he writes to Hobhouse, 'and I believe the rest of the English were equally lucky, for we were all *clapped*.' This was commonplace enough; but his homosexual pleasures were not – at least, not in his own estimation. They set him apart, a traveller more daring, more wicked than 'the rest of the English'. In April 1811 he left Athens, having resisted the temptation to take along with him the daughter of his former landlady. (The 'fair maid of Athens' would have been an expensive luxury at 30,000 piastres, which was the price her mother wanted for her.) After a melancholy break in Malta where his venereal infection was compounded by a bout of fever, he sailed on to England and the extraordinary four years ahead, marked first by the explosion of fame that turned him into one of the most sought-after celebrities in the country and then by the plunge into infamy that was to make him an exile for the rest of his life.

It is clear that his sexual behaviour on this first journey was in a different category from that of the average Grand Tourist, whose transgressions were not essentially subversive. Byron had turned travel into an act of defiance. When he set out in 1809, it was a private act; when he sailed from Dover in 1816, it was a very public one. If society was rejecting him, he was also rejecting society. The gulf that had been opened up by his first journey could only get wider.

Having left England in a blaze of scandal, Byron assumed the role of outcast with energetic disdain. Over the next three years he took full advantage of the sexual privileges of exile, playing in turn the opportunist, the romantic and the debauchee, always with half an eye on the moral conventions he was flouting. Sexual indulgence, duly reported home, became a gauntlet thrown down to the society he had abandoned. The ferry from Dover took him to Ostend. 'As soon as he reached his room,' noted the young Dr Polidori, who was travelling with him, 'Lord Byron fell like a thunderbolt upon the chambermaid.' It was an apt enough way of signalling his escape from the sanctimonious air of England, and a letter to Hobhouse next day reminded him to bring more condoms when he came to join Byron in Geneva. (According to a note Monckton Milnes made in his commonplace book, Byron always kept a condom in his waistcoat pocket.) A few days later, in Cologne, 'the host of our hotel mistook a German Chambermaid – whose red cheeks & white teeth had made me venture upon her carnally – for his wife – & stood swearing at the door like a Squadron of Cavalry ... till the mystery was developed by his wife walking out of her own room – & the girl out of mine'.

Continental chambermaids were probably a less tiring diversion than the importunate Claire Clairmont, who came back into Byron's life the following month when he met the Shelleys in Switzerland. Mary and the poet were themselves sexual refugees of a sort, in flight from the social and domestic pressures that had beset their unconventional partnership in England. Claire Clairmont, Mary's stepsister, had already managed a brief affair with Byron shortly before he left England and was keen to repeat the experience. Byron had taken the Villa Diodati on the south shore of Lake Geneva, and when the Shelley party moved into a neighbouring house, the less than enthusiastic poet found himself again the object of her attentions: 'I never loved nor pretended to love her – but a man is a man – & if a girl of eighteen comes prancing to you at all hours – there is but one way.' To make sure that things were as bad as they seemed, a number of British tourists trained telescopes on the Villa Diodati from the other side of the lake.

The combination of so much sexual wickedness in one place was seized on with relish by public opinion at home. It offered pleasing confirmation of the depravity of these individuals in particular and of abroad in general. For Victorian England it would carry an even starker message about the dubious sexual implications of travel. Well over thirty years later, Ruskin's father could respond to his son's innocent proposal to rent a house in Venice with misgivings that plainly hark back to this scandalous ménage:

> Mama deems it a duty to beseech of you to pause before you plunge too far into the fascinations of Continental life – They never yet I fancy did much good to either man or woman – Woman especially . . . I cannot at once say I entirely approve of hiring House or Palace abroad yet – It sounds Byronish or Shelleyish . . . how few of our best men have dwelt in Foreign Land?

To sound Byronish or Shelleyish was the sign of a sexual reprobate, and for the finely tuned Victorian ear any inclination to live abroad was a dangerous step in this direction.

It was not, of course, just the stories of Lake Geneva that made Ruskin *père* nervous of having his son set up house in Venice, for this was the city, above all others, on which Byron had set his mark. It was here that Childe Harold had stood at the start of the final canto and here that Byron himself lived out the most notorious period of his exile. After five months in Switzerland he paused only a couple of weeks in Milan before moving on through Verona to Venice, which he reached in November 1816. It was to be his base for just on three years, first as a lodger in the house of a merchant in the Frezzeria, near the Piazza San Marco, then as tenant of the Palazzo Mocenigo on the Grand Canal.

At his lodgings in the Frezzeria he swiftly reached an understanding with his landlord's wife, the enchanting Marianna Segati, and she became the first, and one of the most enduring, of a long line of Venetian loves. A month after his arrival in Venice, he reported back to his half-sister Augusta:

> Then I have fallen in love with a very pretty Venetian of two and twenty – with great black eyes – she is married – and so am I – which is very much to the purpose – we have found & sworn an eternal attachment – which has already lasted a lunar month – & I am more in love than ever – & so is the lady – at least she says so – & it seems so, – she does not plague me (which is a wonder –) and I verily believe we are one of the happiest – unlawful couples on this side of the Alps.

Though the tone is humorous, the language of romance is not out of place. Byron was well enough aware of the romantic possibilities of his situation. 'I am going out this evening,' he writes next day to Augusta, ' – in my *cloak & Gondola* – there are two nice Mrs. Radcliffe words for you.' In neither case does the self-mockery quite disguise the pleasure Byron takes in his role. But again it's a pleasure derived partly from its opposition to the respectable domestic alternative. Mrs Radcliffe's name evokes the aristocratic villains of her Gothic fiction, and the romantic pair in the Frezzeria are an 'unlawful couple'. The attraction of the adulterous Marianna is all the greater by contrast with 'that virtuous monster Miss Milbanke', the poet's wife.

The eternal attachment survived on Byron's side for something over a year. He broke with Marianna in March 1818, was suffering from clap again by April, and took a lease on the Palazzo Mocenigo in May. 'I have broke my old liaison with la Segati,' he wrote to his friend and banker Douglas Kinnaird, '& have taken a dozen in stead.' In truth, he had been taking others well before the final break, among them Margharita Cogni, known as La Fornarina, the baker's wife, whom he had come across the previous summer as he rode one evening beside the Brenta. With her tall figure, fine eyes and passionate temperament, La Fornarina became Byron's dominant sexual interest for the rest of his time in Venice. As he put it himself when the relationship was over: 'for two years – in the course of which I had more women than I can count or recount – she was the only one who preserved over me an ascendancy – which was often disputed & never impaired'.

But if Margharita was the lover who presided over this second stage of his life in Venice, the countless others were what gave the period its characteristic tone. Byron's appetite, by his own admission, was voracious and indiscriminate. More significant than the liaisons themselves is Byron's insistence on relating them in letter after letter to friends at home. The boastful catalogues are themselves a form of rebellion – a harsh expression of his contempt for conventional morality. It is as debauchee that the sexual exile makes his most uncompromising statement. 'Since last year,' he writes to Hobhouse and Kinnaird in January 1819, 'I have run the Gauntlet . . . the Tarruscelli – the Da Mosti – the Spineda – the Lotti –

the Rizzato – the Eleanora – the Carlotta – the Giulietta – the Alvisi – the Zambieri – the Eleanora de Bezzi – (who was the king of Naples' Gioaschino's mistress – at least one of them) – the Theresina of Mazzurati – the Glettenheimer – & her Sister – the Luigia & her mother – the Fornaretta – the Santa – the Caligari – the Portiera – the Bolognese figurante – the Tentora and her sister – cum multis aliis . . . I have had them all & thrice as many to boot since 1817.' It's a catalogue of which Leporello would have been proud – in fact, the author of *Don Juan* may well have had Don Giovanni's servant in mind. Byron's cynical conclusion that 'some of them are Countesses – & some of them Cobbler's wives – some noble – some middling – some low – & all whores', is no doubt partly affectation, but it suggests a somewhat joyless pursuit, confirmed by his comment on the opera singer Arpalice Taruscelli: '[I] have fucked her twice a day for the last six – today is the seventh – but no Sabbath day – for we meet at Midnight at her Milliner's'. One is reminded of Byron's later project of writing a tragedy about the Emperor Tiberius, which would exhibit 'the despair which must have led to those very vicious pleasures'.

His letters from Venice contain a stream of hectic bulletins which seem to detail every aspect of his sexual adventures except one – and this, in terms of his identity as rebel, perhaps the most important. It was touched on by Shelley in a letter to Thomas Love Peacock. He expresses his disgust with Italian women and goes on:

Well, L.B. is familiar with the lowest sort of these women, the people his gondolieri pick up in the streets. He allows fathers & mothers to bargain with him for their daughters, & though this is common enough in Italy, yet for an Englishman to encourage such sickening vice is a melancholy thing. He associates with wretches who seem almost to have lost the gait & phisiognomy of

man, & who do not scruple to avow practices which are
not only named but I believe seldom even conceived in
England. He says he disapproves, but he endures.

The unnamed, un-English practices are left to our imagination, but they recall Hobhouse's note that on the earlier
journey the poet did not want 'any Englishman immediately
and constantly near him'. Liberation from the standards of
England and Englishmen is exactly what Byron is claiming by
right of exile. The relative scarcity of English tourists was part
of Venice's attraction. Rome he described as 'infected' with
English, and expanded the same metaphor in a letter to James
Wedderburn Webster: 'Florence and Naples are their
Lazarettoes where they carry the infection of their society ... I
never see any of them when I can avoid it.' In Venice he could
enjoy the outcast's freedom from all the webs of social obligation, expectation and supervision which support, but also
constrain, those who are within the fold. The city fostered
both his greatest poetry (the fourth canto of *Childe Harold*,
Beppo, *Mazeppa*, the early cantos of *Don Juan*) and his wildest
dissipation, as though the sexual excess, the physical degenera-
tion and the literary outpourings were all part of the poet's
imaginative response to Venice itself – the place which, as he
wrote to Moore, 'has always been (next to the East) the green-
est island of my imagination'.

To all appearances, the years that followed turned Byron
into a different figure. His travels took him first to Ravenna,
then to Pisa and Genoa, and finally to Greece again and his
death at Missolonghi. The love of his final years was Teresa
Guiccioli. A pretty nineteen-year-old when he met her in
Venice, she was married to a man forty years older than her
whose sexual tastes ran to unspecified forms of perversion.
Her husband was complaisant and Byron moved on to terms
of intimacy with both him and Teresa's family, the Gambas,
who were deeply involved in the revolutionary politics of the

time. Byron soon found that he had slipped from debauchery into love, and through love into politics. His moves during the last four wandering years in Italy were largely driven by political necessity. Identified as a subversive element by the authorities, he was now spied on professionally for evidence of political rather than sexual misconduct.

The makings of a political subversive had always been there. The use of sexual transgression abroad to define one's resistance to the values of home produces a wide band of tourist experience within which travel, sex and subversion come together. It was already apparent in Byron's first journey. The discovery of habits of thinking and feeling 'truer and more admirable than those he found in England' points directly to his experience of travel as a basis for challenging the norms of his own society. Once tourism becomes primarily a personal enterprise, recorded and valued in terms of its effect on the individual consciousness, the cultural contrasts it reveals are judged according to personal sympathies; they will no longer automatically confirm the superiority of English society or English customs.

Where the contrast is one of sexual tolerance, the tourist may be happy to take advantage of the freedoms offered abroad while maintaining a fundamental allegiance to the standards of home. ('I thought that I might allow myself *one* intrigue in Italy . . .', Boswell had noted.) But if the tourist's allegiance is shaky to start with, then the experience of foreign alternatives is likely to be decisive. This was the case with Byron. The satirical poem 'Don Leon', which was written a couple of decades after Byron's death and purports to be his homosexual autobiography, makes the appeal of foreign lands, 'Where Cupid's wings were free, his hands unbound', quite explicit. It follows Byron to Turkey – 'There venial youths in every stew are found,' – and then presents a striking assertion of the personal liberty offered by a Muslim as opposed to a Christian country:

Hail, freedom, hail! For though the soil I trod,
Still groaning lay beneath the Moslem's rod,
Here first to me her benisons were known,
For mental freedom is to think alone.

(ll.483–86)

The freedom fighter of Byron's last months and the sensualist of the Venice period are perhaps closer to each other than at first appears.

When he went into exile in 1816, Byron went as a rebel against English values, and he chose Italy as the place where his rebel life could be lived. Set in this context, Shelley's comments on his behaviour could hardly be less apposite: of course his unnamed practices wouldn't be conceived in England, of course an Englishman wouldn't engage in such trade – that, for Byron, was the whole point, as it would be for generations of (often homosexual) travellers who came after him, looking for an escape from Anglo-Saxon attitudes and a vantage point from which to challenge them. Byron is their patron saint. By the time he left to promote political rebellion in Greece, he himself had settled into a more or less conventional relationship with Teresa Guiccioli, but the Byronic legend of pre-Guiccioli days was to have a profound effect on the future of tourism.

7

Forbidden Fruit

Byron's life and work bequeathed to the nineteenth century a series of images which surrounded the figure of the wanderer with romantic glamour. The Byronic pose expressed a scornful rejection of everything most obviously Victorian, offering an imaginative truancy that added zest to the normal concerns of the package tourist. 'Every Englishman [abroad],' remarked the sculptor William Wetmore Story in 1863, 'carries a Murray for information and a Byron for sentiment.' Wrapped against the night at the prow of the ship, even the most cautious tourist is a potential Don Juan. Byron's legacy has become part of the air the traveller breathes, from the Victorian youth striking attitudes in front of the Bridge of Sighs to the modern tourist braced with deliberate poise against the swaying of the airport bus. At a resolute distance from the ruck of commonplace tourists, the Byronic traveller carries within him a fantasy of escape from all that defines their ordinariness. It is a dream whose chief ingredient is sexual freedom.

For nineteenth-century tourists, both men and women, Byron had subtly eroticised the whole project of European travel, investing particular tourist sites with thrilling associations but also bringing to the surface the tremors of sensual excitement that are part of the physical and emotional business of changing people and places. The rebel identity that emerges from this has two aspects, corresponding in some measure to the character of Byron's two periods abroad. The first is that of the traveller who rejects the sexual norms of society and goes abroad specifically to enjoy illicit pleasures. The second, more general, is that of the alienated traveller, sick of society or even of civilisation, who looks abroad for a different order of things.

Leaving England in quest of forbidden fruit was nothing new, but Byron had helped to turn it into a conscious tourist motive. Foreign travel in his day was still a cumbersome and expensive business. Boats across the Channel were irregular, coach travel on the other side was slow and often uncomfortable. But all this was about to change. The first regular steamer service across the Channel had opened in 1820 and the following decades saw the spread of rail networks across Europe. Within thirty years Continental travel had become dramatically quicker, cheaper and more widely available. In 1816 Shelley took a leisurely five days to reach Paris from Dover, by 1850 a traveller could get there from London in eleven hours. Foreign travel no longer had to be seen as a long-term project. There were still plenty of people who chose to make extended Continental tours, but a new dimension had been added to the tourist's range of experience. An increasing number of travellers now began to use the Continent as a refuge where pleasure could be snatched in the discreet intervals of a virtuous working life.

This aspect of Victorian tourism is Stevenson's story of Jekyll and Hyde writ large. Jekyll, we recall, was initially troubled by no more than 'a certain impatient gaiety of disposition' which was at odds with his desire to present a grave face to the world: 'hence it came about that I concealed my pleasures'. It is not that he is a hypocrite – both the pleasure-seeker and the respectable doctor are genuine sides of his nature – but there is no social mechanism that allows him to give expression to the pleasure-seeker without compromising the gravity of the doctor. This was precisely the dilemma of many Victorians for whom Continental travel had almost the same effect as the tincture that releases Hyde:

There was something strange in my sensations, something indescribably new, and, from its very novelty, incredibly sweet. I felt younger, lighter, happier in body; within I was conscious of a heady recklessness, a current of disordered sensual images running like a mill race in my fancy, a solution of the bonds of obligation, an unknown but not an innocent freedom of the soul.

To live respectably and yet give free rein to natural impulse, to lose nothing of one's social standing and yet shake off the bonds of social obligation – this is the aim that Jekyll seems to have realised: 'I was the first that could thus plod in the public eye with a load of genial respectability, and in a moment, like a schoolboy, strip off these lendings and spring headlong into the sea of liberty.' His words encapsulate the feelings of those Victorians whose genial respectability at home was exchanged for a sudden plunge into the sea of liberty offered by foreign travel. A summer in Italy or just a weekend across the Channel could be a welcome chance for Hyde to step briefly out of the shadow of Jekyll.

The most immediate focus for such trips was Paris, a city whose reputation was well established by the end of the eighteenth century. 'It is certain,' wrote Thicknesse, 'that men of large fortunes can in no city in the world indulge their passions in every respect more amply than in Paris; and that is the lure which decoys such numbers, and in particular Englishmen, to this city of *love* and folly.' Tourist pleasures were interrupted by war and revolution at the end of the century, but normal service was quickly resumed with the coming of peace. (J.G. Lemaistre recalls hearing one Englishman observe that 'as soon as the peace took place, he would give himself the happiness of passing six weeks in the Palais-Royal without once going out of its gates'.) As an epigraph to his Venetian poem *Beppo*, set in the eighteenth century, Byron quotes the remark that Venice was 'much visited by the young English gentlemen of those times' since it was then 'what *Paris* is *now* – the seat of all dissoluteness'. Things did not get better through the century; by the 1870s Paris had become, for Josephine Butler, 'the great Babylon'. Thomas Cook advised his patrons to shun the city's vices; but the same vices served as a beacon to others. If they wished, tourists could now simply cross the Channel for a few days to let off steam and then return to England.

The popularity of this sort of excursion is indicated by the number of 'bachelor's guides', designed to take the effort out of finding a suitable brothel, which were published in the later years of the century. The newly-arrived tourist no longer had to rely, like Boswell, on picking up addresses from chance acquaintances; he could turn, for example, to *The Pretty Women of Paris, Being a complete Directory or Guide to Pleasure for Visitors to the Gay City* (1883). The facilities, charges and special attractions were all conveniently recorded:

The finest bagnio in the world. Each room is decorated in a different style, regardless of expense. The bathing chamber is sumptuously arranged and may be used in company of a chosen nymph, for the charge of 100 francs. The management issue an illustrated book giving a view of the principal saloons. A negress is kept on the establishment. This is a favourite resort of the upper ton, and many ladies, both in society and out it, come here alone, or with their lovers, for Lesbian diversions.

Among the patrons of this particular spot, at 12 rue Chabanais, was the Prince of Wales, who, like so many of his future subjects, felt a regular need to get away from the pressures of life in Victorian England. According to his biographer, Christopher Hibbert, 'Twice or sometimes three times a year he would slip away to Paris for a few days without his wife'.

The world of the boulevards which attracted the wayward
Prince had by this time acquired a notoriety that made Paris
in the 1880s and 1890s a byword for everything agreeably
sinful. The atmosphere was suffused with erotic invitation: 'In
Paris,' notes Arthur Symons, 'I got utterly tired of that eternal
refrain: "Couchez-avec," always with a note of interrogation.
Sex in Paris is an obsession . . .' An obsession that formed a
constant undercurrent in the life of the cafés and among the
girls who were drawn to it:

> Most of these young unsophisticated girls were fearfully
> fascinating; in the summer so lightly clad that you could
> almost divine their nakedness under their dresses; bodies
> which seemed always so willing to offer their most inti-
> mate charms to anyone who wanted to go home with
> them; faces so eager and wild, so wicked and so innocent,
> so impure and so pure; ripe red lips that might suck your
> soul out of you; mouths so amorous and at the same time
> so full of laughter . . .

Innocent and wicked, pure and impure: in this Parisian fantasy
Symons has reconciled a contradiction at the heart of
Victorian sexual life. The paralysing split between madonna
and whore is here magically healed in a vision of laughing girls
whose depravity is just the other side of their innocence. These
must have been intoxicating images for men bounded by the
social constraints of England in the 1890s. It is hardly surprising if even the most respectable of them were sometimes
tempted to slip across the Channel. Not of course that they
were likely to end up with one of Symons's charming nymphs.
More often they would have come across the sort of figure that
T.S. Eliot, recalling the Paris of 1911, describes in 'Rhapsody
on a Windy Night': the woman who hesitates towards you in
the light of the door, the border of her dress torn and stained
with sand, the corner of her eye twisting like a crooked pin.

But here too there could be a tinge of romance, as John Lehmann, writing of his appetite for casual sex in the Paris of the 1930s, tries to explain: 'Even the squalid little hotels, *maisons de passe*, with their sour-faced, sharp-witted proprietors, partook of it; a way of life so utterly remote from my sheltered upbringing that one might have been in Babylon or Carthage thousands of years ago'. What he responds to is the sensual appeal of exotic squalor that has always drawn travellers to the *quartiers louches* of foreign cities. If, as Havelock Ellis claims, 'it is the prostitute who incarnates the fascination of the city', this is partly because there is not a Dr Jekyll on the planet without some curiosity about the world of Mr Hyde. Even the most sober tourist must sometimes feel a tug of recognition that answers the call from the alleyway. With its brightly-lit thoroughfares and its dark, tempting backstreets, the city is a map of our public and private desires.

Because writers write, we know a disproportionate amount about what they do and think and feel. They are the ones who provide us with evidence. Of the sexual scandals at the end of the nineteenth century, Rupert Croft-Cooke remarks: 'No doubt stockbrokers and lawyers attended the sessions at St John's Wood which attracted Swinburne but nobody knows of it now. No doubt at all – indeed it is recorded in the trials – that Wilde was only one of the victims of his gang of blackmailers, but all the others, referred to primly as "gentlemen" by Counsel, are so much anonymous dust.' Similarly, the vast majority of those who crossed the Channel in pursuit of pleasure have left no trace of their passage. Because A.E. Housman was a celebrated poet, and one who kept a dutiful record of his sexual expenses, we know something of his annual trips to Paris in the years before the First World War – the sailors, ballet dancers and male prostitutes he had there, and the prices he paid for them. But his biographer's summary could stand for all the others who have no memorial: '... his foreign visits meant, above all, freedom – a temporary escape from the conventional morality by which . . . he felt imprisoned'.

Tourists of this kind were rebels only in the sense that they used travel to seek pleasures that were outlawed or disapproved of at home. In other respects, they were determined to remain respectable, which is why they went abroad. The Jekyll and Hyde market has been a large, and rarely acknowledged, feature of modern tourism, created by the desire to purchase a temporary sexual freedom that can be enjoyed without loss of social or moral status. No doubt it involves an element of hypocrisy, but then so do most of the shifts by which we manage to show a respectable face to the world. In its overall effect, it is a practice which sustains rather than undermines the tourist's basic allegiance to domestic values. Rebellion in this context is whatever can be stolen from the demands of propriety.

For others who responded to the call of Paris, a desire for sexual freedom was mixed with a more general assertion of youthful revolt. The American critic Malcolm Cowley, who wrote of Paris in the 1920s as 'a great machine for stimulating the nerves and sharpening the senses', has suggested that one of the articles of the bohemian creed espoused by those living in New York's Greenwich Village after the First World War was the value of changing place: 'By expatriating himself, by living in Paris, Capri or the South of France, the artist can break the puritan shackles, drink, live freely and be wholly creative.' The young Americans who arrived in Paris, dumped their bags and set out to find a mistress were looking not just for sexual experience but also for the gratifying sense that they had earned a place in the nineteenth-century bohemian tradition of artists, cafés, garrets and *grisettes* that constituted the real meaning of Paris. As George Wickes puts it, 'To the middle-aged summer tourist out on a spree Paris may have had the aura of a glorified Folies Bergère; to his son or daughter it suggested the romantic life depicted in George Moore's *Confessions of a Young Man*, Du Maurier's *Trilby*, or Murger's *Scènes de la Vie de Bohème*.'

For young refugees from the United States, Europe held out the double lure of adult independence and adolescent irresponsibility. In this respect it was the antithesis of Prohibition America, which treated them like children while at the same time hedging them around with the domestic responsibilities of adulthood. Travel, as always, was the perfect solution for those who wanted to be free of grown-ups and yet not to grow up themselves. Writing about Henry Miller, George Orwell summed it up with a predictable note of adult disapproval: 'On the whole, in Miller's books you are reading about people living the expatriate life, people drinking, talking, meditating and fornicating, not about people working, marrying and bringing up children; a pity . . .' Orwell speaks for the grown-up world of social and sexual responsibility. It is the argument that Hemingway parodies in *The Sun Also Rises* when Bill Gorton tells the book's hero, Jake Barnes: 'Fake European standards have ruined you. You drink yourself to death. You become obsessed by sex. You spend all your time talking, not working. You are an expatriate, see? You hang around cafés.'

Orwell has drawn up the balance sheet accurately enough, but how you read it depends on your point of view. It is a defining characteristic of the traveller's erotic interests that they are *not* concerned with reproduction. Sex is about pleasure, experiment, excess, self-discovery, not about making families. The life of work, marriage and children, with all its associated values, was exactly what most of the expatriates were trying to escape. They did not want the role of the father; it was a mistress not a wife they were looking for. And there is a sense in which they found her in their relationship with Europe, and especially with Paris. Hemingway caught just this aspect of it in an article he wrote for the *American Mercury* in 1933; 'Paris is very beautiful this fall,' he begins. 'It was a fine place to be quite young in and it is a necessary part of a man's education. We all loved it once and we lie if we say we didn't. But she is like a mistress who does not grow old and she has other lovers now. She was old to start with but we did not know it then. We thought she was just older than we were, and that was attractive then.' The image of Paris as an older woman offering herself to a generation of inexperienced Americans catches the erotic flavour of expatriate life in the Twenties, and carries with it the suggestion that for these young tourists travel was itself a form of sexual expression. Beyond that, however, it recognises the love affair as a temporary deviation from loyalties that were essentially American.

Youthful revolt in England took a similar line. 'Always before,' wrote Evelyn Waugh, 'it has been the younger generation asserting the fact that they have grown up; today the more modest claim of my generation is that we are young.' In *Enemies of Promise* (1938), Cyril Connolly famously elaborated his 'Theory of Permanent Adolescence', according to which the greater part of the British ruling class is trapped by the experience of public school in a pre-adult framework of attitudes and responses; but it's a theory that Connolly tests only against himself and his contemporaries, then in their early thirties. For all the undoubted intensity of the public school experience, the claim that it was unrivalled by anything that happened later in life would have seemed grotesque to most of those who had been through the trenches. What Connolly presents as a generalisation about the British ruling class is in reality a statement about his own generation. On the one hand, there was a desire to stand against the Fathers (reflected at a personal level in the troubled relationship that Waugh and Connolly themselves had with their actual fathers); on the other, there was this nostalgia for the outlook and values of childhood, which went hand in hand with a rejection of all the dreary implications of being mature, responsible, grown-up. Once again, travel, with its natural antagonism to the routine life offered by society, was the obvious answer.

Moreover, the effects of Prohibition in America were matched in England by the determination of a puritanical

Home Secretary, Sir William Joynson-Hicks,* to reinforce the repressive effects of the wartime Defence of the Realm Acts, which had, among other things, introduced licensing hours for the sale of alcohol. ('That is the Englishman's method of procuring happiness,' Mr Keith remarks in Norman Douglas's *South Wind* (1917): 'to deny himself pleasure in order to save his neighbour's soul.') The mood which drove the young abroad was caught by the American writer Robert McAlmon in the opening paragraph of *Being Geniuses Together* which speaks of London in 1920 as 'sodden with despair'. Travel was a gesture of revolt against an atmosphere that still reeked of the Dickensian Sunday: 'I found the smoky heaviness of the city muffling as a dull illness driving one into a despairing delirium.' Throughout the Twenties Paris was the most immediate refuge. 'In February 1929 London was lifeless and numb,' Evelyn Waugh declares at the start of his travel book *Labels* – time to head for Paris.

It is indicative of its role, both social and psychological, during these years that in Anthony Powell's *Agents and Patients* (1936) Chipchase should decide to take the unsophisticated Blore-Smith to Paris for a week or two to 'shake off a few inhibitions there'. The cafés and dancehalls of Paris stood for a sexual freedom hostile to the values of the older generation that wielded power in England and America. But as Hemingway's comments imply, the young with a taste for Bohemia were rarely at odds with society for longer than the time it takes to pass from youth to middle age. In the end, they were excursionists. The focus of a more sustained and bitter rebellion lay elsewhere.

Behind the romantic posturing that created the image of the Byronic traveller, there had been a hard core of opposition to the sexual norms of a hypocritical and punitive society. Out of

---

* Joynson-Hicks was Home Secretary from 1924 to 1929.

this came a tradition of tourists, for the most part homosexual, who have quite consciously used the pursuit of forbidden fruit as a form of guerilla warfare against the conventions of their own society. It is the homosexual tourist, more than any other, who has promoted the interplay of sex, travel and subversion referred to in the previous chapter.

An early offspring of Byronic legend was *Melmoth the Wanderer* (1820), Charles Maturin's Gothic fiction about a doomed figure whose pact with Satan has condemned him to an endless life of exile. When a traveller appeared at a hotel in Dieppe in May 1897 and signed the name Sebastian Melmoth in the register, he was proclaiming himself, with a touch of literary melodrama, both an outcast and a wanderer as well as a martyr. Not coincidentally, he was also the age's most famous homosexual. For years Oscar Wilde had conducted a brilliant campaign of subversion against the complacencies of late Victorian society, defying its expectations, laughing at its solemnities, turning its cherished assumptions upside-down – all from within its ranks. What was not publicly apparent was the extent to which the subversive impulse was fuelled by his homosexuality.

To some, his influence could seem almost Satanic. 'Wilde contrives piously to kill what was left of my soul,' wrote André Gide a few weeks after they had first met in Paris in 1891. And the account he gives of their subsequent meeting in the Algerian town of Blidah portrays Wilde as a sinister figure drawing Gide with mephisthophelian glee into a corruption that is also a realisation of his true self. The two of them travel back to Algiers together after a quarrel between Wilde and Lord Alfred Douglas. At a café there a young Arab boy, one of Douglas's previous boyfriends, comes in and plays the flute. Wilde notices Gide's response to the boy and asks, 'Dear, *vous voulez le petit musicien?*' When Gide chokingly acknowledges the fact, Wilde bursts into 'satanic laughter'. He whispers a few words to the guide and later takes Gide to a house guarded by police, shows him into a room where the little musician is waiting, and then himself goes off with another Arab boy. 'Since then,' Gide comments, 'every time I have looked for pleasure I have been running after the memory of that night.' In the joy of the experience he at last found his natural state: '*je trouvais enfin ma normale*'.

It's an episode that suggests the erotic pull of North Africa, the liberating effect of the encounter on Gide, and the perverse thrill its orchestration has given Wilde. (Gide himself in later life noted the extent to which the discovery of his homosexuality, closely bound up with his discovery of Algeria, pushed him along the path of revolt.) The holiday in Algeria was for Wilde a short respite on the eve of the trials that ended with his imprisonment. Whatever resolutions he formed in prison, the years of exile that followed drew him back into a familiar pattern. His letters from Rome during a brief stay shortly before his death depict a consoling pageant of young Italian boys who form the background to his decline. He cut a sad figure by this time, but in the negligent flaunting of his conquests – Giuseppe, Armando, Arnoldo, Omero, Philippo ('whom I culled in the Borgia room'), Dario and the rest – there is a gleam of defiant contempt for the conventions of the society that had imprisoned him. 'It is not for pleasure that I come here,' he had written from Naples just after his release, 'though pleasure, I am glad to say, walks all round.' It's a pose which depends on Continental disdain for the narrow concept of pleasure that rules in England.

Wilde's downfall had been a piece of legislation that came into force in 1885 as part of the Criminal Law Amendment Act. Known as the Labouchère Amendment after its proposer, Henry Labouchère, it stipulated that

Any male person who, in public or private, commits, or is a party to the commission of, or procures or attempts to procure the commission by any male person of any act of gross indecency with another male person, shall be guilty of a misdemeanour, and being convicted thereof shall be liable at the discretion of the court to be imprisoned for any term not exceeding two years, with or without hard labour.

Before the prosecution of Wilde, shockwaves had already been felt among the upper classes in the scandal of the Cleveland Street brothel in 1889, which resulted in the exile of a number of male prostitutes to Australia and New Zealand and several of their wealthy and noble clients to the Continent. But the Wilde affair was of a different order of magnitude, not least in the boost it gave to international tourism. Frank Harris no doubt exaggerates – 'Every train to Dover was crowded; every steamer to Calais thronged with members of the aristocratic and leisured classes . . .' – but the exodus at the time of Wilde's arrest was real. And the pressure on homosexuals, at least on those who could afford it, to spend as much time abroad as possible continued for another seventy years. Trying to convey the state of mind that took Somerset Maugham and so many others into exile, his friend Glenway Wescott explained to Maugham's biographer: 'What is very hard for your generation to appreciate is that Willie's generation lived in mortal terror of the Oscar Wilde trial'. Whatever the periodic changes in moral rhetoric, sex tourism had been tacitly accepted as a social safety-valve for over two hundred years; in the case of homosexuals, it was not merely sanctioned but enforced.

For those in fear of the law, sex was a renegade pursuit, and the consciousness of this put them at a sharp angle to much of what was taken for granted by the law-abiding majority. This was notably true of Norman Douglas, whose transformation from career diplomat to exiled rebel was set in motion by the discovery of his homosexuality. In Italy, and particularly in Florence, where, according to his friend Pino Orioli, the young Florentines had gaberdine trousers specially tailored to show off their genitals, he found a congenial base from which to wage war on respectability. To the young Joe Ackerley, lunching with him at a café in 1922, he pointed out a youthful waiter: 'Hasn't got a hair on his body, Joe. It slips into him like a knife in butter. When are you coming out here to join us?' Candour is a mode of defiance. Piercing the surface of Douglas's old-world courtesy, it habitually pits the scandalous against the socially conventional.

For most of his long life Douglas used travel as a way of staying beyond the reach of the law without abandoning his sexual preferences. His declared policy when things got awkward was to 'hop it'. The countries of the Mediterranean afforded him a sexual freedom that was part of the wider freedom from the 'murk' of England. Returning to Sant'Agata in 1920, he wrote to Edward Hutton: 'What a relief to come to a place, a green oasis, with views over the sea on both sides, where everybody smiles at you and where you can eat and drink till you bust, and where all the boys look like angels, and mostly are! Yes; I shall be needing cricket belts very soon . . .'* It was an article of faith for Douglas, intimately related to the fact of his exile, that the conventional pieties of English domestic life – pieties about sexual morality, family values, childhood innocence, etc. – were a denial of life, joy and colour. English values needed to be replaced by Mediterranean ones, and the sexual freedom he could enjoy abroad was both a personal motive for his travels and a weapon of offence against these values.

Douglas is unusual among English travellers in admitting the role that sex plays in his response to foreign countries. His schooling in Germany was supplemented during his last two

---

* Of the need for cricket belts, Douglas's biographer Mark Holloway notes, 'These peculiarly English articles of dress played an almost ritualistic part as tokens of Douglas' esteem for his young friends'. (Holloway, 271).

years as a gymnasium student by regular visits to the town brothel, from which he graduated to a 'harem' of local girls. 'A sound education for boys of eighteen to twenty,' he concludes. 'If some of my young English friends could enjoy its advantages, they would not grow up to be the flabby nincompoops they are, in the matter of sex.' His dealings with a variety of pimps and procuresses in a variety of countries are chronicled with urbane relish, whether he's subscribing in advance for a girl in Russia (as Rousseau had done a hundred and fifty years earlier in Venice) or making arrangements to acquire a girl in Naples (only to find that he has acquired her brother as well). 'Why are such delectable places not commoner?' he asks of an agreeable café-brothel that cheered his stay in Smyrna in 1895.

Indignation at Douglas's behaviour, if that is what we feel, should not blind us to the ordinariness of what he describes. He merely recalls the facilities that were available to any traveller with the relatively small amount of money required to pay for them. In his recollections of the ageing Raffaele Amoroso, who 'pimped for the nobility and gentry, and also, on occasion, for royalty', there is a sense of the unexplored continents of desire to which the pimp gives access: 'Once you begin to indulge in certain caprices, he used to say, there are no limits to what can be done; *la libidine non ha fine*; and he made it his business to cater genially, and unscrupulously, and successfully, and rapaciously, for every taste'. Maupassant was one of those who, 'like other intelligent tourists', made use of Amoroso, a man *'dont les relations sont fort utiles aux voyageurs'*, and in *Les Soeurs Rondoli* he wrote of the stupefying propositions such pimps would make: *'tout un programme de plaisirs sensuels compliqués d'articles vraiment inattendus: pour peu que vous aviez envie, ces gens-là vous offriraient le Vésuve!'* Anything is available, anything. On foreign soil, in the company of men like Amoroso, the horizons of desire, at home so clearly defined and anxiously policed, are boundless.

Amoroso is a type familiar to tourists the world over, a man whose every word and gesture seem to erase the moral certainties the traveller brings from home. Evelyn Waugh described him in the figure of Mr Bergebedgian, an Armenian hotelier encountered in Harar: 'I do not think I have ever met a more tolerant man; he had no prejudice or scruples of race, creed, or morals of any kind whatever; there were in his mind none of those opaque patches of principle; it was a single translucent pool of placid doubt; whatever splashes of precept had disturbed its surface from time to time had left no ripple; reflections flitted to and fro and left it unchanged.' For those who are anyway of subversive temper, such men, or sometimes women, are irresistible. Their very existence is a serene comment on the provisional nature of our moral structures. With disarming candour they acknowledge the raw material of human diversity and go about their business, offering a perspective from which moral distinctions become mere differences of taste and presentation. They have the uncomplicated outlook of the dressmaker who supplied Douglas with girls in Naples: 'a woman full of gaiety who took a fancy to me; like many others of her sex she did it for sport, for the fun of the thing. No doubt she earned a small commission; I have known English society ladies earn dreadfully big ones for performing the same service.'

The atmosphere that fosters such moral neutrality has an obvious appeal to those defined by their own society as morally unacceptable. Of his restlessness between the wars J.R. Ackerley wrote, 'This obsession with sex was already taking me, of course, to foreign countries, France, Italy, Denmark, where civilised laws prevailed and one was not in danger of arrest and imprisonment for the colour of one's hair. Many anxieties and strains were therefore lessened abroad.' It was a continuing refrain; a diary entry for June 1950 muses on whether, if his dog* were to die, he should 'pack up this life

---

* This was his beloved bitch, Queenie, who shared Ackerley's domestic life and from whom he was only parted during his occasional infidelities abroad.

and go to some Mediterranean country, where friendship is easy, and pick up a boy'. In England, as he grew older, he no longer thought much about sex, but 'whenever I went abroad I found myself pursuing it again. I did not go abroad much, I preferred to spend my holidays with my bitch, but on the few occasions that I left her, when she was getting old and inactive, and went to France, Italy, Greece and Japan, I looked for sexual adventure and found it.' The trip to Japan in 1960, of which we get glimpses in his letters to Forster and others, took him through the gay bars of Kyoto, where boys, 'sometimes in kimonos', were on offer in the tiny bar-rooms: 'I small bedroom at the back to which you can take one if you fancy him. 25/- about the lowest tariff.' To the traveller, kimonos, of course, make a difference.

Throughout the first half of the century, excursions of this kind, albeit on a more modest scale, were a standard reaction to the legal situation at home, but in one way their relative safety diminished the challenge they represented to orthodox behaviour. From this point of view, danger could be a necessary part of the experience – what Wilde called 'feasting with panthers'. Ackerley records an episode when he was having lunch with his father on a train to Liverpool. Towards the end of the meal a good-looking young waiter gave him a meaning look and a backward glance. Without more ado, Ackerley excused himself to his father and made for the lavatory in the wake of the boy: 'We entered together, quickly unbuttoned and pleasured each other. Then I returned to finish my coffee.' The brazenness that brings illicit sex to within inches of the ordinary world is a sexual strategy that both intensifies the thrill of the participants and mocks the blithe unawareness of everyone else. In this respect it must be rather like spying – as a number of our home-grown spies could probably have confirmed.

What drives the episode is a form of excitement, not necessarily homosexual, associated especially with the curious blend of intimacy and anonymity that belongs to travel. We have only to think of the heroes of Victorian pornography grappling their way through bumpy coach rides and feverish train journeys, or the long tradition of shipboard romance, or the persistent legends of a 'mile-high club'. When John Osborne manages to have sex with his girlfriend on the coach back to Brighton, or John Updike patiently masturbates the woman next to him on a car journey back from New Hampshire, or Emmanuelle melts under a stranger's hands on the plane to Bangkok, or Erica Jong's heroine fantasises the zipless fuck on a speeding train, they are in one sense testifying to the basic affinity between travel and sex that is inscribed in our sexual vocabulary of roving eyes and wandering hands, of exploring, mounting, entering, penetrating, riding, galloping, coming, going all the way and so on; in another, they are linking this to the equally basic affinity between travel and rebellion. The moment of illicit sexual satisfaction is a brief erotic victory over the rest of the world, a successful raid on the kingdom of propriety.

This dangerous edge is not to everyone's taste. Ackerley's preference for finding sex abroad was common during a period when fear and repression among homosexuals were widespread. For those who could not move permanently abroad, or did not want to, there was the option of occasional forays such as those made by Ackerley himself and countless numbers of his contemporaries. At the time, this sort of tourism wore a different public face which obscured its motives, with the result that its importance to the history of twentieth-century travel has been underrated. In his influential book on the period between the wars, *The Auden Generation* (1976), Samuel Hynes explains the preoccupation with travel during the 1930s in terms of three factors: first, popular fashion; second, its appeal as a metaphor of a journey into the unknown; and third, the possibility of adventure. These are valid considerations, but they quite ignore what was often the most pressing reason of all: the perilous sexuality of the traveller. Indeed, it is Valentine Cunningham's claim in *British Writers of the Thirties* (1988) that 'the British homosexuals and their boyfriends – Isherwood and Heinz, Howard and Toni, Spender and Tony Hyndman, John Lehmann – perpetually on the go, always *déraciné*, forever moving on and moved on . . . can be considered to stand as representatives of an extraordinarily restless era'. Homosexuals were one group of travellers whose motivation was indisputably sexual, and this perception of them as representative figures of the period suggests just how big a gap Hynes has left.

The relationship between homosexuality, travel and social rebellion is addressed by Christopher Isherwood in *Christopher and his Kind.* At the start of the book, published in the same year as *The Auden Generation*, he explains what had really taken him to Germany in 1929. Like others at the time, he had lied about his reasons for going abroad, but here he sets out to put the record straight. It was not, as he had suggested, the desire to meet the anthropologist John Layard that had made him so keen to get to Berlin: 'It was Berlin itself he was hungry to meet; the Berlin Wystan [Auden] had promised him. To Christopher, Berlin meant Boys.' This was exactly what had been unmentionable when he wrote *Lions and Shadows* (1938), a fictionalised autobiography of his life between the ages of seventeen and twenty-four. The book provides a useful illustration of how the history of tourism becomes distorted by omission and falsification. Isherwood had in fact made an earlier trip to Germany in 1928, which he says had awakened his sense of the erotic possibilities of travel, but 'the Bremen trip isn't even mentioned in *Lions and Shadows* because Christopher was then unwilling to discuss its sexual significance'. (He later destroyed the diary he kept in Berlin because it was 'full of details about his sex life'.) *Christopher and his Kind* brings into view the motives that had previously been suppressed, and in doing so it speaks for a whole category of British tourists between the wars.

Isherwood's first visit to Berlin, only a few days long, was 'one of the decisive events of my life'. Guided by Auden to a gay bar called The Cosy Corner,* he immediately fell for a blond, blue-eyed German boy he calls Bubi, who, like his later Berlin boyfriends, was a perfect vehicle for expressing rebellion against an English upper-middle-class background. At the end of this first visit to Berlin, Bubi gives Isherwood a gold-plated bracelet which he sees as a badge of his liberation and displays 'challengingly' when he gets home. But it was not enough simply to defy the conventions of proper masculine attire. The experience of Berlin had left Isherwood unable to reconcile himself to a life in England that he felt 'was basically untruthful, since it conformed outwardly to standards of respectability which he inwardly rejected and despised'.

By contrast, Germany held the key to a truthful life. When he returns there, he finds that Bubi is wanted by the police, and a letter from the fugitive thrills him with the feeling that 'he himself had become an honorary member of the criminal class'. (Auden's boyfriend is taken off by police on the same day.) The significance of this feeling, which is also evident in Douglas and Wilde, and perhaps even in some of Byron's dabblings in Venice, is suggested by Isherwood's comment on the social pressures towards heterosexuality: 'Girls are what the State and the Church and the Law and the Press and the Medical profession endorse, and command me to desire. My mother endorses them, too. She is silently, brutishly willing me

---

* John Lehmann describes it as 'filled with attractive boys of any age between sixteen and twenty-one, some fair and curly-haired, some dark and often blue-eyed, and nearly all dressed in extremely short *lederhosen* which showed off their smooth and sunburnt thighs to delectable advantage' (Lehmann, 44), The *lederhosen* had the added convenience of pockets cut off inside.

to get married and breed grandchildren for her. Her will is the will of Nearly Everybody, and in their will is my death.' To be a homosexual is to stand against these dominant forces, and to be a traveller is to put oneself outside their reach. Both are transgressive identities, and their intersection in the figure of the homosexual traveller compounds the potential for sedition.

Byron is probably not a name with which Isherwood would have chosen to associate himself, but an element of Byronic self-dramatisation is clearly present in the persona of heroic exile he adopted for the benefit of himself and his friends: 'He [Christopher] liked to imagine himself as one of those mysterious wanderers who penetrate the depths of a foreign land, disguise themselves in the dress and customs of its natives and die in unknown graves, envied by their stay-at-home compatriots'. The world of homosexual bars and semi-criminal boyfriends was part of this romance, as was his brief flirtation with living in the slums.

Berlin's success in promoting itself as the capital of European decadence has made Germany famous as a resort of homosexuals between the wars, but in practice the more civilised arrangements across the Channel made the whole Continent a welcome refuge for British tourists. When Evelyn Waugh arrived in Athens at the start of 1927 to stay with his friend Alastair Graham, who was sharing a flat with an attaché at the British Embassy, he found an atmosphere imbued with homosexuality. Another Englishman was staying in the flat: 'He wants to seduce Alastair and his talk – and indeed everyone's in Athens – is only of male prostitutes. The flat is usually full of dreadful Dago youths called by heroic names such as Miltiades and Agamemnon with blue chins and greasy clothes who sleep with the English colony for 25 drachmas a night.' Further west, Capri, which first acquired a homosexual following in the 1870s, had been serving as a post-Wilde refuge since the end of the nineteenth century and continued to do so between the wars and beyond. In its heyday, Capri was home to a colourful band of male and female homosexuals that included Douglas himself and the notorious Count Fersen, whose record of pederasty persuaded even the tolerant Capresi to exile him from the island for a few months, as well as Somerset Maugham, E.F. Benson, the Wolcott-Perrys, Mimi Franchetti and Romaine Brooks. As Mrs Ambrogio says in Compton Mackenzie's *Vestal Fire* (1927), 'Everyone's immoral in Capri. It's the air. Dogs. People. All immoral. Can't help it, poor dears.'

Again, I'm drawing on professional writers because they have tended to write and be written about more than any other section of the travelling public, but among those with the money and the leisure to go abroad the same practices and assumptions were widely shared. Homosexual travel between the wars was partly a response to existing laws at home, partly also an expression of the social climate of the time. Goronwy Rees noted that at Oxford and Cambridge in the 1920s and early 1930s, 'homosexuality was, among undergraduates and dons with pretensions to culture and a taste for the arts, at once a fashion, a doctrine, and a way of life'. More specifically, he associates this with the impulse to rebel: it was, he suggests, 'very largely the particular form which the revolt of the young took at the universities at that time'. To accept a homosexual identity ranged one against the massed ranks of the establishment; it also gave one an excellent reason to travel.

The same patterns of homosexual tourism were still in place in the two decades that followed the Second World War. The diaries of Joe Orton reflect a subculture that thinks of travel primarily in terms of sex. After a disappointing visit to Tripoli in March 1967 ('Not a sign of a cock,' he reports in a note to Kenneth Williams), he takes advice from friends. The journalist Henry Budgen warns him that 'Agadir was "nice" but trade difficult because the hotels won't allow dragging back'. Next month, over lunch at Simpson's, the former MP

Sir Ian Horobin tells Orton that he has found an agreeable village in southern Morocco:

'We stayed at a little place and there were boys galore and so nice. Not spoiled like Tangier.' He then said he'd been to Lisbon, 'which also,' he said, lowering his voice, 'is very good. But you must have a flat, of course. These wretched hotels simply won't allow you to take anyone back.'

Undeterred by the warning about Tangier, which enjoyed a long-standing tourist reputation – 'all junkies . . . and pederasts' had been Anthony Burgess's verdict four years earlier – Orton and Kenneth Halliwell took a flat there for May and June.

The most striking aspect of Orton's diary entries for this period is the atmosphere of sexual carnival. He and the other English tourists who drift in and out of the diaries are there for pleasure, and pleasure walks all round. Once again, it's the lure of limitless availability ('Sir, you can have her. It would not be difficult'). After turning down a casual offer of *soixante-neuf* from a young boy who has approached him on the street, Orton sits out on the Boulevard Pasteur drinking Coca-Cola with Kenneth Halliwell and a couple of acquaintances: 'Very boring conversation, but a succession of very pretty boys to look at passing at intervals. And all available!' It is yet another image of the sultan reviewing his harem, but from a writer so sensitive to the insolence of the ruling class, it strikes a curious note. Next day Orton muses on his happiness: 'To be young, good-looking, healthy, famous, comparatively rich *and* happy is surely going against nature, and when to the above list one adds that daily I have the company of beautiful fifteen-year-old boys who find (for a small fee) fucking with me a delightful sensation, no man can want for more.'

This refrain is accompanied by a persistent, and complacent, awareness that such happiness is a rebel stronghold, held in the teeth of conventional opposition. After dinner that evening Orton finds himself drinking with a group of acquaintances at a café where he is seated next to 'a rather stuffy American tourist and his disapproving wife':

> They listened to our conversation and I, realising this, began to exaggerate the content. 'He took me right up the arse,' I said, 'and afterwards he thanked me for giving him such a good fucking. They're most polite people.' The American and his wife hardly moved a muscle. 'We've got a leopard-skin rug in the flat and he wanted me to fuck him on that,' I said in an undertone which was perfectly audible to the next table. 'Only I'm afraid of the spunk you see, it might adversely affect the spots of the leopard . . . He might bite a hole in the rug. It's the writhing he does, you see, when my prick is up him that might grievously damage the rug, and I can't ask him to control his excitement. It wouldn't be natural when you're six inches up the bum, would it?'

However mischievous, it's a bravura performance. Orton takes the respectable middle-class values he imputes to the American couple – one must be polite, one mustn't damage the rug, one wouldn't want to do anything unnatural – and tosses them back in a grotesquely subverted form. In a few sentences he creates a parallel world in which their assumptions define the social niceties of buggery. His world. And that's the point – this foreign territory *is* his world. When one of his companions reproaches him for driving away the Americans and argues that the town needs tourists, Orton rounds on him: '"Not that kind, it doesn't," I said. "This is *our* country, *our* town, *our* civilisation. I want nothing to do with the civilisation they made."' Sexual contentment is dependent not just on being in Tangier but in a Tangier perceived as the antithesis of straight, middle-class western civilisation.

An Alternative Kingdom is necessary because of the laws of the United Kingdom. Orton's assault on the Americans and the angry Declaration of Independence that follows it are prompted by his recognition that at home there is no scope for his way of life. It's a point he makes more than once. After an encounter with a boy he calls 'Yellow-jersey', he gives him five dirham and observes that 'having had a boy of his age in England I'd spend the rest of my time in terror of his parents or the police'. Finally, this is what it comes down to – 'that wch you get for £5 we must risque our necks for'. It's what sent Byron to Greece in 1809 and what sends Orton to Morocco a century and a half later. Walking along the seafront at Brighton with Kenneth Halliwell a month after his return, Orton sees a teenage youth lying face-down on the beach and works himself into a rage at the laws that make him inaccessible: 'England is intolerable ... I hate this tight-arsed civilisation'. In the event, he did not have to put up with it for much longer. Within a fortnight he was dead, murdered by Halliwell.

In the previous month, English law had at last been changed to permit homosexual acts in private between consenting adults. It was an overdue reform, but it would have affected relatively few of the people with whom this chapter has been concerned. The outlaw strain was strongest among those who were looking for something else, with a sharper edge of pleasure than the company of consenting adults. What took them abroad were the boys whose taut bodies would prolong their youth, whose unformed minds would flatter their wisdom, whose adolescent spirits would keep the world at bay.

The tourist in search of forbidden fruit belongs to an important but narrow tradition in which the focus of rebellion is almost entirely sexual. Often the travellers who raged against society's moral hypocrisy remained in other ways firmly committed to the values and material life-style of their class and country. The second model of the tourist-as-rebel, which we turn to now, has far wider implications.

8

Some Sunny Isle

On his way to fight for Greek independence, Byron told a travelling companion that if his efforts failed, he would try 'to obtain by purchase, or otherwise, some small island in the South Sea, to which, after visiting England, he might retire for the remainder of his life'. Those who want to turn their backs on civilisation are sometimes drawn to the harsher places of the earth – the desert, the mountains, the heart of the jungle – but these are destinations for the ascetic: they have more to do with curbing desire than fulfilling it. Rebels in the cause of personal liberty have usually preferred the enticements of the tropical island, and the image that attracts them has remained more or less unchanged for a couple of centuries.

In a small way Byron himself helped to create it. Among his less familiar poems there is one called 'The Island', which takes as its subject the mutiny on the *Bounty* in 1789. After five months in Tahiti, collecting breadfruit trees, the ship was on its way to the West Indies when twenty-five members of the crew, led by Fletcher Christian, took control of it, alleging tyranny on the part of the captain, William Bligh. The mutineers subsequently split up, one group under Christian ending in the Pitcairn Islands, the other returning to Tahiti, where they were later arrested. In itself it was a trivial episode that should have had no significant effect on anything, and yet it has probably gained a stronger hold on the popular imagination than any other voyage in history. Two hundred years later, it still has the power to shape our dreams of travel. For three successive generations of filmgoers, Clark Gable, Marlon Brando and Mel Gibson have turned Fletcher Christian into a screen idol.* Why should the mutiny have worked itself so deeply into our cultural memory? Perhaps because it brings together in dramatic colours three separate threads of fantasy: rebellion against authority, escape to another world, enjoyment of sexual freedom.

Fantasies of erotic escape had been accumulating around Tahiti for some twenty years before the *Bounty* set sail – in fact, since the morning in June 1767 when the *Dolphin*, under the command of Captain Samuel Wallis, dropped anchor in Matavai Bay. At sunrise the following day a flotilla of canoes put out from the shore, with 'a fair young Girl in Each Canoe, who played a great many droll wanton tricks'. In this case the Tahitian girls were merely being used as a diversion for the islanders' planned attack, but once the British had demonstrated their military supremacy by slaughtering a number of Tahitians with round and grape-shot, the girls – 'some a light coper colour oythers a mullato and some almost white' – were made available in earnest: 'The old men made them stand in Rank, and made signs for our people to take which they lyked best, and as many as they lyked and for fear our men hade been Ignorant and not known how to use the poor young Girls, the old men made signs how we should behave to the Young women.' It was a powerful image to take back to England. Here was a place where the usual mechanisms of sexual scarcity, so important to cultural life in the west, seemed unknown.

The few weeks Wallis spent on Tahiti confirmed these first impressions. In the words of George Robertson, master of the *Dolphin*, the sailors 'declared they would all to a man, live

---

* In all, five films of the mutiny have so far been made. Apart from those mentioned, there was an Australian silent film in 1916 and a version starring Errol Flynn in 1933.

on two thirds allowance, rather nor lose so fine an opportunity of getting a Girl apiece', swearing that 'they neaver saw handsomer made women in their lives'. It was an opinion endorsed by Wallis himself: 'The women in General are very handsome, some really great Beauties, yet their Virtue was not proof against a Nail'. The Tahitians' high valuation of anything made of iron had quickly established nails as a currency for buying sexual favours from the women. By 9 July the gunner could inform Robertson that 'the price of the old trade, is now fixt at a thirty penny nail* each time'. Such was the popularity of this trade that by the time Wallis left, most of the men had to sleep on deck for lack of any nails from which to sling their hammocks. According to the account given by Hawkesworth, Wallis was obliged, in order 'to preserve the ship . . . from being pulled to pieces', to forbid anyone to go ashore except for wood or water. Two years later, when Cook reached Tahiti, he instructed that iron was not to be used for the purchase of anything other than provisions.

If Wallis's stay had sketched in the outlines of the myth, the visits of Louis-Antoine de Bougainville in 1768 and James Cook in 1769 completed the picture. De Bougainville supplied the poetry, Cook the factual detail. The Frenchman spent only ten days there, but they gave him enough to create for his European audience a fantasy of untrammelled tropical sensuality that still haunts the western imagination today. As soon as his ships had anchored, a young Tahitian girl from one of the canoes boarded de Bougainville's own ship, the *Boudeuse*. Like an image of the island they had reached, she displayed herself naked to the astonished crew. Next day the sailors went ashore to find that they had stepped into the landscape of an erotic dream. As de Bougainville noted in his journal:

---

* i.e. one of the 3½ inch nails that cost thirty pence for a hundred.

The women are pretty ... This people breathe only ease and sensual pleasure. Venus is the goddess who is worshipped here. The sweetness of the climate, the beauty of the landscape, the fertility of the ground which is everywhere fed by streams and waterfalls, the purety of the air, free from the legion of insects that are the scourge of hot countries – everything inspires voluptuous sensations. Accordingly, I have named it New Cythera.

The iconography is unmistakable – it is the rediscovery of paradise, not as poetic fiction but as a tangible reality.

Almost exactly a year after de Bougainville's departure, Cook's ship, the *Endeavour*, anchored in Matavai Bay, and on the same day Joseph Banks, the expedition's chief natural historian, went ashore to be met by 'the truest picture of an arcadia of which we were going to be kings that the imagination can form'. When John Hawkesworth, commissioned by the Admiralty, came to compile an account of the Pacific Voyages a few years later, it was on the journals of Banks and Cook that he mainly relied. For the twenty-five-year-old Banks, whose scientific interests were supported by a large personal fortune, the expedition was for pleasure as well as business, and he became the first individual to be popularly identified with the sexual fantasy that had enveloped Tahiti. Enough was gathered – and then garbled – from his own journal, as well as from the accounts of others, to make him the object of envy, indignation and satire when details of the voyage became public.

The story went that his breeches had been stolen by natives while he was enjoying a night of love with Queen Purea. (Actually, it was his jacket and waistcoat, and at the time he was sleeping blamelessly in Purea's canoe, but this was a man who had shared a tent with three Tahitian women.) On another occasion, a Tahitian girl presented herself to him 'and quickly unveiling all her charms gave me a most convenient opportunity of admiring them by turning herself gradually round', and then, after repeating the performance on a series of pieces of cloth, she 'immediately marchd up to me . . .' The meaning of the ceremony was never made clear, but readers were not slow to imagine its sequel. This was the sort of sexual frankness that Cook stamped indelibly on the public mind by his account of what had taken place the previous Sunday after the expedition's religious service, when at the gate of the Fort 'a young fellow above 6 feet high lay with a little Girl about 10 or 12 years of age publickly before several of our people and a number of the Natives'. It was, he explains, 'done more from Custom than Lewdness', and the women present, including Queen Oberea [Purea], far from disapproving, advised the girl how she should act her part, though the girl herself seemed in little need of instruction.

Even though Hawkesworth toned down the details of the episode (in the version he gives, the youth is described as 'near six feet high' and the girl 'about eleven or twelve years of age'), it could hardly fail to excite comment when the book came out. The same was true of the dance which Cook and Banks had called 'Timorodee', probably from the Tahitian word for copulation: 'they dance especialy the young girls whenever they can collect 8 or 10 together, singing most indecent words using most indecent actions and setting their mouths askew in a most extraordinary manner'. Public interest in all of this was huge. For the copyright to his *Voyages* Hawkesworth received £6,000 – more than was paid for any other book during the century. Unfortunately for him, the public's appetite for salacious detail was matched by its capacity for moral indignation. Within six months of the book's appearance in June 1773, a barrage of criticism and abuse had speeded Hawkesworth to his grave.

Gossip, pamphlets, lampoons, erotic entertainments, pornographic anthologies and a stream of articles and comment all helped to fix Tahiti in people's imagination as a place of unbridled sensual indulgence. The details given by Cook and

Banks, endlessly rehearsed and often distorted, became part of a mythology of exotic sexual freedom, both fascinating and corrupting:

> One page of *Hawkesworth*, in the cool retreat,
> Fires the bright maid with more than mortal heat;
> She sinks at once into the lover's arms,
> Nor deems it vice to prostitute her charms;

Predictably, it was the danger to society's womenfolk that most exercised the moralists. As 'A Christian' remarked in one of his many anonymous assaults, 'Our women may find in Dr Hawkesworth's Book stronger Excitements to vicious indulgences than the most intriguing French Novel could present to their imaginations'. His picture of libertines throwing aside their copies of *Fanny Hill* to revel in Hawkesworth conveys something of the smoking-room appeal it was also supposed to enjoy. The enterprising Mrs Charlotte Hayes, a well-known brothel-keeper of the time, took the opportunity to stage for a few discerning clients her own performance of the spectacle witnessed by Cook and Banks at the gate of the Fort. Her invitations specified that 'a dozen beautiful Nymphs, unsullied and untainted, and who breathe health and nature, will perform the celebrated rites of VENUS [Hawkesworth's elegant phrase], as practised at *Otaheite*, under the instruction and tuition of Queen OBEREA'. In the event, Mrs Hayes herself tackled the role of Oberea, and the Tahitian evening ended with the aristocratic spectators making their selection from the unsullied nymphs.

It was against this background that the mutiny of 1789 defined the South Seas for the next two centuries as a paradisal alternative to all that was constrained, sunless and oppressive about life in the civilised West. The opposition could not have been more starkly drawn. On one side was the institutional brutality of life in His Majesty's Service: backbreaking work, rigid discipline, ferocious punishments; on the other, a carefree life of childlike leisure and untroubled sensuality. It was the fallen world we know against the unfallen world we dream of. That, at least, was how the contrast passed into legend. And it is not entirely contradicted by Captain Bligh's own account, which acknowledges that the mutineers had the chance 'to fix themselves in the most of plenty in the finest Island in the world where they need not labour, and where the alurements of disipation are more than equal to anything that can be conceived'. The mutinous sailors, he concluded, had 'assured themselves of a more happy life among the Otaheitians than they could possibly have in England, which joined to some Female connections has most likely been the leading cause of the whole business'. The 'female connections' are at the heart of the story, as Bligh readily concedes: 'The Women are handsome – mild in their Manners and conversation – possessed of great sensibility, and have sufficient delicacy to make them admired and beloved . . .' To the wretched mutineers, faced with the hardships of life on an eighteenth-century naval vessel, the temptation must have been strong. But those who chose to stay on Tahiti were merely borrowing time. Two years later, caged on the deck of the *Pandora*, the pursuit ship which had come with grinding inevitability to put an end to their idyll, they witnessed the grief of the island women who had been their partners:

> During the time we staid, the Weomen with whom we had cohabited on the Island Came frequently under the Stern (bringing their Children of which there were 6 born, Four Girls & two Boys, & several of the Weomen big with Child) Cutting their Heads till the Blood discoloured the water about them.

Irrespective of one's loyalties in the affair, the images of Tahiti that emerged from it could hardly be other than appealing. Though Byron sees Bligh, 'the gallant chief', as a wronged man, he enters freely into the mutineers' dreams of escape: 'Young hearts, which languish'd for some sunny isle,/Where summer years and summer women smile'. Neuha, the heroine of his poem, is described in a simile which makes the sexual invitation startlingly direct:

> The sun-born blood suffused her neck, and threw
> O'er her clear nut-brown skin a lucid hue,
> Like coral reddening through the darken'd wave,
> Which draws the diver to the crimson cave.

In our own time the films and books that have interpreted the mutiny for us have all painted slightly different pictures, but in each case the hard obligations imposed by society and its institutions are pitted against the overriding impulse to return to Eden. Regardless of other concerns, there is the same incorrigible sympathy with the rebel hearts languishing for a sunny isle. (What Byron dreamed of, Brando did. The actor later bought his own South Sea island where he could live out the Fletcher Christian fantasy in comfort.)

Long before Hollywood adopted the *Bounty*, Americans had created their own island fantasies out of the same desires. In *Typee* (1846), the first of his South Sea novels, Herman Melville gives a semi-autobiographical account of a renegade sailor who jumps ship in the Marquesas and lives for a time with one of the island tribes. The ship's arrival is greeted by a shoal of young girls swimming out to meet it, their long dark hair trailing beside them as they swim: 'What a sight for us bachelor sailors! how avoid so dire a temptation?' In the evening the deck is illuminated with lanterns, and the girls, tricked out with flowers, put on a Marquesan version of the dances recorded by Cook and Banks. The dances are beautiful in the extreme, Melville allows, 'but there is an abandoned voluptuousness in their character which I dare not attempt to describe'. What follows is the predictable descent into 'every species of riot and debauchery' – 'Not the feeblest barrier was interposed between the unholy passions of the crew and their unlimited gratification'.

But the dream of unlimited gratification is only one side of the coin; the other is the dream of exotic romance. In a valley scarcely distinguishable from Eden the narrator meets Fayaway, one of the long line of Polynesian heroines that begins with Purea. 'Her free pliant figure was the very perfection of female grace and beauty,' Melville writes at the start of an inventory that for a page or more runs from her rich complexion, full lips, rosy mouth, dazzling teeth, flowing hair, unfathomable eyes, delicate hands, shapely feet, to her 'inconceivably smooth and soft' skin. Her dress, inevitably, is 'the primitive and summer garb of Eden'. To her physical perfections are added the womanly tenderness and loyalty that qualify her as the complete romantic heroine. There are serpents in Eden, as Melville's narrator discovers, but the impression we are left with is of an unfallen world in blissful contrast to the corrupt civilisation that threatens it.

Typee is just one example of the mixture of fact, fiction and legend that by the middle of the nineteenth century had moulded the popular image of the South Sea Islands. There had been paradises before, of course. Columbus had long ago imported images of the Golden Age into his account of the Indies, whose inhabitants had gold but 'no iron or steel or weapons' and where the people 'always go naked, just as they were brought into the world', and give 'with marvelous love'. Such remarks clearly prefigure eighteenth-century responses to the Pacific, but with two important differences. In the first place, the South Seas had acquired, partly through the *Bounty* and partly through a steady trickle of renegade traders, travellers and beachcombers, the status of refuge from, and challenge to, the laws and conventions of western society. In the second place, the images of exotic felicity associated with the South Seas, unlike those of earlier periods, now lay almost within reach. Banks revealingly observed of the voyage he was about to take with Cook, 'my Grand Tour shall be one round the whole globe'; and Byron's project, however frivolous, was not unrealisable. Boswell, while talking with Cook at a dinner given by the President of the Royal Society in April 1776, 'felt a strong inclination to go with him on his next voyage', and for Diderot, de Bougainville's *Voyage* was the one account of a journey 'that inspired me with the taste for a country other than my own'. The South Sea islands were more than another dream. A vivid promise of all the sensual freedom that life in the West had suppressed, they were there, just a voyage away, waiting for the traveller.

9

Fuir! là-bas fuir!

The appeal of the South Seas for rebel spirits was emphasised by the contrasting version offered by organised religion. Missionary efforts in the first half of the nineteenth century did much to establish an alternative discourse, within which the noble savage was replaced by the depraved heathen, and the delights of paradise by the sins of the unredeemed. In conversation with the writer John Sterling, Samuel Taylor Coleridge endorsed the party line: 'The missionaries have done a great deal for us in clearing up our notions about savage nations . . . of course there never were such dear, good, kind, amiable people. We know now that they were more detestably licentious than we could have imagined.' His plan to keep the Tahitians permanently in mind of their fallen state and curb the excesses of idleness 'by extirpating the bread-fruit from their island, and making them live by the sweat of their brows' has a premonitory ring of the coming age. It is the language and outlook that created the Victorian Sunday experienced by Arthur Clennam on his return from Marseille. To those who burned to get away, the anathemas pronounced by missionaries and their supporters were fuel to the flames, merely confirming the attractions of a world so remote from the joyless orthodoxy of the time.

Moreover, the beachcomber ideal had behind it the force of Rousseau's scathing analysis of the constraints and corruptions of civilised society. Images of a natural paradise in the South Seas were a perfect foil for the growing distaste felt by many Europeans for the effects of industrialisation. The strain of primitivism that runs through Victorian responses to the Mediterranean was one aspect of this. It was not in general consciously rebellious, but it implied a marked ambivalence towards the tide of industrial progress. Elsewhere, the disaffection was more explicit. Alienation from nineteenth-century urban society – Dickens's melancholy streets in a penitential garb of soot – was repeatedly expressed through fantasies of a primitive setting where life was freer, easier, sunnier than at home. Tennyson's dreams in 'Locksley Hall' of 'Summer isles of Eden lying in dark-purple spheres of sea' are revisited through the century as a refuge from the pressures of an increasingly mechanised and demanding world: 'There methinks would be enjoyment more than in this march of mind, / In the steamship, in the railway, in the thoughts that shake mankind'. And always behind the impulse to escape there is the same insistent erotic keynote: 'There the passions cramped no longer shall have scope and breathing space; /I will take some savage woman, she shall rear my dusky race.' By the end of the poem Tennyson has rejected 'lower pleasures' and brought himself sternly back into line, but the images of exotic freedom are what linger in the reader's memory:

Or to burst all links of habit – there to wander far away,
On from island unto island at the gateways of the day.

Larger constellations burning, mellow moons and happy skies,
Breadths of tropic shade and palms in cluster, knots of Paradise.

It is notable that France, which had the most extensive colonial possessions among the Pacific islands, should also have produced the most powerful response to the intertwined appeal of the exotic and the erotic. Chateaubriand, Lamartine, Gautier, Flaubert, Du Camp, de Nerval, Baudelaire, Rimbaud and a catalogue of less celebrated writers all made their contribution. In some cases the poets travelled to the places they dreamed of, in others they just dreamed. Baudelaire had himself been as far as Mauritius, but his poem 'La Chevelure' imagines the continents of Asia and Africa ('*La langoureuse Asie et la brûlante Afrique*') as an exotic world to be discovered in the scented locks of a woman's hair, her tresses an ebony sea that contains a dazzling dream of the romantic voyage – sails, rowers, pennants and masts. The sexual encounter and the journey melt into each other to form a vision of erotic escape in which sex and travel are one. Throughout the century there is a cross-pollination between the actual experience of travel and the daydreams of an orientalist imagination disenchanted with western society.

By giving popular form to this process, Pierre Loti changed the imaginative landscape of European tourism. Born Julien Viaud, Loti was given his pseudonym by the women of Tahiti during his visit in 1872. He had reached the island at the end of January as a sailor aboard the frigate *La Flore*, but what had really brought him to Tahiti was an imagination stirred by the tales his brother Gustave had sent back from there a dozen years earlier, when Loti himself was only ten. Gustave, fourteen years older than Loti, had lived with a native girl during his time on Tahiti and fathered children by her. His letters home had enthralled the younger boy, as had the illustrated *Voyage en Polynésie* which Gustave gave him. One of the pictures that stayed in his mind, he tells us, was of two young girls on the beach, bare-breasted, with flowers in their hair. It was an image effortlessly matched by reality. His affair with a young Tahitian girl became the basis of *Le mariage de Loti* (1880), the most successful of a series of books that presented fictionalised accounts of his romantic dealings in various parts of the world.

Le mariage builds up a seductive contrast between life in the West and the Tahitian alternative, beginning with the now familiar opposition between a cold, sad winter's day in Europe and the 'tranquil, enervating languor of a summer night' in Tahiti. For the westerner disgusted by the priorities of industry and commerce, 'languor' is a word full of temptation. The fourteen-year-old heroine, Rarahu, has eyes 'full of an exotic languor' which bespeak both her sensuality and the prevailing indolence of a life that, unlike our own, knows nothing of Adam's curse – 'these big children have no suspicion that in our splendid Europe so many poor folk wear themselves out to earn their daily bread'. The relationship into which Loti drifts – 'quite gently I surrendered to this soft existence, abandoning myself to the charms of the South Seas' – deftly packages the standard elements of exotic romance. Rarahu not only exhibits a primitive and shameless sensuality, she also falls deeply and flatteringly in love with the narrator, to the extent that when he leaves the island she in effect dies of a broken heart. Loti has combined in a single figure the twin satisfactions described by Melville: unlimited sensual gratification and romantic love.

But Rarahu is more than a woman; she is the essence of the place and its people, 'a little personification, touching and sad, of the Polynesian race'. Through her, Loti gains access to a pre-civilised world. Again it's the idea broached by Symonds of sex as a mode of travel: to know the sexual partner is to know the place. (Thus Anthony Burgess, arriving in the East for the first time: 'I wandered Singapore and was enchanted. I picked up a Chinese prostitute on Bugis Street. We went to a filthy *hôtel de passe* full of the noise of hawking and spitting, termed by the cynical the call of the East. I entered her and entered the territory.') That Rarahu should be 'touching and sad' reflects the delicious vein of melancholy that runs through the traveller's encounters: 'and yet this charming life could have no tomorrow. It would soon be unravelled by departure and separation.' Transience lends the relationship a bitter-sweet intensity which can never be captured in the routines of domestic life. That is the nature of travel: foreknowledge of the final scene at the dockside, the train station, or the airport terminal colours all that goes before.

As Boswell knew when he left Siena, tearful partings belong to the traveller's romantic heritage. To love and ride away is what it's all about. The queen promotes Loti's relationship with Rarahu, but 'it goes without saying that she was in no way suggesting one of those marriages according to the laws of Europe that chain people for life'. The male traveller must retain his freedom, or he ceases to be a traveller. It is part of his attraction that he is a messenger from another world – almost literally. Loti tells us towards the end that Rarahu still loved him 'in the way that one might love a supernatural being, whom one could scarcely grasp or understand'. It's the sort of adoration that is unlikely to survive prolonged acquaintance.

A comparison of Loti's journal notes from Tahiti and what he made of them in *Le mariage de Loti* shows a deliberate process of romanticising. His girlfriend catches sight of him on his return from a neighbouring island: '"Ave Loti!" she said, and then got up and came over to me.' In the novel this becomes, '"Ave! Loti," she said, clasping me in her arms with all her strength.' In both the journal and the novel he goes for a last walk in the valley, but only in the novel is he accompanied by the girl. And then, as the ship takes him away, he observes 'the whole country and my darling girl were going to disappear, vanishing like the stage-set at the end of a performance ...' In the journal we find exactly the same sentence, but without any reference to the girl. What Loti had set out to do was fuse his own casual experiences with existing myths of the South Seas and create out of them a fantasy of escape for disaffected Europeans.

He succeeded beyond his dreams. For domestic readers, the image of Tahiti with its *'charme tout-puissant de volupté et de nonchalance'* was captivating. 'Your name is everywhere,' Alphonse Daudet wrote to Loti shortly after the book's appearance. 'Everyone is mad about Rarahu.' A wave of popularity produced Loti bonbons and Rarahu ribbons, while reviewers outdid each other to convey the book's exotic charm. 'When you finish it,' wrote a critic in *Le Temps*, 'your soul remains haunted by this marvellous landscape. In a low voice you say over to yourself the names of Papeete and Bora-Bora. You dream of these islands of white coral, of these shores where thousands of palm-trees nod like reeds in the sea-breeze ...' The reviewers enthusiastically recycled Loti's story for the public, adding their own poetic gloss to the mythology of the South Seas:

> There, beside fresh springs, among the scented plants, youths and young girls, scarcely clad, meet in total freedom and abandon themselves to the intoxication of the senses with a voluptuous carelessness. There is no sentiment of reserve, restraint, or even modesty; the native of Tahiti follows omnipotent instinct, which impels youth and beauty to seek each other out, to love each other, to come together.

This is the Tahitian dream in its purest form, and its relevance to readers of the magazine is made explicit in the reviewer's summary of Loti's thoughts: 'Why leave this happy corner of the globe that shelters his love? Would not true happiness be to forget the cares and struggles of civilisation, tasting in peace the sweetness of life, beside a faithful partner, in the bosom of a natural world forever young?'

Loti had brought the fantasy to a new completion. Encapsulated in the relationship between the young naval officer and the native girl are all the traveller's subversive dreams – sexual freedom, romantic love, escape from civilisation, magical access to a new world and a new identity. 'It was reserved to Pierre Loti,' wrote Anatole France, 'to make us taste to the point of drunkenness, of delirium, of stupefaction, the pungent flavour of exotic loves.' A century later *Le mariage de Loti* looks a modest enough achievement, its appeal marred by sentimentality, self-regard and colonialist condescension, but it enlarged the landscape of fantasy. The temptation to travel had been crudely but significantly augmented.

Perhaps the most momentous effect of Loti's novel was on a young French painter called Émile Bernard, who was at the time hoping to set out for a new life in Madagascar with Paul Gauguin. Entranced by *Le mariage de Loti*, he wrote to Gauguin proposing that they change their destination to Tahiti. When Gauguin sceptically pointed out that Loti had plenty of money and was only on shore leave, Bernard sent him the official handbook prepared for the 'Exposition coloniale' of 1889, which itself showed more than a trace of Loti's influence. In particular, its portrait of the typical Tahitian woman has a tone not normally associated with official publications:

> her large, dark eyes are so fine and so clear, her lips, though a fraction too full, create, along with her magnificently white and regular teeth, a look so sweet and innocently voluptuous that it is impossible not to share in the admiration she arouses. In keeping with the fashion, her long, ebony hair falls free or else is divided into two thick plaits which she leaves to bob on her shoulders. Her features are open and serene, with never a shadow of worry or concern.

The influence of Loti is equally evident in a passage from the same page that Gauguin would soon be quoting in a letter to one of his friends: 'While men and women on the other side of the planet must toil to satisfy their needs, battling against cold and hunger, and suffering every kind of privation, the lucky inhabitants of the remote South Sea paradise of Tahiti know only the sweetness of life. For them, to live is to sing and to love.' Gauguin had not taken too much persuading. Before he decided to go to Madagascar, the image of Tahiti had already presented itself as a thrilling alternative to a Europe 'gone rotten'. It was a vision so strongly coloured by erotic possibilities that he could not even keep them out of the somewhat tactless letter he sent his wife at the time, in which he pictures himself surrounded by another family, far from this European scramble for money: 'There, in Tahiti, in the silence of the beautiful tropical nights, I shall be able to listen to the soft murmuring music of my heart in amorous harmony with the mysterious beings around me.' What could be more attractive to 'a European who is dissatisfied with his existence'? When his friend Charles Morice heard of the artist's plans, he responded by declaiming 'Brise Marine', Mallarmé's hymn to the lure of exotic escape: 'Fuir! là-bas fuir! Je sens que des oiseaux sont ivres/D'être parmi l'écume inconnue et les cieux ...' Morice had chosen the perfect epigraph for a venture that marked the culmination of the century's quickening undercurrent of disgust with its own achievements.

This was the start of a story that would cast as long a shadow over tourism in the twentieth century as Byron's had in the nineteenth, providing a template for our fantasies that is if anything more potent today than it was a hundred years ago. An icon of defiant escapism, Gauguin has left us with an array of brilliantly coloured images that are central to the tourist ideal; but like respectable heirs to a dubious fortune, we tend not to enquire too closely into their origins. It is worth looking in more detail at the material out of which these images were constructed.

The Gauguin of legend is a middle-aged, middle-class stockbroker who on a wild impulse abandons civilisation to become an artist, a savage and a free man. He himself was content that it should seem so. The life he led, first in Tahiti and then in the Marquesas, was a tangle of financial worries and rancorous embroilments with the colonial authorities, but this finds no reflection in his paintings. The colonial realities of the late nineteenth century – ugly brick buildings, plank houses with corrugated iron roofs, uniformed Europeans and so forth – are nowhere to be seen, replaced by a primitive landscape which only in its intimations of melancholy gives any hint of the pressures of another world.

The reality was more sordid, but it did nothing to contradict the sexual fantasies which had been a notable spur to Gauguin's journey. His early arrangement with a frivolous mulatto girl called Titi was satisfactory enough in its way – 'There is, in all of them, a love so innate that, whether mercenary or not mercenary, it is still Love' – but when he decides to move out of Papeete, he feels the need for a woman less tainted by European influences. 'I shall find them by the dozen,' he assures himself, dismissing Titi with a promise to send for her later. (He did in fact recall her when the expected dozens failed to materialise, but Titi was not cut out for the country life. Before long she was on her way back to Papeete.) In *Noa Noa* he tells how, in the course of a journey round the island, he was invited into a village by a Maori woman who offered him her daughter as a wife. A tall thirteen-year-old girl is duly brought for his inspection. Gauguin's description of her, directed to his European audience, is a calculated advertisement for the erotic delights of the South Seas: 'Through her excessively transparent dress of pink muslin the golden skin of her shoulders and arms could be seen. Two nipples thrust out firmly from her chest. Her charming face appeared to me different from the others I had seen on the island up to the present, and her bushy hair was slightly crinkled. In the sunshine an orgy of chrome yellows.' He takes her back to his home, where they embark on an existence which Gauguin consciously elevates to the status of prelapsarian idyll: 'I set to work again and happiness succeeded to happiness. Every day at the first ray of sun the light was radiant in my room. The gold of Tehaurana's [Teha'amana's] face flooded all about it, and the two of us would go naturally, simply, as in Paradise, to refresh ourselves in a near-by stream . . . all is beautiful – all is well.'

This was written while Gauguin was back in France, trying to create a market for his pictures. How far it was a product of nostalgia, how far the result of a desire to publicise himself and vindicate his exile is unimportant. Its effect, in conjunction with the paintings, was to turn his life into myth. The book ends with his departure for France: 'When I left the jetty to go aboard, Tehaurana, who had wept for several nights, had sat down on the stone, tired and melancholy; her legs dangled, letting both her big sturdy feet brush the salt water. The flower she had been wearing over her ear had fallen into her lap, faded.' Reminiscent of the desolate girls who watched the *Bounty* mutineers shipped back to England, Teha'amana reaffirms Tahiti as the place above all others where the erotic coexists in harmony with the romantic. For a western culture that has always found it difficult to reconcile the two, this is a beguiling achievement. If travel answers the rebel's desire to be somewhere else, Gauguin's rendering of his life with Teha'amana depicts the final goal – a sensuous vision of the primitive, the exotic and the paradisal that stands at the opposite pole from civilised, familiar, fallen Europe.

In reality, the colours were never quite so bright. On his return to Tahiti in 1895, Gauguin tried to take up with Teha'amana again, but the syphilis which he had probably brought with him when he first came to Tahiti was becoming more evident, and he was troubled by an ankle injury from a fight he'd got into while back in France. Moreover, Teha'amana had married in his absence. She returned to him for a week but soon went back to her new husband, leaving Gauguin to boast somewhat forlornly that life was fine without her:

> Every night skittish young girls invade my bed – three of them yesterday to keep me busy. I'm going to stop leading this wild life, install a responsible woman in the house and get down to work, especially as I feel in good form and I think I'm going to do better work than before.

With his bad ankle and running sores, the painter was becoming a steadily less attractive item, but he nonetheless managed to persuade another more or less willing fourteen-year-old to share his life. Pau'ura never meant as much to him as Teha'amana, but they seem to have reached an accommodation of sorts, even though she spent an increasing amount of time with her friends and family rather than with Gauguin. In a letter home at the beginning of 1897, he wrote complacently about the joys of sitting at his open door, smoking a cigarette and drinking absinth: 'And then I have a fifteen-year-old wife who cooks my simple everyday fare and gets down on her back for me whenever I want, all for the modest reward of a frock, worth ten francs, a month. . . . You have no idea how far 125 francs will go here.'

By 1901 Gauguin had begun to realise that Tahiti could no longer offer him what he wanted – notably, young Polynesian girls. According to friends and neighbours of Gauguin interviewed by Bengt Danielsson, this was the main source of his restlessness. Pierre Levergos is quoted as saying: 'It was in fact the sores that made him leave Tahiti, because no women there would sleep with him any more. The women of the Marquesas were poorer and more savage, and he would have better opportunities there, he said.' The point is confirmed by another friend, Fortuné Teissier, who recalled that Gauguin 'one day returned triumphant from Papeete; he had heard that in the Marquesas you could still buy a girl model for a handful of sweets! He ordered a sackful, and with this honeyed "barter" sought the last corner [of the archipelago]'.

Even with a sackful of sweets he didn't find the going particularly easy. His sores were repulsive, and it was only by dispensing rum and claret in his new house in Atuona – on the lintel he had optimistically inscribed the words 'MAISON DU JOUIR' – that he was able to attract a supply of complaisant women, though they tended to be neither young nor handsome, since the local missionaries had managed to corral most of the younger teenagers in a convent. Gauguin worked with some success to undermine the missionaries' influence – enough, anyway, to secure himself another fourteen-year-old bride. The price demanded by her family was steep (six yards of cotton cloth, seven yards of chintz, eight yards of muslin, ten yards of calico, three dozen ribbons, a dozen pieces of lace, four reels of thread and a sewing machine), but both the girl, Vaeoho, and her parents seem to have been content with the outcome. Once established, Gauguin stayed here on Hivao island for the twenty months that remained to him, fathering a daughter on Vaeoho and continuing, when not embroiled in quarrels with missionaries and colonial administrators, to paint.

Such details of the artist's life in the South Seas make uneasy reading, but they shed light on an impulse which became central to twentieth-century tourism. Gauguin not only brings into focus the romantic primitivism that had been gathering strength since the beginnings of the Industrial Revolution, he also demonstrates that one of its primary motivations was erotic. When Freud asserted that civilisation was paid for by the repression and sublimation of the sexual urge, he did not have to look far for supporting evidence. Nineteenth-century Europe, and Victorian England in particular, had put a higher and higher premium on restraint; every step in the progress of civilisation had been marked by a tightening of the sexual reins. The underlying assumption, which had a long history, was that the gap between savage and civilised corresponded to that between sexual abandon and sexual restraint. Sometimes the implications of this were made explicit: 'the primitive woman . . . was always a prostitute', wrote Cesare Lombroso in 1896, echoing the words of Alphonse Esquiros from half a century before, 'the black woman is naturally a prostitute'. And when Esquiros comments that 'More than anything else, prostitutes love three things in the world: the sun, flowers, and their hair', he is only a step away from traditional images of the South Seas Islanders. In 1911 Octave Simonot was still thinking along the same lines in his attempt to establish the character and appearance of the 'born prostitute', who was thought to have a short attention span, 'as among savages', and an affinity for bright colours, music and sexual relations. The prostitute's sphere, like the tourist's, is the world of pleasure as opposed to the world of work, and in her dedication to pleasure she is linked, as the social historian Alain Corbin has argued, with the child and the savage.

If the Victorian prostitute is a type of the primitive, then the Victorian gents who made use of her were engaging in a kind of sexual tourism; they were going among savages. Conversely, those who travelled to distant and primitive lands were likely to be going among prostitutes. In either case, the impulse away from civilisation was an impulse towards sexual licence. This was the lure of the primitive (reflected more decorously in Victorian responses to the wildness of nature or the rough vitality of the Mediterranean peasantry), and travel, across countries or across classes,* was what gave access to it.

But access came at a price. If Gauguin's pursuit of the primitivist ideal has made him the archetypal hero of escapist fantasy, it has also provided an image of the tourist as exploiter and violator. He arrives in Paradise with syphilis and while protesting his enthusiasm for the native culture does little more than grab what he can from it on his own terms. The primitivist hero and the European exploiter collide most obviously in Gauguin's sexual interests. No painting better expresses the ambiguities of his position than *Manao tupapau*. It shows a young girl lying naked, face-down on a flowered couch, her buttocks slightly raised, her head half-turned towards the spectator; in the background stands a black-clad spirit (*tupapau*). Gauguin was aware from the start of possible controversy ('I did a nude of a young girl. In that position, a mere nothing, and it is indecent . . .'), so sent detailed instructions to his wife Mette on how to explain the picture in a way that would head off criticism. But his sermon on local practices and superstitions could do little to distract from the immediate impact of the painting. It is both erotic and disturbing – disturbing *because* erotic. And the implication in *Noa Noa* that the girl waiting uneasily on the couch was his fourteen-year-old wife added to the provocation. Behind many of the images Gauguin presents of his life in the South Seas, and especially his life with Teha'amana, there is the desire to show himself living out a Lotiesque fantasy to which the childlike

---

* It could be argued that in our own time the prostitutes of the third world have gone some way towards taking the place of the working-class women – servants, milliners, farm girls, factory workers and so on – who were the sexual resource of these well-to-do Victorians. Tourism can be used to buy the sexual privileges of a former age. As the anthropologist Claude Lévi-Strauss remarked in another context, 'The tropics are not so much exotic as out of date' (Lévi-Strauss, 87).

Rarahu figure is central. As the book's popularity had testified, it was a fantasy widely shared. But the stark depiction of a wary, fourteen-year-old girl, naked and inviting, was another matter. Loti's Rarahu taken out of soft focus was still an object of fantasy, but a much more unsettling one.

In this, Gauguin's picture is part a wider ambiguity that has teased western culture since the middle of the nineteenth century. Our attitudes to the child/adolescent as object of desire are shot through with contradictions. The poses of coy invitation that delighted nineteenth-century photographers, that ensured Shirley Temple's success in the 1930s (Graham Greene was sued for claiming that her stardom depended on arousing adult lust), and that are frequently used in today's advertisements, suggest a responsiveness to the child's sexual appeal which is at odds with our public protestations. In recent years an obvious example of this ambivalence has been the ongoing controversy over Vladimir Nabokov's *Lolita*. The outrage that greeted its publication in 1955 surged back powerfully enough in 1997 to make Adrian Lyne's film of the book virtually untouchable. (As Lyne remarked at the time, 'I could make a movie about a 12-year-old girl getting chopped up and eaten and no one in America would say anything.') And yet the subject continues to fascinate. Why else has Lolita's name found a place in our vocabulary?

For anyone who looks at the relationship between travel and sex, it's a fascination that cannot be brushed aside. In so far as moral codes are maintained by the difficulty of breaking them with impunity, the dangers of travel are manifest. Its sexual opportunities are often opportunities for sex with the young, and this has been so for every category of traveller we have considered. The stimulus is power, of course, but also the transgressive nature of travel itself; crossing boundaries is the traveller's occupation. And so is the search for Eden. Above all, the child seems to offer a forbidden way back from the conditions of adulthood to the prelapsarian world which is the traveller's grail. It's a fantasy deeply rooted in our culture but for the most part expressed only through a sentimental and apparently unsexual reverence for the innocence and freshness of children. Travel unlocks other possibilities.

In the light of this, it is not surprising that a child-bride like Rarahu so often figures as the symbol of Tahiti, or that the Tahitians themselves were so often characterised by Europeans as children. Their childishness and innocence are precisely what make them an alternative to the world grown old and corrupt which the traveller has left behind. It is through his union with the child-bride that he consummates his rejection of that world and is himself reborn as a child of nature. But from the start there was an awareness that the sexual idyll could not be separated from the larger process of violation of which it was a part. Even as de Bougainville shaped the original myth, he noted (or perhaps invented) the presence of a symbolic figure who stands aside from the general rejoicing that greets the arrival of the French sailors. The old man's look of speculation and concern, says de Bougainville, 'seemed to announce his fear that these happy days, which had passed for him in the bosom of tranquillity, would be troubled by the arrival of a new race'. It was this figure whom Diderot took as his mouthpiece in the *Supplément au voyage de Bougainville* to warn of the evils that would flow from contact with the Europeans. One of them had already become apparent in the spread of syphilis through the island. Other infections – small-pox, dysentery, tuberculosis, measles, chickenpox, flu – were soon to follow, and with them a spiralling death rate. In 1767, at the time of its 'discovery', Tahiti had a population of some 150,000*; by the end of the century it was down to about 15,000.

---

* This is the figure given by Bengt Danielsson (Danielsson, 83); other writers have put it lower. What is not disputed is the catastrophic nature of the decline.

Paradise is regained, but only at the cost of laying it waste. From this angle it is hard to see the tourist identity as other than destructive: what attracts the Connoisseur at once becomes liable to plunder; the promise of revelation turns the Pilgrim's shrine into a tourist grotto; in defining an alternative paradise, the Rebel initiates a lethal process of colonisation. The history of tourism is the story of desire consuming its object.

10

Playing Gauguin

'Gauguin's Tahiti' was to become the ultimate twentieth-century tourist destination. Ten years after his death, Rupert Brooke arrived there 'to hunt up traces of Gauguin, the painter'. He had left England in May 1913 for a trip to Canada and America after a mild nervous breakdown. By October he was ready to return, but an itch of unfulfilment kept him from home: 'I tossed up – back to England? or out to the South Seas? The latter prevailed,' he wrote to his friend Eddie Marsh from San Francisco. Given the images already in Brooke's mind, it would probably have prevailed anyway. 'Letters will reach me occasionally, I suppose,' he goes on in the same letter. 'And you may figure me in the centre of a Gauguin picture, nakedly riding a squat horse into white surf.' Then the following month, on the boat from Samoa to Fiji, 'You think of me in a loin-cloth, brown & wild, in the fair chocolate arms of a Tahitian beauty, reclining beneath a bread-fruit tree, on white sand, with the breakers roaring against the reefs a mile out, & strange brilliant fish darting through the pellucid hyaline of the sun-saturated sea.'

'You may figure me . . . You think of me . . .' Brooke, visualising himself in the role of noble savage, is keen that others should visualise him in it too. Part of its meaning resides in the envious and admiring attention of the social world whose neurotic complexities the would-be savage has fled. Gauguin is the presiding genius, but mention of the breadfruit tree brings an echo of the *Bounty*, and there are perhaps also thoughts of Robert Louis Stevenson, whose grave Brooke had just visited on Samoa. Stevenson had been living there during the period of Gauguin's first stay on Tahiti, and his writings, though they castigated the effects of European commercial greed, had been making their own contribution to the South Seas legend. As soon as the narrator of Stevenson's 'The Beach of Falesá' (1893) steps ashore, he is approached by the local trader, another European, who confirms the general assumption that an exotic location means available women: 'You can have your pick of the lot for a plug of tobacco.' Taking stock of the crowd of girls about them, the narrator pulls himself up and looks among them 'like a bashaw'. At about the same time, Gauguin was noting that in Tahiti, 'You can easily be your own little Sardanapalus without ruining yourself'. All it takes, he says, is 'an orange and a side-glance'.

The letters Brooke sent home during the six months he spent in the South Seas are a record of his travels, but they are also an indication of how far the whole South Seas mythology had already been absorbed into tourist culture. (The white beaches he anticipated in Tahiti were still in the minds of the producers of Brando's *Mutiny on the Bounty* fifty years later. Disappointed by the dingy volcanic reality of Matavai Bay, they imported hundreds of tons of more suitable white sand from New Jersey, thus keeping the prospect bright for another generation of tourists.) D.H. Lawrence once remarked that 'We travel, perhaps, with a secret and absurd hope of setting foot on the Hesperides, of running our little boat up a creek and landing in the Garden of Eden.' The popular image of the South Sea Islands might have been constructed as a direct answer to Lawrence's melancholy conclusion that this hope was 'always defeated'. Landing in the Garden of Eden was exactly what the South Seas promised, and exactly what Brooke seemed to have done:

Oh Eddie, it's all true about the South Seas! . . . there it is: there it wonderfully is: heaven on earth, the ideal life, little work, dancing singing & eating, naked people of incredible loveliness, perfect manners, & immense kindliness, a divine tropic climate, & intoxicating beauty of scenery.

His ecstatic descriptions over the months that follow combine all the usual ingredients, held together by an exhilarating sense of the recovered liberty of childhood. It was, he wrote to Edmund Gosse, 'quite another world. It's getting back to one's childhood, somehow: but not to the real childhood, rather to the childhood that never was, but is portrayed by a kindly sentimental memory; a time of infinite freedom, no responsibility, perpetual play in the open air, unceasing sunshine, never-tiring limbs, and a place where time is not . . .' This return to the lost Eden of childhood is a familiar theme of travel, but nowhere is it so marked as in writing about the South Seas.

And nowhere is the parallel yearning for the innocence of prelapsarian sex so manifest. Brooke had left behind in England a tangle of romantic relationships – with Noel and Bryn Olivier, with Ka Cox, with Cathleen Nesbitt – that had all been marked by much anguished soul-searching. Further complicated by Brooke's bisexuality, the whole mixture had been scrambled up in the social, literary and political round of Edwardian London. By contrast, social and sexual life in Polynesia had a blissful simplicity, which he tried to express to Violet Asquith:

I suppose you're rushing from lunch party to lunch party, and dance to dance, and opera to political platform. Won't you come and hear how to make a hibiscus wreath for your hair, and sail a canoe, and swim two minutes under water catching turtles, and dive forty feet into a waterfall, and climb a coco-nut palm? It's more worth while.

Once again it's summer isles of Eden against the thoughts that shake mankind. As Brooke realised, he was living out the Tennysonian fantasy of revolt from eighty years before. Writing to Hilton Young in a half-serious attempt to interest him in a South Seas expedition, he falls back on the imagery of 'Locksley Hall': 'Come! It is your only chance of salvation. "Come, and wed some dusky woman, she shall teach your piebald brood: How to wrestle, swim . . ." damn, I can never quote properly.'

By this time, Tennyson's dream of taking some savage woman to rear his dusky race had acquired a topicality that was much in Brooke's mind. Again and again in the last year of his life, he returns to his dislike of the sort of modern women produced by Europe and America, most of them, it seems to him, 'spoilt by feminism and riches'. From Arizona he wrote to Jacques Raverat, 'I shall go back to the South Seas, where women are women, beautiful, intelligent, competent, and real – in the round – three-dimensional (at least): not silhouettes with pince-nez'. It is an Edwardian version of the lament that Alec Waugh would be making in the Twenties and that tourists solacing themselves in the bars of Bangkok are still making today. The social complexities of life in a modern civilisation are mirrored by its sexual complexities. In the revolt against modernity, nostalgia for sexual simplicity – a state of things 'where women are women' – plays a crucial part.

And the crowning fantasy, as always, is the union of sensual gratification and romantic love. In Brooke's case, after a series of 'astonishing medieval adventures with Tahitian beauties', this was realised in the figure of Taatamata, 'a girl with wonderful eyes, the walk of a goddess, & the heart of an angel' whom he met while staying at a hotel about thirty miles outside Papeete. Whether or not, as recent research suggests, she gave birth to a daughter by Brooke a few months before he died, it is apparent from his letters that her company turned the last weeks of his stay on Tahiti into a romantic apotheosis: 'Tonight we will put scarlet flowers in our hair and sing strange slumberous South Seas songs to the concertina and drink red French wine and dance obscure native dances and bathe in a soft lagoon by moonlight . . .'

In retrospect, these scenes have a poignancy that Brooke himself could not have imagined. No escape was ever snatched in the shadow of such a horrifying demonstration of how much there was in Europe to escape from. Nine months later, when the war had already taken countless lives and Brooke was undergoing military training at Blandford in Dorset, he received a letter recovered by divers from the wreck of the *Empress of Ireland*, which had gone down in the St Lawrence Seaway. Dated 2 May 1914 and written in an engaging mixture of French and English, it begins 'My dear Love darling' and goes on to give local news of parties and dances and mutual acquaintances before turning to memories of Brooke:

I wish you here that night I get fat all time Sweetheart you know I alway thinking about you that time when you left me I been sorry for long time. whe have good time when you was here I always remember about you forget me all readly oh! Mon cher bien aime je l'aimerai toujours.

. . . je me rapeller toujour votre petite etroite figure et la petite bouche qui me baise bien tu m'a perceau mon cocur et je aime tourjours ne m'oubli pas mon cher maintenant je vais finir mon lettre. parceque je me suis très occupee le bateau par a l'instant. 5 heures exuse me to write you shot letter. I hope you good health and good time.

I send my kiss to you my darling
xxxxxxxxxxxxxxx mille kiss
Taatamata

It's an awkward document for those who prefer things black and white – the exploited native girl is not really supposed to send breathless, affectionate love letters. 'I puzzled out the French and English misspellings, and, being very tired and slightly drunk, gulped a good deal,' wrote Brooke.

That he should have turned almost at once,* and with some enthusiasm, from beachcombing to battle, need not surprise us. The impulse that sends Byron off to fight in Greece is not so different from the impulse that makes him fantasise about a tropical island. War and travel have certain common attractions. In Brooke's poem 'Peace', written at the start of the First World War, a few months after his return from Tahiti, he sees the young men of his generation turning from a world grown old and cold and weary, and plunging into the conflict 'as swimmers into cleanness leaping'. It was a vision shared by many who saw the war as a way of breaking free of the stale compromises of everyday social and domestic life and recovering what Julian Grenfell called the 'colour and warmth and light' of the natural world:

> The fighting man shall from the sun
> Take warmth, and life from the glowing earth;
> Speed with the light-foot winds to run,
> And with the trees to newer birth;

It did not take many months to see how wrong they had been about the liberating effects of war, but the longing for release from conventional, over-civilised life at home was real enough; it was what had taken Brooke to Tahiti. The language of natural, physical, animal life, which permeates Grenfell's poem, was the language of escape – whether into war or travel.

---

* Brooke's initial attitude to the war was slightly more hesitant than the popular image now suggests. See Jones (1999), 373 ff.

As he faced the approach to death, Brooke's mind perhaps went back to the images that had crowded through it when he was turning for home just a year before:

How I hate civilization & houses & trams & collars. If I got on the *Tahiti* & went back again, shouldn't I find a quay covered with moving lights & lovely forms in white & pink & scarlet & green? And wouldn't Taate Mata be waiting there to welcome me with wide arms? And wouldn't there be coco-nuts to drink, & *pota* & *puhe* & 'curry' & oranges (oh, those oranges!) & mangoes & *avoca* to eat? And wouldn't there be huts & the palms & the trade-winds, & the lagoon to leap into? And . . . and. . . .

Over against the hated civilisation of houses, trams and collars is the world of huts and palm trees and trade winds, with at its centre the native girl waiting on the quay, her arms wide to welcome the foreign traveller. It is a classic statement of the beachcomber fantasy that in various forms has been one of the engines of twentieth-century tourism.

Though he had little of the beachcomber about himself, Somerset Maugham played a significant part in publicising the image. Three years after Brooke came looking for Gauguins, Maugham actually found one – a glass door-panel that Gauguin had painted in a house some miles outside Papeete – and hastily purchased it for a couple of hundred francs. What he also found was material with which to add another layer of colour to the South Seas myth, most obviously in *The Moon and Sixpence* (1919), his fictionalised account of Gauguin's defection to Tahiti. A less well-known story to come out of the same visit was 'The Fall of Edward Barnard'. The narrator, an upstanding young man from Chicago, committed to the world of work and progress, travels to Tahiti to bring his friend Edward Barnard back to a sense of his responsibilities.

He finds Barnard living a life of carefree simplicity, lost to all thoughts of getting on or making his fortune or returning to claim his American fiancée. In their last conversation Barnard outlines the alternative life he plans for himself and the lovely half-caste woman he intends to marry:

> I shall build myself a house on my coral island and I shall live there, looking after my trees – getting the fruit out of the nuts in the same old way that they have done for unnumbered years – I shall grow all sorts of things in my garden and I shall fish. There will be enough work to keep me busy and not enough to make me dull. I shall have my books and Eva, children, I hope, and above all the infinite variety of the sea and the sky, the freshness of the dawn and the beauty of the sunset, and the rich magnificence of the night.

'I shall take some savage woman . . .' The narrator has no answer. He returns to Chicago to marry Barnard's fiancée, with whom he has long been secretly in love. As they embrace for the first time, he has a vision, in grotesque contrast to Edward Barnard's, of the stupendous growth that awaits his family's automobile company. With mechanised warfare turning Europe into a graveyard, Maugham finds it even more difficult than Tennyson to give his vote to the march of mind.

It was this story that was partly responsible for taking Alec Waugh out to the South Seas ten years later, and he provides as good a measure as anyone of the continuing hold of the beachcomber fantasy between the wars. In one of his autobiographical volumes, Waugh recalls discussing Maugham's story with a fellow-novelist: 'We wondered, G.B. Stern* and I, whether an author would not be wise to follow his example.

---

* In *The Coloured Countries* (1930) Waugh names Geoffrey Holdsworth as his interlocutor.

. . . Were we not setting ourselves too hard a pace? Could we not live in Tahiti on 30,000 words a year? Might we not produce better work, under more congenial conditions? Why not quit the rat race?' Waugh may seem an unlikely rebel, but that is the role in which he casts himself, driven to wander by a mixture of professional, social and sexual dissatisfaction. He explains that he was bored with his work in publishing and disenchanted with the social life of London, particularly with the attitudes of contemporary women. His thoughts turned to the world of Edward Barnard: 'The dark ladies of Polynesia with their wreaths of flowers around their necks and their white tiare blossoms behind their ears might well provide the antidote to the capricious tyranny of the ex-debutantes of Mayfair.' Within a few weeks, in June 1926, he was boarding the *Amboise* at Marseille on the first stage of a journey round the world. His goal was Tahiti – or, rather, the mythical place Tahiti had become. He set out as the conscious heir to a century and a half of exotic fantasy.

And Tahiti obligingly responded. From his ship Waugh sees the mountains, the flame trees along the harbour, the yachts at their moorings, the dock lined with laughing Polynesians: 'You can fall in love at first sight with a place as with a person, and I fell in love with Tahiti before I set foot on it.' On the crowded waterfront he sits at a café and is at once drawn into cheerful conversation by a group of Tahitian girls: 'they were always laughing, out of sheer light-heartedness'. With only £11 in his wallet, Waugh faces the prospect of having to leave within a few days on the same ship, but 'as I sat among these laughing people, while the sun sank in a mist of golden lilac behind the crested outline of Moorea, I felt that my life would be half-lived were I to sail five days later'. Only a miracle could prolong his stay in Eden, and a miraculous telegram from his agent duly arrives the afternoon before the ship's departure.

What follows is the fulfilment of the South Seas dream. Having let his ship sail without him, Waugh moves on to the next stage of the cycle and glides into 'the conventional Tahitian romance'. He meets Tania on a local bus one afternoon and then sees her again on the beach that evening among a crowd of women who are laughing, clapping and shouting as the fish nets are hauled in: 'I went across to her. Nothing could have been more natural. I took her back with me to Papeete and established her in my hotel.' She was, predictably, 'warm and sensual', with the astonishing suppleness of the hula dancer: 'This was what I had come across the world to find; . . . a light–hearted romance without complications, without responsibilities, in this Pacific pleasure-loving Eden, where life ran easily, without contention.' The conditions of Paradise – its freedom from complications and responsibilities, its devotion to pleasure – are defined by the sexual experience it delivers.

Having realised the dream, Waugh begins to think back to his conversation with G.B. Stern. Why not make it permanent? Why not live in Tahiti on thirty thousand words a year?

A bungalow on the edge of a lagoon; a couple of hours' writing in the morning, when the sun was low in the sky and the air was cool; with the daytime given up to fishing, swimming, picnicking in the hills off fresh-speared fish, and fruit pulled from the boughs; idling on a veranda in the heavy heat; then the long warm scented night, the dancing and the singing and the final swim.

The picture Waugh paints to himself is idyllic, but it is an idyllic alternative. If it were to become a permanent reality, then the tourist dynamic would kick in again and he would be looking for another alternative. In this context the identity of the Rebel is merely an aspect of the perennial dissatisfaction that keeps the traveller on the move. Loti too had thoughts of leaving everything behind and going off to live with Rarahu on one of the remotest islands, but like Waugh he opted to keep the tension between dream and reality in play rather than to try and live the dream. They are both tourists, and it is the business of the tourist to sample and move on. What keeps the traveller in motion is the possibility that over the next hill, round the next corner, across the next frontier there is something even better. In this pursuit of fantasy, escape is only escape as long as it does not become another reality.

The laughing girls who surround Alec Waugh the moment he steps off the boat are just one more in a line of images that runs straight back to the scenes described by Wallis and Cook, and forward to the guidebooks and holiday advertisements of the twenty-first century. On 16 July 1934 a commemorative monument to Loti was unveiled in the valley of Fataoua. At the ceremony a young Tahitian girl decked the statue with flowers, saying: 'Your little Rarahu is not entirely dead, beloved Loti. I am come here to represent her. I am come here to represent all those Rarahus who are still on the island.' The message could not have been clearer: an island of Rarahus still awaits the tourist. And if not Rarahu, then Neuha or Teha'amana or Taatamata. The native girls who smile coyly from the pages of the travel brochures are indistinguishable, quite deliberately, from those who have welcomed Fletcher Christian ashore in a succession of Hollywood films.

The monument to Loti was a recognition of how much he had done to put Polynesia on the tourist map. Even when Waugh set sail, the South Seas were already becoming a cliché: 'Long before you get to them you know precisely what you are to find. There have been Maugham and Loti and Stevenson and Brooke.' A couple of years after Waugh wrote this, Nathanael West parodied the fantasy in *Miss Lonelyhearts* (1933) – the thatch hut, the slim young maiden, the languorous evenings by the blue lagoon: 'And so you dream away the days, fishing, hunting, dancing, swimming, kissing, and picking flowers to twine in your hair . . .' This is the longed-for escape from 'the city and its teeming millions', but its time has gone: 'The South Seas are played out and there's little use in imitating Gauguin.' Played out because too commonplace. As we shall see, the mass market took over the escapist fantasy but spat out the already diluted element of rebellion. In 'native-style' huts with air-conditioning and modern plumbing, primitivism is a matter of stage decoration. Thanks to jet planes and paid holidays, anyone who has the money can play Gauguin for a fortnight.

At this point, far from being a challenge to western values, the flight to exotic islands becomes a neo-colonialist expression of them. Middle-class western tourists, like middle-class colonial administrators of the nineteenth century, are catapulted into a situation where they can live like royalty, with native servants on hand to furnish every requirement. And this boost in status, discreetly advertised by the brochures (pictures of uniformed flunkies at the poolside and smiling natives displaying craftwork for sale in the local village, the promise of 'true island hospitality from a charming people' and so on), brings with it a corresponding sexual power. At one level this is simply the ability of the rich to buy sex from the poor, but it can also be experienced, more satisfyingly, as confirmation of the visitor's racial, cultural or sexual superiority. Rupert Brooke's unappealing habit of addressing his girlfriends as 'child' perhaps hints at this source of attraction in the Polynesian women. Given a tradition that regarded all Polynesians as natural children, the male/female relation of dominant adult to submissive child, which intelligent women in Edwardian England were already repudiating, could be reaffirmed through the racial relation of westerner to Polynesian. In a modern world of triumphant women and lost empire, the male western tourist is often grateful for similar mercies.

We are a long way from Gauguin here, but perhaps not quite as far as he would have liked to think. Ever since Joseph

Banks stepped ashore to admire the 'arcadia of which we were going to be kings', the South Seas myth had had its roots in assumptions of colonialist superiority. You cannot survey the native women like a bashaw, or set out to play Sardanapalus, without implicating yourself in those assumptions. A scene in Gauguin's *Avant et après* describes a young girl called Vaitauni, who has 'the roundest and most charming breasts you could imagine', going almost naked to bathe in the river. A gendarme, however, is watching and will later charge her with a misdemeanour 'in revenge for having troubled his senses and so outraged public morals'. By contrast, the painter responds with virile frankness: 'I set off for some amusement in the river. We have both of us laughed, without bothering about fig-leaves . . .' In this opposition between freewheeling sensuality and repressive authority, Gauguin, the artist/rebel/beachcomber, places himself on the side of the Tahitians. As a European gone native, the beachcomber is always likely to be at odds with the colonist, but Gauguin's allegiance is less than convincing. In the end, his keys to this sexual playground are the money he gets from Europe and the status he enjoys as a member of the colonising race.*

For the beachcomber, the pleasures of the primitive have always depended partly on having a white skin. His role is made possible by an imbalance of cultural and economic power, and however much local camouflage the tourist applies, this is still a determining factor. At one point the narrator of *Christopher and his Kind* gets round to questioning the morality of hiring boys for sex, as he and his friend Francis

---

* It's notable in this context how often the tourist's preference, Gauguin's included, is for mulatto girls/women rather than for those with darker skins, as though what's sought is a version of the exotic that has already been half-colonised. Mary Louise Pratt (*Imperial Eyes*, 100–101) has noted that lovers in New World romances were 'rarely "pure" non-whites or "real" slaves' but typically mulattoes or mestizos.

used to do in Berlin: 'Christopher had found it charming to watch Francis bargaining with the natives of the jungle. Francis himself didn't have the ugliness of an exploiter because his own state of degradation put him on a level with the natives and made him sympathetically picturesque. But this was a colonial situation, nonetheless.' Sex turns even the Rebel into a colonialist. The same, of course, is true for the Connoisseur and the Pilgrim. It is one of the ways in which the thread of sexual motivation exposes patterns of relationship between rich guest and poor host that the official framework of tourism tends to mask.

In the case of tourism outside Europe and the United States, there is a further argument that the whole western love affair with the exotic is itself imbued with a kind of colonialism. Since the publication of Edward Said's *Orientalism* (1978), much has been written on the subject, sometimes in language of mind-warping obscurity. Few would now deny that western travellers have created versions of foreign countries, particularly oriental ones, that suit their own political convenience and reflect their own cultural prejudices. It is also true that these distorted images have often been a vehicle for sexual fantasy. But this only explains so much. To argue, as Michael Bronski does in *Culture Clash* (1984), that the English fascination with cultures perceived as more primitive, and therefore sexually enticing, was 'based in and inseparable from deeply rooted standards of white British racism and political and cultural imperialism', is to end up with half the truth. As the example of Gauguin demonstrates, it's perfectly possible to be at the same time a rebel against dominant values and an exploiter of them. The increasing numbers of women who use travel to exotic places – the Caribbean, Bali, Greek islands, the Gambia – for sex with the locals are in one sense successful rebels against a convention that has defined this as a male pursuit, but their sexual independence implicates them in what is undeniably a colonialist exchange. A feature in the women's magazine *Marie Claire*, which described women in their fifties and sixties on holiday in the Gambia 'strolling hand in hand with beautiful young men', quoted one woman as saying, 'It was very empowering as a woman to be able to have my pick of a bunch of beautiful men'. Her comment neatly brings together both the sense of personal liberation and the cultural inequality that makes it possible – she is in a position of sexual power only because the men are in a position of cultural subordination.

This may be true enough, but it says little about the reality of whatever relationships she formed, any more than my comments on Brooke explain the relationship that produced the scrambled, touching letter from Taatamata. Quirks of individual circumstance and psychology continually elude the embrace of cultural theory. Of course the pursuit of exotic sex is bound up with racist and imperialist assumptions, as it was with Gauguin and Brooke, as it is with the tourists of today, but just as often it's bound up with the desire, which must at some level spring from a dissatisfaction with home, to penetrate and be penetrated by another person, another place, another culture. Moreover, the sheer excitement of what is different has a force of its own, independent of particular cultural ideologies. 'It is only fair to say,' Anthony Burgess remarks, after cataloguing the charms of eastern women, 'that Orientals, especially for some reason, Sikhs, have found ecstasies in Bayswater unprocurable in the lands of spice.' The lines of desire run both ways. On the point of leaving Trinidad for England in the 1950s, one of Sam Selvon's characters in *The Lonely Londoners* is encouraged by a friend, 'Boy, it have bags of white pussy in London, and you will eat till you tired . . .' By and large, the West has had the money, and westerners have done the travelling, but if we want confirmation that the lure of exotic sex is not simply a function of wealth and an imperialist culture, we can go back to the first Tahitian who ever made his way to the West. His motive, according to one of those who travelled with him – and subsequent events offered ample corroboration – was primarily a desire for '*des femmes blanches*'. Nothing in tourism cuts more clearly across boundaries of period, race, class and gender than the kinship of the exotic and the erotic.

PART FOUR

The Triumph of the Senses

I I

The Cult of the Sun

Our tourist literature is reassuringly slow to change. Pick up a guide to one of the countries around the Mediterranean and it will be filled with much the same helpful information about museums and churches, gardens and galleries, as its predecessors of a century ago. The difference now is that most people heading for the Mediterranean would happily acknowledge that they are more interested in the quality of the beaches. The mere size of the industry ensures that there is still a busy market for anything that gets three stars in the guidebook, but tourism's centre of gravity has shifted decisively from the cultural to the sensual. And this process has reshaped the traditional tourist identities.

It is already implicit in the beachcomber motif of the early twentieth century. Images of Brooke swimming after turtles, of Edward Barnard gazing at tropical sunsets, of Waugh picnicking in the hills off fresh-speared fish are signs of what was happening. They point towards the primacy of pleasure – a notion of travel that puts hedonism at the top of the agenda. To tourists at the beginning of the twenty-first century this may seem too obvious to need stating, but though self-indulgence has always been an aspect of travel, it is only in the past hundred years that the idea of going abroad purely for pleasure has come out of the shadows. Wider social trends clearly play their part, but in the context of tourism there has been one essential factor, the defining tourist activity of the twentieth century: sun-worship.

Contrary to popular belief, the Victorians did not dislike suntanned skin. According to John Pemble, they 'generally admired and envied brown complexions, which struck them as healthy and sexually attractive'; and he quotes a string of persuasive extracts to illustrate the point. Among them he notes Lucie Duff Gordon's admiration for the colour of the Arabs, 'just like dark clouded amber, semi-transparent'; the heroine's exclamation in Wiliam Morris's *News from Nowhere*, 'Look if I don't need a little sun on my pasty white face!'; and Dickens's Little Dorrit returning from the South with 'the ripening touch of the Italian sun . . . visible upon her face', which has the effect of making her 'something more womanly'. He might have added Charles Darwin's observation on the dark skins of the Tahitians: 'It has been remarked that it requires little habit to make a dark skin more pleasing and natural to the eye of the European than his own colour. A white man bathing by the side of a Tahitian was like a plant bleached by the gardener's art compared with a fine dark green one growing vigorously in the open fields.' The appreciation of the tanned body is both aesthetic and sexual; but over against it are the repeated warnings of risk from fever and sunstroke. The orthodoxy of the time – rightly, as it has turned out – made exposure to the sun a dangerous business.

So no hint of sun-worship breaks the surface of Victorian tourism until almost the end of the century, and then, appropriately enough, it comes from a man who was on the point of becoming an outcast. Meeting André Gide in Algeria early in 1895, Oscar Wilde declares: 'I no longer want to worship anything but the sun. Have you noticed that the sun detests thought . . .' As so often, Wilde was ahead of his time, and in Gide he found a receptive audience. The Frenchman had grown up in a devoutly Protestant household under the repressive influence of a mother whose puritanical code seemed increasingly at odds with the impulses of his own nature. In 1893, at the age of 23, Gide finally set off for North

Africa, determined to find some means of resolving the conflict. This prospect of resolution, he tells us, was the 'golden
fleece' that led him on, not any desire to see a new country.

What quickly becomes apparent is that the pursuit of the
golden fleece is linked to sex, and sex to the sun. With conscious symbolism Gide had tried, and at the last moment
failed, to leave behind the Bible which until then had been his
daily reading. Under the desert sun he looks for another sort
of revelation – first, with a young Arab boy called Ali who
seduces him on the outskirts of Sousse. In a passage that was
for many years omitted from the standard English edition of
his works, Gide describes how Ali, naked as a god, fell against
him among sand-dunes lit by the declining sun: 'How beautiful the sand was! In the divine splendour of the evening, what
radiance clothed my joy!' Eager to educate himself in the life
of the senses, Gide goes to the winter resort of Biskra in
Algeria, where in the evening the sumptuously dressed Oulad
Naïl girls, with their gold necklaces and high coiffures, sit
waiting for passers-by at the foot of the stairways that lead up
to their rooms. In his autobiography he recalls how three years
later he walked through the same streets with a Swiss doctor
who exclaimed in disgust that he wished he could bring
young people there to give them a horror of debauchery. 'Ah!
how little he knew of the human heart!' writes Gide, 'at least
of mine ...' To Gide these exotic creatures are like the Queen
of Sheba. There are people, he says, who are drawn to what is
like themselves, others to what is different. He, like all whose
nature impels them to travel, belongs to the latter: 'the strange
entices me as much as the familiar repels. To put it another
way, and more precisely, I am drawn by the lingering presence
of the sun on bronzed skins.' The sun itself, even its fading
signature, is an aphrodisiac.

Like other temptations to travel, it stands against the habits
and values of the family home. Apollo is a youthful god, and
dedication to the sun is an escape from the laws of the parent.

(In his *Journal* Gide noted the fashionable comparison between Oscar Wilde and the Sun God.) When a liaison with one of the Oulad Naïl girls, Mériem, is interrupted by the arrival of Gide's mother, who has dragged herself from Paris in her anxiety about his health, he and his travelling companion, Paul Laurens, worry that she will interfere with the process of 'reeducating our instincts'. In the event, the tears of Gide's mother not only put a stop to his relationship with Mériem, they also capsize his clandestine attempt, 'far from the hotel', to find relief with Mériem's cousin: 'Caresses, provocations, nothing worked; I remained silent, and left her without having been able to give her anything except money'. Finally, the Mother is defeated by the power of the Sun. When spring comes to Biskra, Gide goes out one day for a longer walk than usual, feeling in himself that he has escaped the valley of the shadow of death, that for the first time 'I was being born into real life'. As he walks, he is suddenly overwhelmed by the world of the senses around him and surrenders to Apollo in a moment of ecstatic abandonment: 'Take me! Take all of me, I cried. I belong to you. I obey you. I give myself up to you.' This was the climax of his first visit to Algeria. The following year he was back, confirmed in the new religion of which he was to become the prophet.

Naturally bookish, Gide did not take easily to the life of the senses. When he met Wilde in Blidah, he was still very much the neophyte, ready to follow the promptings of the older man. A couple of years later, in *Les nourritures terrestres* (1897), he explained his development in terms that immediately recall Wilde's comment on the sun's hostility to thought: 'While others publish or work, I, on the contrary, have spent three years travelling to forget what my head had learnt.' As Gide goes on to emphasise in *L'Immoraliste* (1902),* sun-worship is

---

* John Weightman names it as the first novel to depict the practice of sunbathing. See Weightman, 12.

antagonistic to the claims of art, culture, the intellect, anything except the supremacy of the senses – 'Nothing discourages thought as much as this persistent blue sky'. Academic literature on tourism has made great play with its quasi-religious nature – tourist sites as holy places, cultural artefacts as objects of worship, tourist souvenirs as relics etc. – and there is clearly a case for putting sun-worship in the same context. More usefully, though, we might see it in antithetical terms: against the religion of the spirit it sets up an anti-religion of the senses. For the first time, sun-worship gives full status to the sensual as opposed to the cultural attractions of tourism.

In this respect, it is vital to the relationship between travel and sex. Gide's account picks up threads from each of the preceding sections: in the process of dedicating himself to the sun, he proclaims his independence from home and family; he pursues self-discovery through sensual experience; and he rejects the socially established moral norms in the name of the primitive and instinctual. By recasting the existing tourist roles in an explicitly sensual form, sun-worship marks the emergence into daylight of those underground streams which had nourished tourism from the start.

It is while staying at Ravello that Michel, Gide's hero in *L'Immoraliste*, first takes up sunbathing: 'The sight of the beautiful, brown, sun-burned skins which some of the carelessly clad peasants at work in the fields showed beneath their open shirts, made me long to be like them'. By contrast, his own thin arms, stooping shoulders and white skin bring tears of shame. He walks to some grassy rocks outside the town:

> When I got there, I undressed slowly. The air was almost sharp, but the sun was burning. I exposed my whole body to its flame. I sat, lay down, turned myself round. I felt the ground hard beneath me; the waving grass brushed me. Though I was sheltered from the wind, I shivered and

thrilled at every breath. Soon a delicious burning enveloped me; my whole being surged up into my skin.

A decade before D.H. Lawrence, this is sex with the sun. That the sensations of the skin should become the seat of being is central to the meanings that sunbathing was to acquire – erotic, amoral, libertarian. But if the tanned skin of the tourist denotes sensuality, this is not merely because getting a tan is itself a sensual process; just as important is the long tradition that associates dark skin with primitive sexuality. From this point of view, the crass racial assumptions of the nineteenth century have passed on an unrecognised legacy in the cultural significance we give to suntan. It is not coincidental that the period in which sunbathing first became popular was also a period of fashionable enthusiasm for jazz music, black entertainers and African art. To a get a tan was, and to some extent still is, to borrow a cultural sign of the savage and the sensual.

The recognition that sun and sex go together was not a discovery of modern tourism. Arriving in Marseille at the start of one of the great tourist journeys of the nineteenth century, Flaubert had felt through his thin shoes the warmth of the Canebière stones and his calves had stiffened at the thought of the burning beaches. The warm air, he tells us, carried to his heart the sensual pleasures of the East. These reactions are symptoms of the '*volupté virile*' which overtakes him at the prospect of this Mediterranean port. For the traveller from the North, the touch of the sun is always the first, voluptuous intimation of unfamiliar pleasure.

Not that this had usually been regarded as a good thing. 'It is certainly true,' noted Philip Thicknesse in the eighteenth century, 'that the nearer we approach to the sun, the more we become familiar with vice of every kind.' Theories about the effect of climate on character had been advanced by Aristotle and, before him, Hippocrates, but in modern Europe it was only in the mid-sixteenth century, the great age of exploration, that such ideas came back into circulation, partly through the Dutch physician Levinus Lemnius whose major work, *The Touchstone of Complexions* (1576), was much concerned with the influence of climate and geography on temperament. (Women, he explains in a fairly characteristic passage, are more inclined to 'fleshly concupiscence and bodily lust' in summer than winter 'because in summer, heat enkindleth moisture and stirreth up Venus'.) As travel became more widespread, interest in these ideas grew. In his *Voyages en Perse* (1686), Jean Chardin speaks of 'the naturalness of lust to the Persian climate . . . which is generally hot and dry', and Montesquieu later noted in *De l'esprit des lois* (1748), that 'There are climates where the impulses of nature have such force that morality has almost none'. Among tourists at the time, this was a commonplace assumption.* 'My blood was inflamed by the burning climate, and my passions were violent,' Boswell wrote in explanation of his libertinism in Naples. And elsewhere, 'Besides I do assure you the climate of Italy affects me much. It inflamed my hot desires.' A couple of centuries later, E.M. Forster was giving the same explanation of his behaviour in India. 'I did not suffer from the heat in other ways,' he writes, 'but it provoked me sexually.' For Daniel Defoe, we remember, 'Lust chose the torrid zone of Italy', while Byron's 'The Girl of Cadiz' offered a predictable contrast to the frigidity of her English counterparts, 'But, born beneath a brighter sun,/For love ordained the Spanish maid is . . .' Which was exactly the experience of Don Juan: 'What men call gallantry, and gods adultery,/Is much more common where the climate's sultry.'

These links have long been reflected in our vocabulary. 'Hot' was already being used as a synonym for lustful in the early 1500s, and the sexual connotations of 'warm' and 'cold' edge into the language towards the end of the same century,

---

* Interestingly, the first English translation of Montesquieu's book was produced by Thomas Nugent, author of *The Grand Tour*.

both recorded in early works by Shakespeare. At the beginning of the eighteenth century, Alexander Pope, whose satirical comments on the Grand Tour were noted earlier, was one of the first to use 'sultry' in an erotic sense. The Oxford English Dictionary quotes a finely ambiguous line from his 'Windsor Forest' (1713), describing Pan in pursuit of Syrinx: 'His shorter breath, with sultry air, /Pants on her neck ...' Three centuries later, our own usage has if anything intensified the sexual force of this vocabulary.

To support the association between the heat of the sun and the heat of lust, the nineteenth century could draw on a range of dubious scientific opinion about climate that interlocks with the equally dubious notions about race already mentioned. In 1819, J.J. Virey remarked in an essay in the *Dictionnaire des sciences médicales* that the 'voluptuousness' of black females attains 'a degree of lascivity unknown in our climate, for their sexual urges are much more developed than those of whites'. The same point is made later in the century by Richard Burton: 'In these hot-damp climates the venereal requirements and reproductive powers of the female greatly exceed those of the male; and hence the dissoluteness of morals would be phenomenal, were it not obviated by seclusion, the sabre and revolver.' Misgivings on this score even extended to the moral effect of overheated Victorian factories. In a survey published in 1836, P. Gaskell warns against 'the stimulus of a heated atmosphere', particularly on young girls: 'Indeed, in this respect, the female population engaged in mill labour, approximates very closely to that found in tropical climates; puberty, or at least sexual propensities, being attained almost coeval with girlhood.'

By the early twentieth century, when the English translation of Julius Rosenbaum's *The Plague of Lust* appeared, arguments about the sexual effect of climate had lost none of their appeal. In this wide-ranging history of venereal disease in antiquity, Rosenbaum comments that 'Paederastia appears, as is the case with all sexual perversions, to owe its origin to the stimulation of the Asiatic climate, the mother of exuberance and voluptuousness'. He goes on to explain that 'the genital organs of Asiatic women – a fact true also of Italian and Spanish women – like their whole bodies, exhibit great looseness'. The natural receptiveness of the women is matched by the precocious inclinations of the men: 'The son of the South is like a tree growing in rich, rank soil; he ripens betimes to the sexual life, but equally early is constrained to abandon it again'. Some consolation, perhaps, for the slow-starting northerner.

Hot climates invite a relaxation in dress, and the stubborn northern assumption has always been that shedding clothes goes hand in hand with shedding morals. As travellers move away from the frigid lands of the North, they unbutton metaphorically as well as literally. It is under the burning sun that our modern tales of moral disintegration – of death in Venice or adultery on the plantation – have their natural home. The inhabitants of these places, growing in rich, rank soil, were naturally disposed to sexual activity. For many Europeans the bare breasts of African or Asian women could be confidently read as a sign of availability. Exotic potboilers of the postwar years still signalled the temptation of tropical lust with covers picturing sultry native girls whose swelling breasts were barely concealed by the obligatory rags. If the closing decades of the century taught us to tread a little more carefully, we nonetheless continue to think in much the same terms, as a cluster of popular films and books attest. In Lawrence Kasdan's film *Body Heat* (1981), the hero's downfall is brought on as much by the dripping sexuality of the hot days and languorous nights as by the charms of the murderous heroine. It's the old story: hot countries excite the blood.

Like the fashion for visiting spa towns and, later, seaside resorts, sunbathing called medical evidence in its support. Gide's Michel himself had taken to it partly in an attempt to remedy his nervous debility, and the curative powers of the sun received endorsement in the 1920s from the celebrated Swiss physician, Auguste Rollier. The translation of his *Heliotherapy*, with its contrasting illustrations of ugly physical deformities and rows of convalescent sunbathers on Alpine balconies, gave influential support to a growing trend. In a Foreword to the English edition of 1923, Caleb Williams Saleeby declared that 'the restoration of sunlight to our malurbanized millions, now blackened, bleached and blighted in slums and smoke, is the next great task of hygiene in our country'. This restates the opposition between urban gloom and healing sunlight, but it is hardly the language of the sensualist. Talk of the 'great task of hygiene' places the author in a more austere tradition, and it would be misleading to suggest that sun-worship in the 1920s was synonymous with hedonism. Those who emphasised the healthful properties of the sun were often careful to distance themselves from any taint of impropriety. The early naturists, for example, elaborated a fiercely puritanical code of practice in order to assert their respectability.

But among tourists, considerations of health and virtue were secondary. As a reason for doing what is pleasurable, medical arguments, like moral ones, have always been suspect. 'Many having no disease but that of love ... come hither for remedy, and many times find it,' wrote Fynes Moryson of those going to Baden, ostensibly for the waters, at the end of the sixteenth century. Medical opinion played its part in promoting sun-worship, but the new fashion owed more to an instinctive recognition of the sun as a source of well-being. In the 1920s, inhabitants of Northern Europe had more than enough cause to be aware of this. The First World War had left people with an overwhelming thirst for escape into sunlight. Reading the literature of the period, one gets the impression that the war, but for a few brief interludes, had blotted the sun out of existence. 'Move him into the sun' is the opening line of Wilfred Owen's 'Futility', which contrasts the life-giving power of the sun with the context of victorious death created by the war. To turn one's face to the sun was to turn it away from the darkness of the previous decade.

Even more devastated and more disillusioned than Britain, Germany embraced the sun with fervour. It was, says Stephen Spender in a famous passage, 'a primary social force':

> Thousands of people went to the open air swimming baths or lay down on the shores of the rivers and lakes, almost nude, and sometimes quite nude, and the boys who had turned the deepest mahogany walked amongst those people with paler skins, like kings among their courtiers.

To these young Germans 'the life of the senses was a sunlit garden from which sin was excluded'. We are back in Eden. The world that Spender describes, in which the goal is to enjoy whatever is free – 'sun, water, friendship, their bodies' – is anti-intellectual, physical, almost animal. And dominated by the sun:

> The sun healed their bodies of the years of war, and made them conscious of the quivering, fluttering life of blood and muscles covering their exhausted spirits like the pelt of an animal: and their minds were filled with an abstraction of the sun, a huge circle of fire, an intense whiteness blotting out the sharp outlines of all other forms of consciousness, burning out even the sense of time. During their leisure, all their powers of thought were sucked up, absorbed into the sun, as moisture evaporates from the soil.

'Have you noticed that the sun detests thought . . .?' It is not difficult to trace the line that runs through from Gide to Spender's young Germans. Or to the Austrian youths whose similarly unfettered sexuality was experienced by John Lehmann in the 'arcadian place of sun and water and sensual invitation' where he used to sunbathe beside the Danube.

Among those who had felt most keenly the oppression of life in wartime England was D.H. Lawrence, whose writings return with obsessive frequency to the erotic power of the sun. For someone with weak lungs, the stifling emotional atmosphere of the time had a physical equivalent that was almost an echo of the trenches: 'I dare not come to London, for my life,' he wrote to his friend Samuel Koteliansky in 1916. 'It is like walking into some horrible gas, which tears one's lungs.' And a few months later, again to Koteliansky, 'I can't live in England any more. It oppresses one's lungs, one cannot breathe.' Writing to his sister a couple of years before his death, he again lamented the impossibility of settling in England: 'If only this climate were not so accursed, with a pall of smoke hanging over the perpetual funeral of the sun, we could have a house in Derbyshire and be jolly. But I always cough – so what's the good.'

For Lawrence, healing exposure to the sun was itself a sexual experience. In a story written in 1927 he describes the heroine's secret retreat to the flat roof of the stables, where she takes off her clothes and lies in the sun, feeling the bitterness of her heart begin to dissolve: 'Luxuriously, she spread herself, so that the sun should touch her limbs fully, fully. If she had no other lover, she should have the sun! She rolled over voluptuously.' The scene is a rerun of what Lawrence had described fifteen months earlier, at the end of 1925, in another short story just called 'Sun'. It tells of a woman who leaves her husband in America and on doctor's orders goes to Sicily, where she abandons herself to a passionate affair with the sun: 'He faced down to her with blue body of fire, and enveloped her breasts and her face, her throat, her tired belly, her knees, her thighs and her feet'. This solar adultery restores her health but can last only until the 'blanched, etiolated little city figure' of her husband comes to return her to 'the vast cold apparatus of civilisation'.

Lawrence's story brings together the three strands that most obviously contribute to twentieth-century sun-worship: the sun as antithesis of the industrial city, as bringer of health, and as liberator of the senses. They are all elements with which Lawrence himself was in tune. A hater of the city, a prophet of sensual awareness, a consumptive whose later life was a long journey in search of health, he was well placed to speak for the new religion in every respect but one: Lawrence was essentially a puritan and the new religion was essentially about pleasure. He ends up as high priest of a practice he came to detest precisely because it was the hallmark of the hedonist. 'Oh, the joy-hogs!' thinks Constance Chatterley as she makes her way among the European tourists. 'Oh "enjoying oneself"! Another modern form of sickness.' And when she gets to Venice, she finds a place given up to it:

> It was pleasant in a way. It was *almost* enjoyment. But anyhow, with all the cocktails, all the lying in warmish water and sun-bathing on hot sand in hot sun, jazzing with your stomach up against some fellow in the warm nights, cooling off with ices, it was a complete narcotic. And that was what they all wanted, a drug: the slow water, a drug; the sun, a drug; jazz, a drug; cigarettes, cocktails, ices, vermouth. To be drugged! Enjoyment! Enjoyment!

As early as 1928, Lawrence takes on board the whole hedonistic consumer culture of twentieth-century tourism and finds it wanting. Nothing that happened across the rest of the century would have led him to change his mind.

'Sun' was not published in unexpurgated form until three years after Lawrence wrote it, when the American expatriate Harry Crosby paid him a hundred dollars for it in twenty-dollar gold pieces emblazoned with the sun. It was brought out in a deluxe edition by the Black Sun Press in Paris, and Crosby, having sent Lawrence two copies in gold boxes, went to elaborate lengths to secure the promised gold coins and have them smuggled out of America and finally delivered to Lawrence in Italy. More than a little mad, Crosby was the most sun-obsessed of the whole sun-obsessed inter-war generation.* With a sun tattooed on his back and a sun ring on his finger, he saw his life as a fierce pursuit of solar liberation: 'I want a long straight road into the Sun and a car with the cut out wide open speeding a mile a minute into the Sun with a princess by my side'. The road into the sun led in December 1929 to a friend's apartment in New York, where he killed both the princess and himself.†

According to Robert Graves and Alan Hodge in *The Long Weekend* (1940), it was the hot summer of the previous year that had popularised sunbathing in England. The exact date is open to question, but it is certainly true that by the time Crosby died sun-worship had become part of the tourist culture. And those who were doing most to promote it would prove in the long run to be neither doctors, prophets nor pederasts but an assortment of pleasure-seekers who had made a refuge for themselves in the south of France.

From the exile of wartime London, Cyril Connolly pictured himself in happier days 'Peeling off the kilometres to the tune of "Blue Skies", sizzling down the long black liquid reaches of Nationale Sept, the plane trees going sha-sha-sha through the open window, the windscreen yellowing with crushed

---

* Paul Fussell has noted the 'plethora of "sun" titles' among books published at the time (including Crosby's own *Chariots of the Sun*), which bear witness to this obsession. See Fussell, 139.

† Crosby was found in the apartment of the painter Stanley Mortimer. He had apparently shot both himself and Josephine Bigelow, the mistress he called his Fire Princess.

midges, she with the Michelin beside me, a handkerchief binding her hair . . .' They are heading south, of course. Connolly's Mediterranean is still a place of pilgrimage, but not in the way it was for Symonds or Forster; its sensual pleasures have no need of a spiritual dimension to justify them. It is also a place for the rebel, where colonies of artists and dropouts can rail against bourgeois values, and the well-to-do can get back to nature and dress like fishermen and labourers; but the gestures towards rebellious primitivism are for the most part just that. More obviously than either of these, it is, in Connolly's presentation of it, a place for the connoisseur. The colours, textures, smells, sights, sounds of the Riviera are summoned from memory with glittering precision as he thinks back to early morning on the Mediterranean – the bright, pine-scented air, the gleaming tarmac of the Route Nationale, the spring-summer green of the plane trees:

> swifts wheeling round the oleander, waiters unpiling the wicker chairs and scrubbing the café tables; armfuls of carnations on the flower-stall, pyramids of lemon and aubergine, *rascasses* on the fishmonger's slab goggling among the wine-dark urchins; smell of brioches from the bakers, sound of reed curtains jingling in the barber's shop, clang of the tin kiosk opening for *Le Petit Var*. Our rope-soles warm up on the cobbles by the harbour where the *Jean d'Agrève* prepares for a trip to the Islands and the Annamese boy scrubs her brass.

He sees again the cooks from the yachts stepping ashore with their market baskets, the cats scrounging among the fish-heads, the dancing sea reflected on the café awning. It is a lover's poem whose gem-like images are drawn from the early days of Connolly's first marriage, when he was living at Sanary, a few miles west of Toulon. There is no social or moral context here, no personal agenda beyond the response to immediate physical sensation. The effect depends on powers of aesthetic discrimination which note sensual detail with an expert's eye. Paul Valéry talked of Nice as 'a combination of stimulants to the senses such as I have seen nowhere in the world', and Connolly's hymn to the Riviera morning could be a gloss on his words.

To speak in general terms of the Riviera or the Côte d'Azur is to ignore the fact that this stretch of coast between Menton and Hyères is made up of a series of towns each with its own history, character and tourist clientèle; but there is no call here to enlarge on these distinctions, for the two things crucial to the subject of this chapter were shared by all of them – sun and sea. Since Lord Brougham first established himself in Cannes in the 1830s to escape the cold and damp of England ('Fogland', as he referred to it), visitors had been drawn from the North by the promise of warmth; but it was only in the twentieth century that the religion of the sun transformed the whole coast into a place of worship for a mixed band of foreigners: literary celebrities, American expatriates, exiled European royalty, indigent artists and writers. Even as an undergraduate, Connolly had appointed himself a keeper of the flame. While at Oxford, he founded the 'Cicada Club', devoted to the proposition that the Mediterranean was best visited during the hottest months of the year – an outlandish claim, by the standards of the day.

The Americans, however, were the visitors who had done most to shape the new character of the Côte d'Azur. It started in 1922 (the year the Blue Train made its first run to the Riviera) when Gerald Murphy and his family went down to the Cap d'Antibes to stay at the Château de la Garoupe, which had been rented by his friend Cole Porter. At the time, the Riviera was still, as it had been since the eighteenth century, a winter resort whose season ran from September to April. Over the next few years, partly through the influence of the Murphys, this began to change. The small beach of La Garoupe was raked clear of seaweed (largely by Gerald), the owner of the Hotel du Cap was persuaded to stay open through the summer, the Murphys bought a villa there and invited their friends. Suddenly the hot months had become fashionable. 'There was no one at Antibes this summer,' Fitzgerald wrote in September 1925, 'except me, Zelda, the Valentinos, the Murphys, Mistinguet, Rex Ingram, Dos Passos, Alice Terry, the MacLeishes, Charles Bracket, Maude Kahn, Esther Murphy, Marguerite Namara, E. Phillips Oppenheim, Mannes the violinist, Floyd Dell, Max and Chrystal Eastman, ex-Premier Orlando, Etienne de Beaumont – just a real place to rough it and escape from all the world. But we had a great time.'

Fitzgerald's *Tender is the Night* (1934) depicted the atmosphere of stylish hedonism that was the keynote of tourist life on the Riviera, and in the figures of Dick and Nicole Diver he borrowed recognisable aspects of the Murphys themselves. 'We'll live near a warm beach,' Nicole says, 'where we can be brown and young together.' Writers from a harsher climate rarely allow their characters to get away with a project like that; what follows is the story of Dick's disintegration. (The fate of the young novelist in Hemingway's unpublished novel *The Garden of Eden* is of a piece with this, his corruption foreshadowed by his wife's insistence that they tan themselves as deeply as possible.)

The erotic dimension which had been more or less submerged in earlier forms of tourism was on open display among the hedonists. It was the relaxed lifestyle of the Côte that begot the tourist triad of the twentieth century – sun, sea and sex. About to embark on an affair with one of Dick's friends, Nicole concludes that it is really the fault of her situation: 'All summer she had been stimulated by watching people do exactly what they were tempted to do and pay no penalty for it'. In much the same way, while the Fitzgeralds were staying at Antibes, Zelda had drifted into an affair with the French aviator Édouard Jozan. 'Pretty much of anything went at Antibes,' Fitzgerald wrote later of the final years of the decade. There were emotional casualties, but it was a life seductively free of the normal constraints. In an elegiac letter to the Murphys just after Fitzgerald's death, Zelda picks up this sense of pleasure there for the taking: 'Those tragicly ecstatic years when the pockets of the world were filled with pleasant surprizes and people still thought of life in terms of their right to a good time are now about to wane'. The romantic flavour of the good times is conveyed by Fitzgerald in a late fragment from his notebooks which again suggests a hedonistic recasting of the impulses of the Connoisseur. He describes the scene at a café in Cannes, 'vivid with dresses just down from Paris and giving off a sweet pungent odor of flowers and chartreuse and fresh black coffee and cigarettes, and mingled with these another scent, the mysterious thrilling scent of love. Hands touched jewelled hands over the white tables; the vivid gowns and the shirt fronts swayed together and matches were held, trembling a little, for slow-lighting cigarettes.'

The inter-war generation that invented the modern Riviera was probably the last to take seriously the charge that its 'combination of stimulants to the senses' was bad for the moral health. In *The Rock Pool* (1936) Connolly portrayed a group of Bohemians living on the Riviera in a village based on Cagnes. His hero, an Oxford-educated stockbroker with literary aspirations, is willingly drawn into their world, which revolves mainly around sex, alcohol and the need for money. Naylor's personal decline follows quickly, but where the stories of Fitzgerald and Hemingway point the obvious moral about lotus-eating and corruption, Connolly's voice is ultimately on the side of the Mediterranean. Early in his stay Naylor begins to sense the grip of his conventional English background loosening: 'gradually he felt the crust of it breaking, the weight of manners and tradition giving way, the disapproval, so tactfully voiced, of ushers, parents, friends and tutors counting for what it was worth, and a new, unembittered, impulsive, and terrible

Naylor free at last'. He has a long way to go, both in terms of what he learns and what he loses, but Connolly's conclusion is that the price of this freedom is worth paying.

In reviewing the book, George Orwell objected to the apparent suggestion 'that there are only two alternatives: lie in bed till four in the afternoon, drinking Pernod, or you will infallibly surrender to the gods of Success and become a London social-cum-literary backstairs-crawler'. This slightly misses the point. The book's purpose is not to formulate a pattern for the good life but to contrast two modes of response, associated respectively with home and abroad, England and the Mediterranean, North and South. It is a kind of travel book, and, as tends to be the case, the horrors of travel are outweighed by the joys of freedom. Perhaps Connolly's mother got closer than Orwell to the truth when she told her son in a letter from South Africa that it reminded her of 'your reading to me out of your diary about the Garden of Eden'. It might seem a perverse version of the lost Paradise, and yet the outlines are still there. The 'Mediterranean madness' analysed by Connolly in *The Rock Pool* – a form of moral tolerance which gives way to sudden acts of violence that dissolve into gossip and easy tears – is not so very different from what transforms the lives of Forster characters like Eustace Robinson and Lucy Honeychurch.

The Americans, the Bohemians, the leisured upper classes and the liberal sprinkling of celebrities all contributed to the development of the Riviera between the wars. In August 1931 the hoteliers on the Côte made a general agreement to stay open through the summer, and from then on laments about its changing character gather strength. This was only a faint intimation of what was to come: the pleasures enjoyed by the privileged classes during these years were laying the foundations of the postwar package holiday. As always, the end of war brought a longing for sunshine and an impatience of restraint. 'Thirst for the sun! Thirst for the hot sand! Thirst for clocks that run slow!' the photographer Jacques Lartigue noted in his diary in 1946. Ten years later, Roger Vadim provided the stuff of fantasy for a new generation of tourists with *Et Dieu créa la femme* (1956). The film which launched Brigitte Bardot's career as a screen goddess also sealed the reputation of the Côte d'Azur as an erotic playground. Abandoning herself to sun and sex in Saint Tropez, Bardot offered a compelling image of the Mediterranean's liberated life-style. It was this world, along with the fantasies created around it, that was to sustain the package tourist industry through the next half-century.

The prewar Riviera had confirmed hedonism as the dominant strain of twentieth-century tourism. What happened after the war was a brilliantly successful attempt to package the ingredients of Riveria tourism for a mass market brought into being by higher wages, increased mobility and longer paid holidays. In the spring of 1950 Gérard Blitz put up an advertisement in the Paris métro which showed simply the sun, the sea and his telephone number. This was the start of the Club Méditerranée, which across the next four decades grew into the largest holiday resort company in the world. Blitz, a diamond-cutter from Belgium in prewar days, had been running a rehabilitation centre for the survivors of concentration camps and was convinced that sport and relaxation in the sun could help people to put behind them the experiences of the war. What he set out to do was extend this prescription to the population at large. The Club Méditerranée was in this sense, like so many impulses towards the sun, an outcome of war. (In more ways than one – the first Club Med village, on Majorca, consisted chiefly of army surplus tents furnished with military cots.) From the start, the ethos of Club Med was defined by three overlapping constituents: the basic physical elements of sun, sea, food and wine; the deliberate evocation of a Polynesian, pre-industrial way of life; the overriding concern with pleasure and self-fulfilment, focused on the body.

True to its original advertisement, Club Med built most of its enclosed villages at sites round the Mediterranean, where sun and sea could be guaranteed. Within this setting the Club aimed to produce an atmosphere of prelapsarian leisure. It established a reputation for excellent food, accompanied by unlimited wine. Inside the villages money was replaced by a currency of coloured beads, and holidaymakers were expected to use first names and the more intimate '*tu*' form when addressing one another. The commercial nature of the operation was masked by a language which referred to the staff as '*gentils organisateurs*' and the clients as '*gentils membres*'. More specifically, the Club adopted Polynesian-style thatched huts as its standard architecture and the sarong as its preferred form of dress. (From 1959, those booked for a holiday could buy Tahitian sarongs from the Club's own mail-order catalogue.) In 1955 the Club opened a village on Tahiti, which it advertised, tellingly, as 'a pilgrimage to the source'. The same year, an article in the Club magazine, *Le Trident*, pictured the *gentils membres*, or 'Polynesians', dreaming of their future holiday – 'the arch of the beach, the Polynesian huts under the palms, men pushing their dug-out canoes into the surf, chasing young girls wearing flowers, and fishing all day'.

Club Med was drawing on a store of imagery that, as we saw in Chapter 9, had taken deep root during the nineteenth century. Echoes of Loti and Gauguin are never far away; this is the earthly paradise they created in imagination. But Club Med had formulated a version of it perfectly adapted to the needs of the second half of the twentieth century: the sarongs, thatched huts and coloured beads, abstracted from any social context, are stage-props in a play that enables the client to enjoy the role of carefree native without forgoing the attractions of European culture and cuisine. Purged of the inconveniences associated with reality, the return to Eden is available at an all-inclusive price. It was a marketing coup that depended on a dream of escape from precisely the consumer world of which it was a classic product. Club Med sold itself quite explicitly as an 'antidote to civilisation'. This was where you came to slough off the trappings of modern urban life and rediscover the essential self: 'No constraint, no obligation. Barefoot, dressed in shorts, a sarong, bathing trunks if you like, you completely forget so-called civilised life . . . A boat. A harpoon. Off to fish.' In all of us there was a noble savage wanting to get out. Interviewed for a BBC series broadcast in 1996, the Club's Director of Development, 'Dudule', explained, 'The Club's philosophy is that everyone must find a way to be free in his mind, in his body and with other people. One can be natural and do things one would not do in everyday life.'

In the vocabulary of tourism, any mention of freedom is likely to contain a coded promise of sexual adventure. Dudule's sub-Gidean philosophy of naturalness and personal freedom reflects the Club's image as a place of sexual liberation, where erotic adventure can be taken for granted. In a world given over to play rather than work, to the physical rather than the intellectual, to the natural rather than the socially conditioned, where the body, tended and displayed with narcissistic concern, is the focus of so much attention, sexual preoccupations are bound to be close to the surface: 'All that people know of each other is their first name, the colour of their eyes, the contours of their shoulders, the suppleness of their walk. There's only so much one can say about the size of the fish, the brilliance of the sea and the heat of the sun, and then what's left? One subject, one alone, always the same, never exhausted, always renewable: love. . . . Winning a smile, exchanging caresses, become, quite naturally, the supreme goal of existence.' Small wonder that, according to Ellen Furlough, 'Club Med villages came to have a reputation as places with "an erotic morality" involving many "brief encounters"'.

In important ways Club Med was the prototype of all the similar ventures which came on the scene over the next twenty years. As the package industry grew and the range of its clients extended down the social scale, so its products diversified, but the basic inducements – sun, sea, sex and liberation from everyday life – remained the same. What was on offer in the seaside resorts that became the focal points of mass tourism was a world of perpetual play which the tourist could buy into for a couple of weeks. It is fitting that the Riviera of the Twenties and Thirties should have been a favourite refuge for the Prince of Wales – a place where one could strip off not just clothes but everything that locked one into a public role. The Prince in shorts and sandals, cruising the Mediterranean with his American mistress, was an image of a new sort of tourist freedom that hinged on the open repudiation of one's workaday identity. By celebrating an ideal of leisure in which routines were abandoned, normal codes of dress and conduct suspended, and the priorities of the working world turned upside down, the Riviera life had begun to effect a marriage between the ancient traditions of carnival and the modern practice of tourism.

Fundamental to both was the promise of respite from a working life whose oppressive tedium was exemplified by its sexual controls. It is a promise that in one form has traditionally been located in the figure of the prostitute. Writing about prostitution in France, Alain Corbin has argued that towards the end of the nineteenth century it offered the provincial bourgeois male not just sexual entertainment but access to a more exotic world: 'The brothel became a place of escape, a place to get away from one's ordinary life, a place where one could make up for the austerity of life at home' – in other words, a place that fulfilled much the same function as the modern holiday resort. And this was not a purely French phenomenon. Havelock Ellis in his *Studies in the Psychology of Sex* (1897–1928) refers to the influence of prostitution 'in adding an element . . . of gaiety and variety to the ordered complexity of modern life, a relief from the monotony of its mechanical routine, a distraction from its dull and respectable monotony'.

The need for moments of 'orgiastic relief' from this monotony is exactly what is now answered by the tourist carnival.

An affinity between the worlds of the traveller and the prostitute has long been recognised. Corbin notes, for example, the tendency in the nineteenth century to equate vagabondage among young men with prostitution among young women, both of which were seen as opposed to the values of settled bourgeois life and the work that sustains it. It has always been the tinkers, players, acrobats and artists, the entertainers from fairground and circus, the birds of passage of one sort and another who have brought disruption with them. They represent an alternative to the routines of work, introducing a whiff of other worlds that stirs the blood of those who are bound to a daily grind. Carnival gave licence to this stirring of the blood, and the prostitute, described by Corbin in carnivalesque terms as a figure who 'symbolises disorder, excess, and improvidence', was essential to its operation. When it was suppressed through the seventeenth and eighteenth centuries, its anarchic impulses retreated to the social and geographical margins, glimpsed, for example, in seaside traditions of naughtiness and vulgarity but no longer acknowledged as central to the rhythms of social life.

The explosion of postwar travel brought it back, with all its potential for subversion. One reason why the hippies seemed such a threat to conventional society was because they represented holiday values uncontained by the structures of the working world. They were in a sense the ultimate product of our tourist traditions – Connoisseurs, Pilgrims and Rebels all in one. Richard Neville, nibbling aphrodisiac chocolate in Thailand, coming face to face with himself on the lonely trek from Marrakesh, contemptuously dismissing the Taj What-everitis, sharing a joint with a dazzling blonde tramp outside Kabul, runs through the whole spectrum. The hippie commitment to a world of leisure, pleasure and childhood fun presented the tourist values not as a two-week truancy but as a viable way of life. For a decade or so it made travel look dangerous again, until the world of work reasserted its dominion and Carnival was restored to the status of a temporary aberration.

This, of course, is where the package holiday comes in: it has proved a perfect device for both expressing and containing people's rebellion. It was, in theory, a feature of Carnival that for a short time the tables were turned so that the underdog could enjoy the privileges of the overlord – commanding service, eating and drinking to excess, taking sexual pleasure at will. This is now the promise of the package holiday. In *The Politics and Poetics of Transgression* (1986), Peter Stallybrass and Allon White note how Carnival 'attacks the authority of the ego . . . and flaunts the material body as a pleasurable grotesquerie – protu-berant, fat, disproportionate, open at its orifices'. Anyone who has seen young Britons at play around the Mediterranean will have no difficulty in making the connection: drunkenness, self-exposure and a defiant rejection of decorum are required ele-ments of the holiday. Like sexual promiscuity, they are the stuff of Carnival.* In our own time it is the holiday sunshine that has provided the context for this Carnival, lining beaches and espla-nades with an array of human flesh that displays all the protu-berances, grotesqueries and disproportions one could want. Sun-worship is all about exposure of the body; it thrusts on us an awareness of the physical in ourselves and other people, eroding the hierarchies asserted by conventional dress and sub-stituting a display of competitive outrageousness in shorts, shirts, hats and dresses that flaunt their gorgeous vulgarity. (Cyril Connolly's bizarre fondness for Hawaiian shirts was in its way an emblem of subversive carnival allegiance in the older man, the badge of the sun-worshipper.) But the pleasures of Carnival, however extravagant, are enjoyed under licence and only for a defined period; the orgy of sun, sea and sex is an experience that

---

* A report published in 1997, *Young People and International Travel*, found, to no one's surprise, that the young were twice as likely to have sex with a casual partner on holiday as at home [*THES*, 8 August, 1997, p. 7].

implies both a revolt from and an affirmation of the norms of daily life.

Club Med's original line looks a bit dated now. In the age of the post-modern tourist, it takes more than a sarong and a thatched hut to make people play the role of noble savage without a certain ironic detachment. We're expected to be in on the game, worldly enough to regard the inauthenticity of the experience as itself a source of satisfaction. Or is this merely our excuse for enjoying the less sophisticated pleasures a previous generation could take without self-consciousness? Either way, the idea behind Club Med was adaptable. The key to its success was the deftness with which Blitz, and later Gilbert Trigano, had identified a number of the most persistent tourist fantasies and matched them with a consumer product. One way of looking at the whole process would be to see it as a dress rehearsal for the future of virtual tourism envisaged by science-fiction films like *Westworld* and *Total Recall*, in which a synthetic environment generated by technology is tailored to the imaginative requirements of the holidaymaker. Any world, any pleasure, can be placed at the tourist's disposal. It was the dual achievement of Club Med, replicated since then by countless other companies, first to create a context in which the tourist identities of the past could be purchased off the peg, and second to recognise that what underpinned their appeal was the promise of erotic freedom. As one of the *gentils membres* you could, for a brief space, be Connoisseur, Pilgrim or Rebel as the inclination took you. Today the experience is familiar to us. Skipping from brochure to brochure, the tourist can browse at will across the inheritance of the past three centuries, selecting whatever role appeals. Earlier paradigms of travel have in effect been swallowed by the single definitive category of travel as consumer item.

This book has tried to identify some of these paradigms and to explore the sexual motives that often underlie them. But the neat categories are of course a kind of fiction. The realities of tourist motivation and experience mingle them inextricably. No one recognised this more clearly than Gide, or gave more haunting expression to the pulse of erotic excitement that transforms the traveller's landscape. For all the importance he ascribes to his sexual experiences abroad, it's clear that the central link between sex and travel is not to do with the meeting of bodies but with the working of the imagination. His erotic memories of North Africa in *Amyntas* (1906) and *Si le grain ne meurt* (1926) owe as much to the context – the noise of the cafés, the smell of kif, the stairway lamps, the narrow apartments, the little cups of coffee – as to the actual encounters. There is a sense of ambient mystery that both concentrates lust and at the same time diffuses it into a wider desire to be absorbed by the strangeness of another world. It is a reflection of the limitless possibilities of self-definition that travellers share with novel readers. An Arab stands poised to open an unknown door: 'I would like to be that Arab, and for what is awaiting him to await me'. Another doorway, this time in the *quartier toléré* of Blidah. Gide's desire 'crosses it at a bound'. Beyond is a dark garden, narrow and deep, 'just glimpsed in passing, while a woman calls out to me'. It is not the woman but the secret, mysterious garden that prompts the traveller's desire. Impossible to say, as he walks these shadowy, scented streets, where the thirst for new experience, or the thrill of revolt against his background, or the longing to escape into the exotic, or the determination to get to the bedrock of his own nature ends, and sexual desire begins.

Notes

Introduction

1 *'is love, eroticism'*: Hesse, 24.
2 *of women travellers*: see, for example, Allen; Birkett; Foster; Robinson; Russell.
3 *'sensations of movement'*: Freud, 202.
3 *'under it'*: Byron, VI, 232.
4 *'afforded by travel'*: Casanova, IX, Chapter 1.
4 *stranger of the opposite sex*: Bates, 270.
4 *'greater sexual freedom'*: Mączak, 237.
4 *'of the English nation'*: Ellis, 295.
7 *administration and the like*: some of these areas have been considered at length elsewhere. See, among others, Ballhatchet; Hopwood; Hyam; Kabbani; McClintock; Schick. Schick's book has a detailed bibliography on the subject.

Chapter One: The European Tour

11 *'into one's own society'*: Wilton and Bignamini, 188.
11 *'the prettyest Women'*: ibid., 25.
12 *'homosexual indiscretion'*: ibid., 83.
12 *'amorous adventures'*: ibid., 57.
12 *'where the Colosseum is'*: ibid., 32.
12 *'acquisition of valuable contacts'*: ibid., 271.
13 *'the complete gentleman'*: Nugent, Preface (3rd edition).
14 *'with spirit whor'd'*: Alexander Pope, *The Dunciad*, IV, 311–316.
15 *'Lewdness and Debauchery'*: first issue of *The Gentleman's Magazine*. See Redford, 17.
15 *'Justice and Religion'*: Dykes, 200 (Verse XIV, Remarks).
15 *'with an experienced mistress'*: see Black, 196.

15 *'propitiously received'*: letter to his son, 25 January 1750.

15 *'belle passion inflames you'*: ibid., 29 March 1750.

15 *'the means to please'*: ibid., 18 March 1751.

16 *'health, education, and rank'*: ibid., 5 June 1750

16 *'serve as volunteers'*: ibid., 6 June 1751.

16 *'when sober'*: ibid., 12 September 1749.

16 *'the year round'*: ibid.

17 *'after their return'*: Evelyn, II, 332 (6 February 1645).

17 *'decorated their libraries'*: Black, 191.

17 *'rest of their favours'*: see Black, 40–41.

17 *'men and manners'*: letter to Lady Pomfret, March 1740.

18 *'to their own country'*: Smollett, Letter XXIX.

18 *'behind the scenes'*: Boswell (1952), 250.

18 *'on the* turf*'*: see Black, 256.

19 *'on the other'*: Hurd, 25.

19 *'debaucht pleasures'*: see Brauer, 173.

19 *'dangerous a season'*: Sheridan, 24–5 (Chapter 2).

19 *'virtue and morality'*: see Black, 209.

19 *'service to your country'*: letter from William Johnson Temple, 31 July 1763.

21 *Thicknesse*: quotations in this chapter are from Thicknesse (1777), Letter XIV.

24 *'are most contagious'*: Hall, 11–12.

24 *'a little tainted'*: Thraliana, II, 640 (27 June 1786).

25 *'village of Italy'*: Lithgow, 43 (Chapter 1).

25 *'persuaded to marry'*: see Redford, 19.

25 *'Rapes and Sodomy'*: Daniel Defoe, 'The True-Born Englishman', ll. 96–97.

26 *'procure for him accordingly'*: Anon. (1728), Chapter 3.

26 *'London in ix yeare'*: Ascham, 87.

26 *'Brothell house of Europe'*: see Redford, 56.

26 *'Lyon of the Deeps'*: Pope, The Dunciad, IV, ll. 307–308.

27 *'pleasing dalliances'*: Coryate, 'Observations of Venice'.

27 *'the nation knows'*: Oliver Goldsmith, 'The Traveller', ll. 123–124.

27 *'place to me'*: Byron, Beppo, Stanza 41.

Chapter Two: Boswell's Travels

29 *'rites of love'*: Boswell, Journal, 13 March 1763.

29 *'and he disappeared'*: Boswell (1934), I, 472.

30 *'to have dignity'*: Boswell, *Journal*, first week of August 1763.

30 *'Father's inclinations'*: letter to John Johnston, 23 September 1763.

31 *'a Dutch girl'*: letter from George Dempster, 23 August 1763.

31 *'reserved, and chaste'*: Pottle (1966), 130.

31 *'forbids girls'*: Boswell, *Journal*, 15 April 1764.

31 *'all ideas change'*: ibid., 23 April 1764.

32 *'Amsterdam, private'*: ibid., 29 May 1764.

32 *'Edinburgh divine'*: ibid., 28 May 1764.

33 *'dull dog of Utrecht'*: ibid., 6 July 1764.

33 *'man for me'*: ibid., 7 July 1764.

34 *'went home late'*: ibid., 17 July 1764.

34 *'sickly theory'*: ibid., 18 July 1764.

34 *'fine a fellow as possible'*: ibid., 20 July 1764.

34 *'my own plan'*: ibid., 6 August 1764.

34 *'as perfect as possible'*: ibid., 9 August 1764.

35 *'be with Temple'*: ibid., 21 July 1764 (memorandum).

35 *'what I saw'*: ibid., 3 September 1764.

35 *'sent her off'*: ibid., 11 September 1764.

36 *'be a man'*: ibid., 11 October 1764 (memorandum).

36 *'Command self'*: ibid., 12 October 1764.

36 *'a matter of geography'*: Burton (1856), Chapter 4.

37 *'way of shopkeepers . . .'*: Thicknesse, Letter 14.

37 *'Cardinal Vicar'*: Boswell (1955), 7.

37 *'making love to their wives'*: Boswell, *Journal*, 14 December 1764.

37 *'least disguise'*: ibid., 8 January 1765.

38 *'inferior beings'*: ibid., 10 January 1765.

38 *'an easy attack'*: ibid.

38 *'summer afternoon'*: letter to John Johnston, 28 September 1765.

39 *'business of this place'*: See Walpole, Vol. XXXVII, p. 323, footnote 6.

39 *'the Apollo Belvedere'*: Goethe, 200.

39 *'making love to a Turk'*: Boswell, *Journal*, 3 July 1764.

39 *'came home'*: ibid., 15 July 1764.

40 *'caused by disease'*: ibid., 15 October 1764.

40 *'Quite adventure'*: Boswell (1953), 245.

40 *'Italian countess'*: Boswell, *Journal*, 10 January 1765.

40 *'fine Roman'*: Boswell (1955), 51.

40 *'Florentine lady'*: Boswell, *Journal*, 12 May 1765 (memorandum).

40 *'Venetian courtesans'*: Boswell (1955), 11.

40 *'soul and body'*: ibid., 122.

40 *'Quite brutish'*: Boswell, *Journal*, 25 February 1765.

40 *about five shillings*: Boswell (1955), 54 (footnote 5).

40 'all danger': ibid., 6.

41 'seraglio around him': Boswell, Journal, 3 August 1764.

41 'to provide for': see Black, 200.

41 'wild schemes': Boswell, Journal, 3 August 1764.

41 'variety of women': ibid., 14 December 1764.

42 'write to you': ibid., 11 December 1764.

42 'time to time': ibid., 13 August 1764.

43 'condoms for Siena': Boswell (1955), 123.

43 'say no more': ibid., 125.

44 'risked nothing': ibid., 16–17.

44 'heard so much of': ibid., 17.

44 'care nothing': Boswell, Journal, 29 September 1765.

44 'bad inn': ibid.

45 'thirteen in all': ibid., 12 February 1766.

46 'true English': ibid., 21 January 1765.

46 'at Minorca': ibid., 21 December 1765.

46 'did no harm': ibid.

47 'inn at night': Boswell, Journal, 22 January 1765.

48 'hold the opera-glass': Byron, V, 229–30.

48 as the spectacle unfolds: Casanova, V, Chapter 3.

49 sixteenth century: Mączak, 251.

49 'as if she were a bitch': Walter, IV, Chapter 14.

49 'proved prohibitive': Evelyn Waugh (1976), 29 December 1925.

50 'remnant of a statue': Moore (1781), I, Letter XLV.

51 'comme animal etc.': Connolly, Unpublished Journal, September–October 1922. See Lewis, 98.

51 'often made up': Greene (1961), 59.

51 'deny her man': ibid., 14–15.

51 'in description': ibid., 14.

51 'always a delight': Burgess (1987), 386.

52 'older than twelve': ibid.

52 'hardly worthwhile': Greene (1961), 54.

52 'for £16': Brendon, 134.

52 'flowers unpicked': see Ohse, 16.

Chapter Three: A New Concept of Travel

56 'better than we do': Sterne, 109.

57 'objects I see': Goethe, 40.

57 'grapes and figs': ibid., 7.

57 *'or picture can give me'*: I quote the translation given in Boyle, 417.
57 *'hardly recognise'*: Goethe, 198.
58 *'more sensuously'*: Friedenthal, 245.
58 *'in the first place'*: Boyle, 506.
58 *'found in England'*: Massie, 71.
59 *and gardening*: see Gay (1986), 255ff. (Chapter 5).
59 *'English men'*: Charles Kingsley, 'Ode to the North-East Wind'.
59 *'one's brain'*: Gower, 1 January 1889.
59 *'overworked people'*: Dickens, *Little Dorrit* (1855–57), Chapter 3.
60 *'Come and eat! Will you?'*: letter to Maria Gisborne, 19 July 1820.
61 *'from the North'*: Buzard, 134.
61 *'By the Fire-Side'*: from *Men and Women* (1855).
62 *'of her charms'*: letter to Edmund Gosse, 24 April 1887.
62 *more women tourists*: see Pemble, 77.
62 *'great spectacle'*: Lever, 231.
62 *'overbearing insolence'*: ibid., 233.
62 *'purse-strong insistance'*: ibid.
62 *'and facetious'*: ibid., 231.
63 *'English mothers'*: Trollope, II, 341–422 (Letter XX).
63 *'Swiss Puritanism'*: George Eliot, *Middlemarch* (1871–2), Chapter 20.
64 *'through her after-years'*: ibid.
64 *'what to enjoy'*: Owenson, II, 170.
64 *'stood before it'*: Kemble (1847), II, 11–12.
64 *'feeling of existence'*: Sewell, II, 345 (Chapter 78).
64 *'dreamy rapture'*: Jameson (1826), 261 (8 March).
65 *'charm of Englishwomen'*: ibid., 50–51 (10 October).
65 *'dream of beauty'*: Trollope, II, 133 (Letter VII).
65 *'a gondola life'*: Owenson, III, 370.
65 *'for existence sake'*: ibid., 385.
66 *'and physical powers'*: Burton (1893), I, 9.
66 *'his waking senses'*: see Withey, 238.
66 *'luxury and peace'*: letter of 7 January 1850.
67 *'encouraged self-gratification'*: Foster, 30. I owe a number of references in this chapter to Shirley Foster's work.
67 *'on our way'*: Birchall, 55–56 (5 March 1873).
67 *'rumble with thunder'*: Mme de Staël, *Corinne* (1807), Bk XIII, Chapter 4.
68 *'much longer'*: letter to William H. Channing, 19 February 1841.
68 *'ways I need'*: letter to Caroline Sturgis, 16(?) November 1846.
69 *'and sublime pleasure'*: Jameson (1826), 226 (23 February).
69 *'in its bosom'*: Kemble (1878), III, 305.

69 'feel *its power*': Finch, 365.

69 'escaped *from bondage*': Jameson (1838), II, 52–3.

70 'ecstasy *could suggest*': Kemble (1835), 147–48 (entry for 10 November 1832).

70 'and *my ecstasies*': see Faith, 34.

70 'amorous *awareness*': Barthes (1985), 264.

71 'generally *intoxicated*': see Frank, 261.

71 *finally stays*: ibid., 273.

72 'coffee *and pipes*': ibid., 284–85.

72 'well-proportioned *limbs*': Kemble (1847), I, 215.

72 'eminently *picturesque*': ibid., II, 87.

73 'beastly *creatures*': ibid., I, 132–33.

Chapter Four: The Tourist Grail

75 'of *my life*': Symonds (1984), 240.

75 'very *seriously*': ibid.

76 'to *my senses*': ibid., 253–54.

76 'upon *my life*': ibid., 254.

76 'ever *met with*': ibid., 262.

76 'law *and custom*': ibid., 268.

77 'a spiritual and a sensual': Symonds (1883), 6.

77 'bodily *love as wantonness*': ibid., 50.

78 'dared *to demand it*': Symonds (1984), 266.

78 'as *they top the bridge*': letter to Edmund Gosse, 9 November 1890.

79 'and *unquiet rapture*': Symonds (1984), 271–72.

79 'sensation *over me*': Symons, 116.

79 'pathetic *in the man*': ibid., 272.

80 'more *solid basis*': Symonds (1984), 275.

80 'ephemeral *lovers*': ibid., 274.

80 'abundantly *supported*': letter to Havelock Ellis, 29 September 1892.

80 'southern *blue eyes*': Lawrence (1961), 268.

80 'just *going to be married*': ibid., 271.

81 'when *erect*': Symonds (1984), 177.

82 'instruction *to myself*': ibid., 276.

82 'sold *his beauty*': ibid., 275.

83 'that *of their own countrymen*': Moore (1779), I, Letter X.

83 'clubs *of their own countrymen*': Hurd, 103.

83 'at *the tavern*': letter to his son, 10 May 1748.

83 'displaying *their own*': Quoted Withey, 92.

83 'with *Mediterranean people*': Pemble, 266.

84 *"slept with one of them"*: letter to Charles Kains-Jackson, 24 April 1892.

Chapter Five: Sexual Pilgrims

86 *'some time to thaw'*: letter to Goldsworthy Lowes Dickinson, 25 March 1902. See Beauman, 108.

87 *something of a celebrity*: see Smith, 62–3.

87 *'Let yourself go'*: Forster (1977), 26.

88 *'began to be happy'*: ibid., 20.

88 *'in a son-in-law!'*: Forster (1971), 17.

88 *'of their engagement'*: ibid., 22.

88 *'blood swell out'*: ibid., 24.

89 *'working-class foreigner'*: Isherwood, 10.

90 *'naked and unrebuked'*: letter to Goldsworthy Lowes Dickinson, 28 July 1916.

90 *'it would be something'*: letter to Edward Carpenter, 12 April 1916. See Beauman, 300.

90 *'parted with respectability'*: letter to Florence Barger, 16 October 1916.

90 *'never like this'*: letter to Florence Barger, 8 October 1917.

90 *'gratitude, or pity'*: entry in Forster's *Locked Journal*, 11 May 1922. See Beauman, 301.

93 *'could call to account'*: Forster (1983), 324.

94 *'pearl would be handed to me'*: Kerouac, 11.

94 *'the road is life'*: ibid., 211.

94 *'roared south'*: ibid., 138.

94 *'every direction for girls'*: ibid., 140.

95 *'never knew existed'*: Neville, 168.

95 *'face to face with'*: ibid., 174.

95 *'desert journey'*: ibid.

96 *'a physical need'*: Lehmann, 75–6.

96 *'in this belief'*: ibid., 104.

96 *'that place is holy'*: Seabrook, 45–6.

97 *'a physical urge'*: Forster (1983), 320.

97 *'had intercourse'*: see Danielsson, 129.

98 *victim and villain*: see, for example, Cohen; Heyzer; Odzer; Skrobanek.

99 *'what she liked'*: Garnett, 39.

101 *'with more romance'*: see Ware, 139. I am grateful to Lyn Thomas for this reference.

101 *'a Gambian lover'*: ibid., 140.

Chapter Six: Byron Abroad

106 *'at Monteriano'*: Forster (1971), 88.
108 *'abroad permanently'*: Rousseau, 175.
108 *'Apostle of Paederasty'*: Byron, I, 210.
109 *'meet in Asia'*: ibid., I, 207.
109 *'unrestrictedly in Turkey'*: see Doris Langley Moore, 244.
109 *too many books*: apart from general biographies, specialist books on the subject include Cheetham; Crompton, whose concern is specifically with Byron's homosexual interests; Massie; Nicolson; Quennell.
110 *'complexion from the heat'*: Byron, II, 4.
110 *'till night'*: ibid., II, 12.
110 *'all clapped'*: Byron, II, 46.
110 *30,000 piastres*: ibid.
111 *'upon the chambermaid'*: Polidori, 33.
111 *'waistcoat pocket'*: Pope-Hennessy, 61.
111 *'girl out of mine'*: Byron, V, 76–7.
112 *'but one way'*: ibid., 162.
112 *'Foreign Land'*: letter from John James Ruskin, 27 November 1849.
113 *'of the Alps'*: Byron, V, 141.
114 *'words for you'*: ibid., 145.
114 *'a dozen in stead'*: Byron, VI, 42.
114 *'never impaired'*: ibid., 193.
115 *'since 1817'*: ibid., 92.
115 *'& all whores'*: ibid.
115 *'at her Milliner's'*: ibid., 40.
115 *'very vicious pleasures'*: Byron, VIII, 37.
116 *'but he endures'*: letter to Thomas Love Peacock, 17/18 December 1818.
116 *'can avoid it'*: Byron, VI, 65.
116 *'of my imagination'*: Byron, V, 129.
116 *forms of perversion*: see Origo, 29–30. One of the reasons given by Teresa for leaving the Count was that she was unable to be as 'vilely complaisant' as he required.
117 *'found in England'*: Massie, 71.

Chapter Seven: Forbidden Fruit

119 *'for sentiment'*: Story, I, 7.
120 *in eleven hours*: see Faith, 42.
120 *'my pleasures'*: Stevenson, V, 57.

121 *'freedom of the soul'*: ibid., 60.

121 *'sea of liberty'*: ibid., 62.

121 *'love and folly'*: Thicknesse (1768), Letter XVII.

121 *'out of its gates'*: Lemaistre, Letter XI.

122 *'the great Babylon'*: see Corbin, 217.

122 *'without his wife'*: Hibbert (1976), 92.

123 *'full of laughter'*: Symons, 147.

124 *'thousands of years ago'*: Lehmann, 113.

124 *'fascination of the city'*: Ellis, 299.

124 *'anonymous dust'*: Croft-Cooke, 11.

125 *'felt imprisoned'*: Graves, 163.

125 *'wholly creative'*: Cowley, 61.

125 *'Vie de Bohème'*: Wickes, 150.

126 *'a pity . . .'*: Orwell, I, 543–44.

126 *'hang around cafés'*: Hemingway, 133.

127 *'was attractive then'*: see Wickes, 166.

127 *'we are young'*: Evelyn Waugh (1977), 7.

128 *'his neighbour's soul'*: Douglas (1987), 180.

128 *'inhibitions there'*: Powell, 69.

129 *'of my soul'*: see Delay, II, 147.

130 *'memory of that night'*: Gide (1955), 337.

130 *path of revolt*: see Dollimore, 339.

130 *'Borgia room'*: letter to Robert Ross, 27 April 1900.

130 *'walks all round'*: letter to Carlos Blacker, 23 September 1897.

131 *'without hard labour'*: see Weeks, 14.

131 *'leisured classes'*: Harris, I, 250.

131 *'the Oscar Wilde trial'*: Morgan, 38.

132 *'to join us'*: Parker, 55.

132 *'cricket belts very soon'*: letter to Edward Hutton, 27 March 1920. See Holloway, 280.

133 *'matter of sex'*: Douglas (1934), 46.

133 *'not commoner'*: ibid., 167.

133 *'for every taste'*: ibid., 262.

133 *'le Vésuve!'*: ibid., 263.

134 *'left it unchanged'*: Evelyn Waugh (1985), 76.

134 *'the same service'*: Douglas (1934), 240.

134 *'lessened abroad'*: Ackerley, 134.

135 *'pick up a boy'*: see Parker, 263.

135 *'and found it'*: Ackerley, 218.

135 *'the lowest tariff'*: letter to E.M. Forster, 21 September 1960.

135 *'finish my coffee'*: Ackerley, 134.

136 *back to Brighton*: see Osborne, 210.
136 *from New Hampshire*: see Updike, 118.
136 *possibility of adventure*: see Hynes, 228–9.
137 *'restless era'*: Cunningham, 347–8.
137 *'Berlin meant Boys'*: Isherwood, 10.
137 *'sexual significance'*: ibid., 10.
137 *'his sex life'*: ibid., 37.
138 *'and despised'*: ibid., 13.
138 *'criminal class'*: ibid., 15.
139 *'is my death'*: ibid., 17.
139 *'stay-at-home compatriots'*: ibid., 47.
139 *'25 drachmas a night'*: Evelyn Waugh (1976), 1 January 1927.
140 *'poor dears'*: see Linklater, 124.
140 *'way of life'*: Rees, 201.
140 *'dragging back'*: Orton, 108 (8 March 1967).
141 *'take anyone back'*: ibid., 139 (18 April 1967).
141 *'and pederasts'*: Burgess (1990), 70.
141 *'all available!'*: Orton, 184 (24 May 1967).
141 *'want for more'*: ibid., 186 (25 May 1967).
142 *'up the bum, would it?'*: ibid., 187 (25 May 1967).
143 *'or the police'*: ibid., 207 (11 June 1967).
143 *'tight-arsed civilisation'*: ibid., 259 (28 July 1967).

Chapter Eight: Some Sunny Isle

144 *'remainder of his life'*: Browne, 64.
145 *'wanton tricks'*: Robertson, 154 (24 June 1767).
145 *'Young women'*: ibid., 166 (27 June 1767).
146 *'in their lives'*: ibid., 167 (27 June 1767).
146 *'proof against a Nail'*: quoted Rennie, 86–7. Rennie's excellent book
      has led me to much of the material cited on early European contacts
      with Tahiti.
146 *'each time'*: Robertson, 185 (9 July 1767).
146 *'pulled to pieces'*: Hawkesworth, I, 468.
147 *'New Cythera'*: Bougainville, *Journal*, 7 April 1768. See Taillemite, I,
      317–18.
147 *'imagination can form'*: Banks, I, 252 (13 April 1769).
148 *'immediately marchd up to me'*: ibid., 275 (17 May 1769).
148 *'of the Natives'*: Cook, I, 93–4 (14 May 1769).
148 *'extraordinary manner'*: Banks, I. 351.
148 *during the century*: see Dening, 262.

149 *'prostitute her charms'*: Anon. (1773), 13.

149 *'present to their imaginations'*: quoted Dening, 263.

149 *'of Queen OBEREA'*: Anon. (1779), II, Chapter 24.

150 *'anything that can be conceived'*: quoted Dening, 8.

150 *'the whole business'*: ibid.

150 *'admired and beloved'*: ibid.

150 *'water about them'*: Morrison, 123.

151 *'dire a temptation'*: Herman Melville, *Typee* (1846), Chapter 2.

151 *'attempt to describe'*: ibid.

152 *'unlimited gratification'*: ibid.

152 *'garb of Eden'*: ibid., Chapter 11.

152 *'with marvelous love'*: Christopher Columbus, Letter to Sanchez. See Campbell, 176.

153 *'the whole globe'*: Banks, I, 23.

153 *'on his next voyage'*: Boswell (1934), III, 7.

153 *'other than my own'*: Diderot, 210.

Chapter Nine: Fuir! là-bas fuir!

154 *'we could have imagined'*: Sterling, xx–xxi.

154 *'sweat of their brows'*: Southey, II, 243, letter to John Rickman, 23 December 1803.

156 *flowers in their hair*: Loti (1922), 111.

157 *'their daily bread'*: Loti (1924), 47.

157 *'charms of the South Seas'*: ibid., 17.

157 *'of the Polynesian race'*: ibid., 188.

157 *'entered the territory'*: Burgess (1987), 373.

158 *'departure and separation'*: Loti (1924), 127.

158 *'chain people for life'*: ibid., 21.

158 *'grasp or understand'*: ibid., 184.

158 *reference to the girl*: Lefèvre, 26–65.

159 *'et de nonchalance'*: Loti (1924), 115.

159 *'mad about Rarahu'*: see Lefèvre, 108.

159 *'in the sea-breeze'*: ibid., 110.

159 *'to come together'*: ibid., 111.

159 *'world forever young'*: ibid., 112–3.

160 *'flavour of exotic loves'*: see Szyliowicz, 52.

160 *'of worry or concern'*: Henrique, IV, 25.

161 *'to sing and to love'*: ibid. Gauguin quoted it in a letter to the Danish artist J.F. Willumsen. See Danielsson, 31.

161 *'beings around me'*: letter of February 1890. See Gauguin (1949), 184.

161 *'dissatisfied with his existence'*: see Danielsson, 31.

162 *colonial realities*: see Danielsson, 57.

162 *'it is still Love'*: Gauguin (1954), 9.

163 *'an orgy of chrome yellows'*: ibid., 36.

163 *'all is well'*: ibid., 38.

163 *'fallen into her lap, faded'*: ibid., 52.

164 *'better work than before'*: letter to Daniel de Monfreid, November 1895.

164 *'how far 125 francs will go here'*: see Danielsson, 190–1.

165 *'opportunities there, he said'*: ibid., 228.

165 *'last corner [of the archipelago]'*: ibid.

166 *'always a prostitute'*: see Corbin, 302.

166 *'naturally a prostitute'*: ibid., 374 (note 43).

166 *'flowers, and their hair'*: ibid. (note 42).

167 *'and it is indecent'*: letter to his wife Mette, 8 December 1892.

168 *'say anything'*: *Independent*, 12 December 1997, 'Eye' Section, 13.

169 *'of a new race'*: Bougainville, 192–3 (Part II, Chapter 2).

Chapter Ten: Playing Gauguin

171 *'Gauguin, the painter'*: letter to his mother, 28 October 1913.

171 *'into white surf'*: letter to Eddie Marsh, 1 October 1913.

171 *'the sun-saturated sea'*: letter to Eddie Marsh, 15? November 1913.

172 *'plug of tobacco'*: Stevenson, XIII, 5.

172 *'without ruining yourself'*: Gauguin (1931), 62.

172 *more suitable white sand*: see Dening, 179.

172 *'in the Garden of Eden'*: Lawrence (1961), 343.

173 *'beauty of scenery'*: letter to Eddie Marsh, 15? November 1913.

173 *'where time is not'*: letter to Edmund Gosse, 19 November 1913.

173 *'more worth while'*: letter to Violet Asquith, mid-December 1913.

174 *'never quote properly'*: letter to Hilton Young, April 1914.

174 *'feminism and riches'*: letter to Cathleen Nesbitt, April 1914.

174 *'silhouettes with pince-nez'*: letter to Jacques Raverat, April 1914.

174 *'with Tahitian beauties'*: letter to Eddie Marsh, 7 February 1914.

174 *'heart of an angel'*: ibid., 7 March 1914.

175 *'lagoon by moonlight'*: letter to Cathleen Nesbitt, 7 February 1914.

176 *'gulped a good deal'*: letter to Dudley Ward, 13 or 14 January 1915.

176 *'to newer birth'*: Julian Grenfell, 'Into Battle'.

177 *'And . . . and . . .'*: letter to Eddie Marsh, April 1914.

178 *'magnificence of the night'*: Maugham, 66.

179 *'quit the rat race'*: Alec Waugh (1962), 211.

179 *'ex-debutantes of Mayfair'*: ibid., 215.

179 *'set foot on it'*: ibid., 234.
179 *'sheer light heartedness'*: ibid., 235.
179 *'sail five days later'*: ibid.
180 *'Tahitian romance'*: ibid., 238.
180 *'in my hotel'*: ibid.
180 *'without contention'*: ibid., 239.
180 *'the final swim'*: ibid.
181 *'still on the island'*: Lefèvre, 151.
181 *'Stevenson and Brooke'*: Alec Waugh (1930), 19.
181 *'twine in your hair'*: West, 248.
182 *'imitating Gauguin'*: ibid.
183 *'bothering about fig-leaves'*: Gauguin (1931), 5–6.
184 *'a colonial situation, nonetheless'*: Isherwood, 31.
184 *'cultural imperialism'*: Bronski, 26–7.
185 *'bunch of beautiful men'*: Ware, 147.
185 *'the lands of spice'*: Burgess (1987), 386–7.
185 *'till you tired'*: Selvon, 74.
186 *'des femmes blanches'*: Journal of Charles-Félix-Pierre Fesche. See Taillemite, II, 92.

Chapter Eleven: The Cult of the Sun

190 *'healthy and sexually attractive'*: Pemble, 123–4.
190 *'in the open fields'*: Moorehead, 90.
190 *'detests thought'*: Gide (1933), 486.
191 *'clothed my joy!'*: Gide (1955), 295.
191 *'at least of mine'*: ibid., 300.
191 *'on bronzed skins'*: ibid., 301.
192 *'reeducating our instincts'*: ibid., 304.
192 *'anything except money'*: ibid., 307.
192 *'born into real life'*: ibid.
192 *'give myself up to you'*: ibid.
192 *'my head had learnt'*: Gide (1927), 19.
193 *'long to be like them'*: Gide (1960), 55.
194 *'surged up into my skin'*: ibid.
194 *thought of the burning beaches*: Flaubert, 'A bord de la cange'.
194 *'vice of every kind'*: Thicknesse (1777), Letter XIV.
195 *'stirreth up Venus'*: Lemnius, Book I, Chapter 10.
195 *'generally hot and dry'*: quoted Grosrichard, 217.
195 *'has almost none'*: Montesquieu, I, 255.
195 *'passions were violent'*: Boswell (1955), 6.

195 '*my hot desires*': letter to John Johnston, 19 July 1765.

195 '*provoked me sexually*': Forster (1983), 311.

195 '*torrid zone of Italy*': Defoe, 'The True-born Englishman' (1701), l. 96.

196 '*than those of whites*': Gilman, 231–2.

196 '*and the revolver*': see McLynn, 177.

196 '*coeval with girlhood*': Gaskell, 103. I am grateful to Ella Dzelzainis for this reference.

197 '*and voluptuousness*': Rosenbaum, I, 111.

197 '*abandon it again*': *ibid.*, II, 118.

198 '*many times find it*': Moryson, *An Itinerary*, 'Comments upon Baden'.

199 '*among their courtiers*': Spender, 107.

199 '*from the soil*': *ibid.*, 107–8.

200 '*sensual invitation*': Lehmann, 104.

200 '*tears one's lungs*': letter to S.S. Koteliansky, 4 September 1916.

200 '*one cannot breathe*': *ibid.*, 19 January 1917.

200 '*so what's the good*': letter to Ada Clarke, 26 October 1925.

200 '*rolled over voluptuously*': Lawrence (1989), 486.

200 '*her thighs and her feet*': *ibid.*, 426.

200 '*etiolated little city figure*': *ibid.*, 442.

201 '*apparatus of civilisation*': *ibid.*, 432.

201 '*form of sickness*': Lawrence (1961), 267.

201 '*Enjoyment! Enjoyment!*': *ibid.*, 270.

202 '*a princess by my side*': see Wolff, 273.

202 '*handkerchief binding her hair*': Connolly (1961), 83.

203 '*scrubs her brass*': *ibid.*, 83–4.

204 '*nowhere in the world*': see Blume, 12.

204 *Cicada Club*: see Quennell (1976), 118.

205 '*a great time*': letter to John Peale Bishop, 21 September 1925. See Mizener, 185.

205 '*brown and young together*': Fitzgerald (1955), 67.

205 *as deeply as possible*: see Blume, 73.

205 '*no penalty for it*': *ibid.*, 310–11.

206 '*went at Antibes*': Fitzgerald (1965), 335.

206 '*about to wane*': see Vaill, 306.

206 '*slow-lighting cigarettes*': Fitzgerald (1945), 110.

207 '*free at last*': Connolly (1947), 62.

207 '*backstairs-crawler*': Orwell, I, 256.

207 '*about the Garden of Eden*': see Lewis, 11.

208 '*clocks that run slow*': see Blume, 140.

209 '*pilgrimage to the source*': *Le Trident*, no. 41, March 1956. See Furlough, 69.

209 *'fishing all day'*: ibid., 68–9.
210 *'Off to fish'*: see Peyre and Raynouard, 60.
210 *'in everyday life'*: The Tourist, BBC2, 28 January 1996.
210 *'goal of existence'*: Peyre and Raynouard, 124.
210 *'many "brief encounters"'*: Furlough, 73.
211 *'life at home'*: Corbin, 60.
211 *'dull and respectable monotony'*: Ellis, 287.
212 *prostitution among young women*: see Corbin, 374 (note 37).
212 *'excess and improvidence'*: ibid., 7. Corbin is at this point summarising the views of the nineteenth-century doctor, Alexis-Jean-Baptiste Parent-Duchâtelet, author of a celebrated study of prostitution in Paris.
213 *'open at its orifices'*: Stallybrass and White, 183.
215 *'to await me'*: Gide (1925), 151.
215 *'woman calls out to me'*: ibid., 140.

Select Bibliography

The following bibliography is restricted to books and articles referred to in the notes.

Ackerley, J.R. *My Father and Myself*, London, 1968

Allen, Alexandra *Travelling Ladies: Victorian Adventuresses*, London, 1983

Allen, Margaret Vanderhaar *The Achievement of Margaret Fuller*, University of Pennsylvania Press, 1979

Andersen, Wayne *Gauguin's Paradise Lost* (1971), London, 1972.

Anon. *An Epistle from Mr. Banks, Voyager, Monster-hunter, and Amoroso, To Oberea, Queen of Otaheite*, 2nd edition, 1773

Anon. *Nocturnal Revels: Or, The History of King's Place, & other Modern Nunneries*, London, 1779

Anon. *Plain Reasons for the Growth of Sodomy in England*, London, c. 1728

Ascham, Roger *The Scholemaster* (1570), ed. John E.B. Mayor (1863), New York, 1967

Bacon, Francis *Essays*, London, 1597

Ballhatchet, Kenneth *Race, Sex and Class Under the Raj*, London, 1980

Banks, Joseph *The 'Endeavour' Journal of Joseph Banks*, ed. J.C. Beaglehole, Sydney, 1962

Barthes, Roland 'Of What Use is an Intellectual?' (1977), reprinted in *The Grain of the Voice*, London, 1985

Bates, E.S. *Touring in 1600: a study in the development of travel as a means of education* (1911), London, 1987

Beauman, Nicola *Morgan: A Biography of E.M. Forster*, London, 1993

Birchall, Emily *Wedding Tour, January–June 1873*, ed. David Verey, Gloucester, 1985

Birkett, Dea *Spinsters Abroad: Victorian Lady Explorers*, Oxford, 1989

Black, Jeremy *The British Abroad: The Grand Tour in the Eighteenth Century*, Stroud, 1992

Blume, Mary *Côte d'Azur: Inventing the French Riviera*, London, 1992

Boswell, James *Boswell in Holland 1763–1764*, ed. Frederick A. Pottle, London, 1952

Boswell, James *Boswell on the Grand Tour: Germany and Switzerland 1764*, ed. Frederick A. Pottle, London, 1953

Boswell, James *Boswell on the Grand Tour: Italy, Corsica, and France 1765–1766*, eds. Frank Brady and Frederick A. Pottle, London, 1955

Boswell, James *Boswell's London Journal 1762–1763*, ed. Frederick A. Pottle, London, 1950

Boswell, James *Life of Johnson* (1791), Oxford, 1934

Bougainville, Louis Antoine de, *Voyage autour du monde par la frégate du roi la Boudeuse, et la flûte l'Étoile*, Paris, 1771

Boyle, Nicholas *Goethe, The Poet and the Age*, Vol. 1, Oxford, 1991

Brauer, George C. Jr. *The Education of A Gentleman*, New York, 1959

Brendon, Piers *Thomas Cook: 150 Years of Popular Tourism*, London, 1991

Bronski, Michael *Culture Clash: The making of gay sensibility*, Boston, Mass., 1984

Brooke, Rupert *The Letters of Rupert Brooke*, chosen and edited by Geoffrey Keynes, London, 1968

Browne, James H. 'Voyage from Leghorn to Cephalonia with Lord Byron, and a Narrative of a visit, in 1823, to the seat of war in Greece', *Blackwood's Edinburgh Magazine*, No. 217, Vol. 35 (January 1834), pp. 56–67

Burgess, Anthony *Little Wilson and Big God*, London, 1987

Burgess, Anthony *You've Had Your Time*, London, 1990

Burton, Richard *First Footsteps in East Africa*, London, 1856

Burton, Richard *Personal Narrative of a Pilgrimage to Al-Madinah and Meccah* (1855–56), London, 1893

Buzard, James *The Beaten Track: European tourism, literature and the ways to culture, 1800–1918*, Oxford, 1993

Byron, George Gordon, Lord *Byron's Letters and Journals*, ed. Leslie A. Marchand, London, 1973–1982

Campbell, Mary *The Witness and the Other World: Exotic European Travel Writing, 400–1600*, New York, 1988

Casanova de Seingalt, Giacomo *Histoire de ma vie* (written 1789–98), trans. Willard R. Trask, London, 1967–72

Cheetham, Simon *Byron in Europe*, Wellingborough, 1988

Cohen, Erik 'Open-ended prostitution as a skilful game of luck; opportunity, risk and security among tourist-oriented prostitutes in a Bangkok *soi*', in *Tourism in South-East Asia*, ed. Michael Hitchcock et al., London, 1993

Connolly, Cyril *The Rock Pool*, London, 1947

Connolly, Cyril *The Unquiet Grave* (1944), London, 1961

Corbin, Alain *Les filles de noce: Misère sexuelle et prostitution aux 19ᵉ et 20ᵉ siècles* (1978), trans. Alan Sheridan as *Women for Hire: Prostitution and Sexuality in France after 1850*, Cambridge, Mass. and London, 1990

Coryate, Thomas *Coryat's Crudities, Hastily Gobled up in five moneths travells*, London, 1611

Cowley, Malcolm *Exile's Return* (1934), London, 1961

Croft-Cooke, Rupert *Feasting with Panthers: a new consideration of some late Victorian writers*, London, 1967

Crompton, Louis *Byron and Greek Love: homophobia in 19th-Century England*, London, 1985

Cunningham, Valentine *British Writers of the Thirties*, Oxford, 1988

Danielsson, Bengt *Gauguin in the South Seas* (1964), London, 1965

Delay, Jean *La jeunesse d'André Gide*, Paris, 1957

Dening, Greg *Mr Bligh's Bad Language: Passion, Power and Theatre on the Bounty*, Cambridge, 1992

Diderot, Denis *Supplément au voyage de Bougainville* (1796), ed. G. Chimard, Paris, 1935

Dollimore, Jonathan *Sexual Dissidence: Augustine to Wilde, Freud to Foucault*, Oxford, 1991

Douglas, Norman *Looking Back*, London, 1934

Douglas, Norman *South Wind* (1917), Harmondsworth, 1987

Dykes, Oswald *The Royal Marriage*, London, 1722

Eisler, Benita *Byron: Child of Passion, Fool of Fame*, London, 1999

Ellis, Havelock *Studies in the Psychology of Sex*, Vol. IV (1906), New York, 1936

Evelyn, John *The Diary of John Evelyn*, ed. E.S. De Beer, Oxford, 1955

Faith, Nicholas *The World the Railways Made*, London, 1990

Finch, Marianne *An Englishwoman's Experience in America*, London, 1853

Fitzgerald, F. Scott *Tender is the Night* (1939), Harmondsworth, 1968

Fitzgerald, F. Scott 'Echoes of the Jazz Age' in *The Bodley Head Scott Fitzgerald*, Vol. III, London, 1965

Fitzgerald, F. Scott *The Crack-Up*, ed. Edmund Wilson, New York, 1945

Flaubert, Gustave 'A bord de la cange' (1880) in *Notes de voyages en Orient*, Paris, 1910

Forster, E.M. *'Albergo Empedocle' and Other Writings*, New York, 1971

Forster, E.M. *A Room with a View* (1908), London, 1977

Forster, E.M. *Selected Letters of E.M. Forster*, Vol. I (1879–1920), ed. Mary Lago and P.N. Furbank, London, 1983

Forster, E.M. *The Hill of Devi*, London, 1983

Forster, E.M. *Where Angels Fear to Tread* (1905), London, 1971

Foster, Shirley *Across New Worlds: Nineteenth-Century Women Travellers and their Writings*, London, 1990

Frank, Katherine *Lucie Duff Gordon: A Passage to Egypt*, London, 1994

Freud, Sigmund *The Standard Edition of the Complete Psychological Works of Sigmund Freud*, trans. James Strachey, Vol. VII, London, 1953

Friedenthal, Richard *Goethe, His Life and Times* (1963), London, 1965

Fuller, Margaret *The Letters of Margaret Fuller*, ed. Robert N. Hudspeth, Cornell University Press, 1983–1995

Furlough, Ellen 'Packaging Pleasures: Club Méditerranée and French Consumer Culture, 1950–1968', *French Historical Studies*, Vol. 18, No. 1 (Spring 1993), pp. 65–81

Garnett, David, 'Frieda and Lawrence' in Stephen Spender (ed.) *D.H. Lawrence: Novelist, Poet, Prophet*, London, 1973

Gaskell, P. *Artisans and Machinery* (1836), London, 1968

Gauguin, Paul *Lettres de Gauguin à sa femme et à ses amis*, ed. Maurice Malingue, 2nd edition, Paris, 1949

Gauguin, Paul *Noa Noa* (1901, modified by Charles Morice; 1954, unmodified) trans. Jonathan Griffin, Oxford, 1961

Gauguin, Paul *Avant et après* (1918), trans. Van Wyck Brooks as *The Intimate Journals of Paul Gauguin* (1923), London, 1931

Gay, Peter *The Bourgeois Experience: Victoria to Freud*, Vol. I, *The Education of the Senses*, New York, 1984

Gay, Peter *The Bourgeois Experience: Victoria to Freud*, Vol. II, *The Tender Passion*, New York, 1986

Gide, André *Amyntas* (1906), Paris, 1925

Gide, André *L'immoraliste* (1902), trans. Dorothy Bussy, Harmondsworth, 1960

Gide, André 'Oscar Wilde' in *Oeuvres Complètes*, Vol. III, Paris, 1933

Gide, André *Les nourritures terrestres* (1897), Paris, 1927

Gide, André *Si le grain ne meurt* (1926), Paris, 1955

Gilman, Sander 'Black Bodies, White Bodies: Toward an Iconography of Female Sexuality in Late Nineteenth-Century Art, Medicine, and Literature' in *'Race', Writing, and Difference*, ed. Henry Louis Gates Jr., Chicago and London, 1986

Goethe, J.W. *The Italian Journey* (1816–29), trans. W.H. Auden and Elizabeth Mayer, London, 1962

Gower, Ronald *Old Diaries 1881–1901*, London, 1902

Graves, R.P. *A.E. Housman: The Scholar-Poet*, London, 1979

Greene, Graham *In Search of a Character*, London, 1961

Grosrichard, Alain *Structure du sérail: La fiction du despotisme Asiatique dans l'Occident classique* (1979), trans. Liz Heron as *The Sultan's Court: European Fantasies of the East*, London, 1998

Grosskurth, Phyllis *John Addington Symonds: A Biography*, London, 1964

Hall, Joseph *Quo Vadis? A Just Censure of Travell as it is commonly undertaken by the Gentlemen of our Nation*, London, 1617

Hamilton-Smith, Elery 'Four Kinds of Tourism?', *Annals of Tourism Research*, Vol. XIV (1987), pp. 332–344

Harris, Frank *Oscar Wilde: His Life and Confessions* (1916), New York, 1918

Hawkesworth, John *An Account of the Voyages Undertaken by the Order of His Present Majesty for Making Discoveries in the Southern Hemisphere*, London, 1773

Hemingway, Ernest *Fiesta [The Sun Also Rises]* (1927), London 1962

Henrique, Louis (ed.), *Les colonies françaises*, Paris, 1889

Hesse, Hermann *Wandering* (1920), trans. James Wright, London, 1972

Heyzer, Noeleen *Working Women in South-East Asia*, Milton Keynes, 1986

Hibbert, Christopher *Edward VII, A Portrait*, London, 1976

Hibbert, Christopher *The Grand Tour* (1969), London, 1974

Holloway, Mark *Norman Douglas*, London, 1976

Hopwood, Derek *Sexual Encounters in the Middle East*, Reading, 1999

Hurd, Richard *Dialogues on the Uses of Foreign Travel*, London, 1764

Hyam, Ronald *Empire and Sexuality: The British Experience*, Manchester, 1990

Hyde, H. Montgomery *The Other Love: an historical and contemporary survey of homosexuality in Britain*, London, 1970

Hynes, Samuel *The Auden Generation: literature and politics in England in the 1930s*, London, 1976

Isherwood, Christopher *Christopher and his Kind, 1929–1939* (1976), London, 1977

Jameson, Anna *Winter Studies and Summer Rambles in Canada*, London, 1838

Jameson, Anna B. *Diary of an Ennuyée*, London, 1826

Kabbani, Rana *Imperial Fictions: Europe's Myths of Orient* (1986), London, 1994

Kemble, Frances Anne (Mrs Butler) *A Year of Consolation*, London, 1847

Kemble, Frances Anne (Mrs Butler) *Journal of a Residence in America*, Paris, 1835

Kemble, Frances Anne (Mrs Butler) *Record of a Girlhood*, London, 1878

Kerouac, Jack *On the Road* (1957), London, 1958

Lassels, Richard *The Voyage of Italy*, London, 1686

Lawrence, D.H. *Phoenix*, ed. Edward D. McDonald, London, 1961

Lawrence, D.H. *The Letters of D.H. Lawrence*, ed. James T. Boulton *et al.*, Cambridge, 1972–1993

Lawrence, D.H. *Lady Chatterley's Lover* (1928), Harmondsworth, 1961

Lawrence, D.H. 'The Lovely Lady' (1927) and 'Sun' (1928) in *Selected Short Stories*, Harmondsworth, 1989

Lefèvre, R. *Le mariage de Loti*, Paris, 1935

Lehmann, John *In the Purely Pagan Sense* (1976), London, 1985

Lemaistre, J.G. *A Rough Sketch of Modern Paris*, London, 1803

Lemnius, Levinus *The Touchstone of Complexions*, London, 1576

Lever, Charles 'Continental Excursionists' in *Blackwood's Edinburgh Magazine*, Vol. XCVII, February 1865, pp. 230–233

Lévi-Strauss, Claude *Tristes Tropiques* (1955), trans. John and Doreen Weightman, London, 1973

Lewis, Jeremy *Cyril Connolly: A Life*, London, 1997

Linklater, Andro *Compton Mackenzie: A Life* (1987), London, 1992

Lithgow, William *The Rare Adventures and Painful Peregrinations of William Lithgow* (1632), London, 1974

Loti, Pierre *Le roman d'un enfant* (1890), Paris, 1922

Loti, Pierre *Le mariage de Loti* (1880), Paris, 1924

McAlmon, Robert *Being Geniuses Together*, London, 1938

McClintock, Anne *Imperial Leather: Race, Gender and Sexuality in the Colonial Contest*, New York, 1995

McLynn, Frank *Burton: Snow upon the Desert*, London, 1990

Mączak, Antoni *Travel in Early Modern Europe* (1878), trans. Ursula Phillips, Cambridge, 1995

Marchand, Leslie A. *Byron: A Biography*, London, 1957

Massie, Allan *Byron's Travels*, London, 1988

Maugham, W. Somerset *Complete Stories*, Vol. I, London, 1951

Mizener, Arthur *The Far Side of Paradise*, Boston, 1949

Montagu, Mary Wortley *The Complete Letters of Lady Mary Wortley Montagu*, Vol. II, ed. Robert Halsband, Oxford, 1966

Montesquieu, Charles-Louis de Secondat *De l'esprit des lois* (1748), trans. Thomas Nugent, New York, 1949

Moore, Doris Langley *The Late Lord Byron* London, 1961

Moore, John *A View of Society and Manners in France, Switzerland, and Germany*, London, 1779

Moore, John *A View of Society and Manners in Italy*, London, 1781

Moorehead, Alan *The Fatal Impact: An Account of the Invasion of the South Pacific 1767–1840*, London, 1966

Morgan, Ted *Somerset Maugham*, London, 1980

Morrison, James *The Journal of James Morrison*, ed. O. Rutter, London, 1935

Moryson, Fynes *An Itinerary*, London, 1617

Neville, Richard *Playpower* (1970), London, 1971

Nicolson, Harold *Byron: The Last Journey*, London, 1924

Nugent, Thomas *The Grand Tour* (1749), London, 1778

Odzer, Cleo *Patpong Sisters*, New York, 1994

Ohse, U. *Forced Prostitution*, Edinburgh, 1984

Origo, I. *The Last Attachment*, London, 1949

Orton, Joe *The Orton Diaries*, ed. John Lahr, London, 1986

Orwell, George *The Collected Essays, Journalism and Letters*, London, 1968

Osborne, John *A Better Class of Person*, London, 1981

Owenson, Sydney [Lady Morgan] *Italy*, London, 1821

Parker, Peter *Ackerley*, London, 1989

Pemble, John *The Mediterranean Passion: Edwardians and Victorians in the South*, Oxford, 1987

Peyre, Christiane and Raynouard, Yves *Histoire et légendes du Club Méditerranée*, Paris, 1971

Polidori, John *The Diary of Dr John William Polidori, 1816*, London, 1911

Pope-Hennessy, James *Monckton-Milnes: The Years of Promise 1809–1851*, London, 1949

Porter, Dennis *Haunted Journeys: Desire and Transgression in European Travel Writing*, Princeton University Press, 1991

Pottle, Frederick A. *James Boswell: the earlier years, 1740–1769*, London, 1966

Powell, Anthony *Agents and Patients* (1936), London, 1966

Pratt, Mary Louise *Imperial Eyes: travel writing and transculturation*, London, 1992

Quennell, Peter *Byron in Italy*, London, 1974

Quennell, Peter *The Marble Foot*, London, 1976

Redford, Bruce *Venice and the Grand Tour*, New Haven and London, 1996

Rees, Goronwy 'A Case for Treatment: The World of Lytton Strachey', *Encounter*, Vol. XXX, March 1968, pp. 71–83

Rennie, Neil *Far-Fetched Facts: The Literature of Travel and the Idea of the South Seas*, Oxford, 1995

Robertson, George *The Discovery of Tahiti*, ed. Hugh Carrington, London, 1948

Robinson, Jane *Unsuitable for Ladies: An Anthology of Women Travellers*, Oxford, 1994

Robinson, Jane *Wayward Women: A Guide to Women Travellers*, Oxford, 1990

Rollier, H.A. *Heliotherapy* (1923), London, 1927

Rosenbaum, Julius *The Plague of Lust, Being a History of Venereal Disease in Classical Antiquity* (1845), Paris, 1901

Rousseau, G.S. *Perilous Enlightenment*, Manchester, 1991

Russell, Mary *The Blessings of a Good Thick Skirt: Women Travellers and their World*, London, 1986

Ryan, Chris *Recreational Tourism: a social science perspective*, London, 1991

Schick, Irvin C. *The Erotic Margin: Sexuality and Spatiality in Alteritist Discourse*, London, 1999

Select Bibliography

Seabrook, Jeremy *Travels in the Skin Trade*, London, 1996

Selvon, Sam *The Lonely Londoners* (1956), London, 1972

Sewell, Elizabeth Missing *Ivors*, London, 1856

Sheridan, Thomas *British Education*, London, 1756

Skrobanek, Siriporn *et al. The Traffic in Women*, London and New York, 1997

Smith, Timothy d'Arch *Love in Earnest: some notes on the lives and writings of the English 'Uranian' poets from 1889 to 1930*, London, 1970

Smollett, Tobias *Travels Through France and Italy*, London, 1766

Southey, Robert *Life and Correspondence*, London, 1850

Spender, Stephen *World Within World*, London, 1951

Stallybrass, Peter, and White, Allon *The Politics and Poetics of Transgression*, London, 1986

Stanhope, P. *The Letters of Philip Dormer Stanhope, 4th Earl of Chesterfield*, ed. Bonamy Dobrée, London, 1932

Sterling, John *Essays and Tales*, ed. J.C. Hare, London, 1848

Sterne, Laurence *A Sentimental Journey Through France and Italy* (1768), Harmondsworth, 1967

Stevenson, Robert Louis *The Works of Robert Louis Stevenson*, Vol. XIII, Heinemann, 1924

Story, William Wetmore *Roba di Roma*, London, 1863

Sweetman, David *Paul Gauguin*, London, 1995

Symonds, J.A. *A Problem in Greek Ethics* [London], 1883

Symonds, J.A. *Memoirs*, ed. Phyllis Grosskurth, London, 1984

Symons, Arthur *The Memoirs of Arthur Symons*, ed. Karl Beckson, University of Pennsylvania Press, 1977

Szyliowicz, Irene L. *Pierre Loti and the Oriental Woman*, New York, 1988

Taillemite, E. *Bougainville et ses compagnons autour du monde 1766–1769*, Paris, 1977

Thicknesse, Philip *A Year's Journey Through France and Part of Spain*, London, 1777

Thicknesse, Philip *Useful Hints To Those Who Make The Tour of France*, London, 1768

Thrale, Hester Lynch (Mrs Piozzi) *Thraliana, Vol. II (1784–1809)*, ed. Katherine Balderston, Oxford, 1951

Trollope, Frances *A Visit To Italy*, London, 1842

Updike, John *Self-Consciousness*, London, 1989

Vaill, Amanda *Everybody was so Young: Gerald and Sara Murphy: a lost generation love story*, London, 1998

Voase, Richard *Tourism: The Human Perspective*, London, 1995

Walpole, Horace *The Yale Edition of Horace Walpole's Correspondence*, Vol. XXXVII, ed. W.S. Lewis, London, 1974

Select Bibliography

'Walter' *My Secret Life* (c. 1890), Ware, 1995

Ware, Vron 'Purity and Danger: race, gender and tales of sex tourism' in *Back to Reality? Social Experience and Cultural Studies*, ed. Angela McRobbie, Manchester, 1997

Waugh, Alec *The Coloured Countries*, London, 1930

Waugh, Alec *The Early Years of Alec Waugh*, Farar, Straus & Co., 1962

Waugh, Evelyn *A Little Order: a selection from his journalism*, ed. Donat Gallagher, London, 1977

Waugh, Evelyn *Diaries*, ed. Michael Davie, London, 1976

Waugh, Evelyn *Remote People* (1931), Harmondsworth, 1985

Weeks, Jeffrey *Sex, Politics and Society* (1981), London, 1989

Weightman, John 'The Solar Revolution: Reflections on a Theme in French literature', *Encounter*, Vol. XXXV, December 1970, pp. 9–18

West, Nathanael *Miss Lonelyhearts* (1933) in *The Collected Works of Nathanael West*, Harmondsworth, 1975

Wickes, George *Americans in Paris*, New York, 1969

Wilde, Oscar *The Letters of Oscar Wilde*, ed. Rupert Hart-Davis, London, 1962

Wilton, Andrew, and Bignamini, Ilaria (eds.) *Grand Tour: The Lure of Italy in the Eighteenth Century*, London, 1996

Withey, Lynne *Grand Tours and Cook's Tours* (1997), London, 1998

Wolff, Geoffrey *Black Sun* (1976), London, 1977

Acknowledgements

Warm thanks to Andrew Gibson and Rachel Bowlby, who were kind enough to read a draft of the book and make valuable suggestions. I'd also like to thank Jonathan Dollimore, Ella Dzelzainis, Alan Sinfield, Lyn Thomas, and the staff of Sussex University library. At John Murray, Grant McIntyre's help with all aspects of the book has added to the pleasure of writing it. Finally, as always, special thanks to my wife, Ayumi.

Index

Index

Browning, Elizabeth Barrett, 63,
Browning, Oscar, 86
Browning, Robert, 61
Budgen, Henry, 140
Buol, Christian, 76–8
Burgess, Anthony, 51–2, 141, 157,
    185
Burton, Richard, 36, 37, 65–6, 107,
    196; *Personal Narrative of a
    Pilgrimage to Al-Madinah and
    Meccah*, 65–6
Butler, Josephine, 122
Buzard, James, 61–2, 92
Byron, George Gordon, Lord, 3, 23,
    48, 58, 105–18, 119–20, 121, 128–9,
    138, 139, 143, 144, 150–1, 153, 161,
    176, 195; *Beppo*, 27, 116, 119–20;
    Childe Harold, 113, 116; *Don Juan*,
    3, 116; 'The Island', 144, 151;
    Mazeppa, 116

Cairo, 49, 66, 71
Cambridge, 108–9, 140
Capote, Truman, 80
Capri, 125, 139–40
Carpenter, Edward, 61, 90
Casanova, Giacomo di, 4, 48
Channel 4, 101
Chardin, Jean: *Voyages en Perse*, 195
Chateaubriand, François-René de,
    156
Chaucer, Geoffrey, 4
Chesterfield, Philip Dormer Stanhope,
    4th Earl of, 15–16, 83
Christian, Fletcher, 144–5, 181
Civil War, the English, 104
Clairmont, Claire, 63, 112
Cleveland Street Scandal, 131
Club 18–30, 101
Club Méditerranée, 208–10, 214
Cogni, Margarita, 114
Coleridge, Samuel Taylor, 154
Columbus, Christopher, 152
Congo, 51–2

Connolly, Cyril, 51, 127, 202–4, 206–7,
    213; *Enemies of Promise*, 127; *The
    Rock Pool*, 206–7
Constantinople, 41, 110
Conway, Henry Seymour, 39
Cook, Captain James, 146–9, 151, 153,
    181
Cook, Thomas, 62, 122
Corbin, Alain, 166, 211–12
Coronation Street, 101
Corvo, Baron (Frederick Rolfe), 80
Coryate, Thomas, 13, 26–7
Côte d'Azur *see* Riviera
Cowley, Malcolm, 125
Cox, Katherine ('Ka'), 173
Croft-Cooke, Rupert, 124
Crosby, Caresse, 99
Crosby, Harry, 201–2
Cunard, Nancy, 99
Cunningham, Valentine: *British Writers
    of the Thirties*, 137

Damiens, Robert François, 48
Danielsson, Bengt, 164, 169
Darwin, Charles, 190
Daudet, Alphonse, 159
Davos, 76–8
Day, John, 26
Defence of the Realm Acts, 128
Defoe, Daniel, 25, 195; 'The True-
    Born Englishman', 25
Dempster, George, 31
Dewas, Maharajah of, 93, 97
Dickens, Charles, 59, 128, 155, 190;
    Bleak House, 74; *Little Dorrit*, 59
Dickinson, Goldsworthy Lowes, 86
Diderot, Denis, 153, 169; *Supplément au
    voyage de Bougainville*, 169
Digby, Jane, 98
Diodati, Villa, 112
Disraeli, Benjamin, 55
'Don Leon', 117–18
Douglas, Lord Alfred, 109, 129, 130,
    138

242

Index

Index

Index

Index

Index